Deadliest Enemies

Deadliest Enemies

Law and Race Relations
on and off Rosebud Reservation

Thomas Biolsi

With a New Introduction

University of Minnesota Press
Minneapolis • London

First University of Minnesota Press edition, 2007

Published by arrangement with the University of California Press

Published by the University of Minnesota Press
111 Third Avenue South, Suite 290
Minneapolis, MN 55401-2520
http://www.upress.umn.edu

Library of Congress Cataloging-in-Publication Data

Biolsi, Thomas, 1952–
    Deadliest enemies : law and race relations on and off Rosebud Reservation /
Thomas Biolsi, with a new introduction. — 1st University of Minnesota Press ed.
        p. cm.
    Originally published: Berkeley : University of California Press, 2001.
    Includes bibliographical references and index.
    ISBN 978-0-8166-4971-6 (pb : alk. paper)
    1. Indians of North America—Legal status, laws, etc.—South Dakota—Rosebud Indian
Reservation. 2. Dakota Indians—Legal status, laws, etc. 3. Rosebud Indian Reservation
(S.D.)—Ethnic relations. 4. Indians of North America—Legal status, laws, etc. I. Title.
    KFS3505.5.R67 B56 2007
    342.78308′72—dc22

                                                                    2006100530

Printed in the United States of America on acid-free paper

The University of Minnesota is an equal-opportunity educator and employer.

14 13 12 11 10 09 08 07   10 9 8 7 6 5 4 3 2 1

To Miyako-san

Contents

Maps and Tables

MAPS

TABLES

Acknowledgments

The research on which this book was based was generously supported by an American Council of Learned Societies grant-in-aid, an American Philosophical Society Philips Fund grant, a Harry Frank Guggenheim fellowship, a National Endowment for the Humanities summer stipend, two Portland State University research and publication grants, and a Portland State University faculty development grant. I am also indebted to Portland State University for a sabbatical leave during which I wrote the bulk of this book.

I have known people on Rosebud Reservation and its environs for years and count many there as friends, without whom I never would have become interested in the subject of this book, much less been in a position to study it. To protect the privacy of my interview subjects, I have not named them here. I regret that I cannot list these people and specify the material contributions they made to this project, but I trust that they will recall our interviews and will know my sincere thanks for their help.

I wish to thank the Rosebud Sioux Tribal Council and its officers for making the research possible with their hospitality and support. In particular I thank Alex Lunderman, who was tribal president, and Mike Boltz and Linda Marshall, who were council members while I conducted research. Whitney Meek, tribal revenue officer, was ever patient with my questions and willing to explain complex matters to a novice. Sherry Red Owl, tribal education director, has helped me a great deal with this project over the years. I am indebted to my *hunka* cousin, Gerri Night Pipe, tribal secretary, who helped me locate documents among the tribal records. Todd Bear Shield and Bernadette Prue also helped me find records at the tribal office. I extend my thanks to Toni Vargas who not only is a friend but who always had suggestions for my research. The Antelope Community was my home for seven months during 1993, and I appreciate the invitation to attend—and vote at—community meetings. I am especially indebted to the kindness of the late Levi Antoine, and Howard Fuller, former community chairpersons. I would like to thank Victor Douville, Russell Eagle Bear, Duane Hollow Horn Bear, and Albert White Hat of the Lakota Studies Department at Sinte Gleska University, who have always welcomed me and shared their knowledge generously. Marcella Cash and Terry Gray helped me locate documents at the Lakota Archives and Historical Research Center of Sinte Gleska University. I am indebted to the late Simon Broken Leg, the late Lloyd One Star, and the late Ted Thin Elk, for coaching me on treaty law over the years. The city council of Mission welcomed me and supported my research, and I am especially indebted to Mayor Jack Herman and Patti Busch. Richard Howard, South Dakota secretary of transportation, visited with me and kindly provided copies of documents from his office files. Aileen Hosek and Marsha Hodge were very patient with me as I searched through the records of the Winner County Courthouse. Jan Lien helped me find records in the Lyman County Courthouse. At the South Dakota State Historical Society, I benefited from the skills of Ann Jenks, Laura Glum, and Lavera Rose. Attorneys Krista Clark, B. J. Jones, Terry Pechota, John Simpson, and Tom Tobin not only shared their expertise with me but also made their office files available. Thanks also to attorneys Bob Gough of Rosebud and Melody McCoy of the Native American Rights Fund, and to law professors Rick Collins of the University of Colorado and Frank Pommersheim of the University of South Dakota, all of whom tried hard to straighten me out on the fine points of Indian law. I am also very appreciative of the valuable time I spent with Vine Deloria, Jr., of the University of Colorado.

Connie Cash transcribed my interviews with great skill and professionalism. Several of my colleagues were kind enough to read parts of this manuscript and offer suggestions that, I am sure, made the book better than it would have been. I have in mind Johanna Brenner, Michele Gamburd, David Johnson, and Craig Wollner of Portland State University, and Akhil Gupta of Stanford University. I am especially indebted to David Wilkins of the University of Minnesota, who taught me a great deal about Indian law and politics (both through his writing and through conversation) and who carefully read multiple drafts and offered insightful feedback. I am also sincerely thankful to David Nugent of Colby College who not only read and helped me through the "sticking points" but listened to me describe the evolution of my research and this book over the years. My friend David has had much to do with the way I thought through this material and with the way I think as a scholar. Indeed, he taught me to "do it dialectically." His influence on this book, and on my life, is indelible.

While it is impolite to brag about one's relatives, I must mention here my *hunka* sister, Rose Cordier. Rose has served as a tribal vice president and tribal council representative and has otherwise long been involved in government and politics. I have learned a great deal from Rose about tribal government and Indian-white relations (as well as cooking soup, fry bread, and secret-recipe *wojapi!*), and she has always gone out of her way to facilitate my work. She and her children—Frances Beauvais, Robert Beauvais, Lisa Beauvais, Brooke Beauvais, and adopted son Lewis Good Voice Eagle—have for many years left the light on at their home in Antelope for me. It is no exaggeration to say that my career as an anthropologist and a college professor who "specializes in" Native American studies has been made possible by Rose's teaching, support, generosity, and kindness over the years. One of the honors I am most proud of in my life is my adoption by Rose as her brother in 1993.

I am also indebted to my immediate domestic unit. Chibby has taught and given me things no mere two-legged could; he naps at my side as I write these acknowledgments. Finally, my partner, Miyako Inoue, has made this book both intellectually possible and personally worthwhile. She heard it all in its various versions a million times over the years, and always encouraged and supported me. More than that, though, I have learned a great deal about critical theory from her, and this has made a fundamental intellectual difference in my book. Without Miyako, there would be no book, and this work is dedicated to her.

The author's royalties are assigned to Sinte Gleska University.

Note on sources. References have been redacted to omit personal names in order to protect the privacy of the parties named.

Introduction to the New Edition

Indian Law and White Innocence

> You know very well that we are exploiters. . . . [A]ll of us without exception have profited by colonial exploitation. This fat, pale continent ends by falling into what Fanon rightly calls narcissism. . . . And that super-European monstrosity, North America? Chatter, chatter: liberty, equality, fraternity, love, honor, patriotism, and what have you?
>
> —JEAN-PAUL SARTRE, preface to Frantz Fanon's *The Wretched of the Earth*

> The more ethnohistory we know, the more clearly "their" history and "our" history emerge as part of the same history. Thus, there can be no "Black history" apart from "White history," only a component of a common history suppressed or omitted from conventional studies for economic, political, or ideological reasons.
>
> —ERIC WOLF, *Europe and the People without History*

It seems a "no brainer" these days that wherever one finds racial difference, one will also find racial inequality and racial struggle. It is now widely recognized that race and racial difference are constructed social facts instituted and reproduced in the pursuit of privilege and struggle against it. No one would be surprised, for example, to learn that the legal statuses of "Indian" and "degree of Indian blood" have had a long history of being used against Indian people for the purpose of transferring Indian resources into the hands of white people, or that Indian people have fought long and difficult battles to "rearticulate" (Omi and Winant 1994 [1986]) the meaning of these statuses in ways that are responsive to their interests. Nor would anyone be surprised to hear from Indian people that local whites living on reservations or in reservation border towns are racist toward Indians. The blistering anti-Indian racism of whites depicted in Sandra Osawa's 1994 film *Lighting the Seventh Fire* (see also Bobo and Tuan 2006) about the struggle to exercise treaty-based fishing rights in northern Wisconsin is, while arresting to the viewer, somehow not surprising given our understanding of the geography of race and racism in the contemporary United States. Reservations and border towns are the contact zones where racial domination and resistance get played out in direct interactions, and it seems unremarkable that Indians and whites in such places are likely to confront each other, as the Supreme Court put it in 1896, as "deadliest enemies" (*U.S. v. Kagama*, 118 U.S. 375, at 384). Who would be surprised that some Indian (and some non-Indian) people have called South Dakota, with its nine reservations, the "Mississippi of the North"?

This book seeks to problematize the commonsense understanding of Indian-white relations just sketched. While we are clearly on firm ground insisting that race be understood as instituted and enacted for the purposes of securing and contesting privilege, a complete picture of racial privilege, injustice, and struggle cannot be limited to a focus on local, intersubjective contact zones, nor is the local contact zone naturally or inevitably hostile (if only because racial difference is always already imbricated with other systems of difference: class, gender, and region among the most obvious, which always make interracial alliance a potentiality). Thus, racially "hot" contact zones need to be explained by putting them into a larger, synthetic framework: we need to recognize how local contact zones and their racial politics are orchestrated and how this orchestration implicates nonlocal racial inequality, inequality that—because it is not local, immediate, and intersubjective—may not even appear as race relations. Put differently, who gets let off the hook and who gets hooked into racial struggle in the prevailing geography of Indian-white relations? This book argues that the active localizing of "race relations" in (arbitrary) contact zones is *part of the strategy by which racial privilege is secured translocally and at a continental scale.* This wider racial hierarchy needs sustained attention in the critical study of Indian-white relations if we are to understand white privilege and the contemporary positioning of indigenous peoples in useful ways.

Deadliest Enemies is a historical and ethnographic study of how Indian and white people on and near Rosebud Reservation in South Dakota (home of the Sicangu Lakota, or Rosebud Sioux) get positioned as local enemies by structuring forces beyond their control, even if not beyond their awareness. More pointedly, this book is a study of the making of racial inequality, but it is not premised on the idea that the key to the racial domination of Native American people is to be found in local white racism. It is important that I be clear about my point of departure. The point of this book is not that whites in South Dakota are racially innocent or that they are not the beneficiaries of white privilege. Rather, the point is that they are *no more racist and no more beneficiaries of white privilege at the expense of Indian people than other whites in the United States.* And perhaps less. Indeed, the book argues that it is whites far from the reservation and far from South Dakota (even whites who teach in universities, such as myself, and who might be inclined to write off South Dakota "rednecks" as the northern equivalent of the paradigmatic white racist in Mississippi) who have a much more formidable white privilege at stake regarding Native peoples.

SETTLER SOCIETY AND CONTINENTAL WHITE PRIVILEGE

On Indigenous Peoples' Day, 2005 (formerly Columbus Day), I attended a small noon event sponsored by Indian students and staff members near Sather Gate (the birthplace of the Free Speech Movement) at the University of California, Berkeley. As the lunchtime crowd thronged past the handful of Indian people with a microphone, an Indian student opened the event by announcing, "Welcome to stolen land." I was impressed by the simultaneous marginality of the whole event amid the bustle of a campus of 33,000 students (of whom only 200 are Native, and only a fraction of that number constitute the active Native community on campus) and the incontrovertible truth—marginalized though it may be—of the founding of the University of California on the homeland of indigenous people wiped (almost) off the landscape. The destruction of the California Indians is, in fact, well documented (Heizer 1993 [1974]; Hurtado 1988). So is what is commonly called the "New World Holocaust," in which the Native population of North America decreased from more than 7 million to 250,000 as a result of "contact" (see Thornton 1987). "You know very well," Sartre tells us from the grave, as do all the Native people, living and dead: The fact of Euro-American barbarism that made the "settlement," "development," and the very "history" of the United States possible is commonsensically understood and commonly acknowledged, but consigned in mainstream thinking to the historically inert, the past. I was stunned into awareness of this transparent (in the sense of ordinarily invisible, like a glass ceiling) horizon of generalized white benefit from Native destruction while I was teaching at Portland State University in Oregon in the 1990s, shortly after relocating from the East, where I seldom encountered Indian college students. In Portland, where I did regularly have Indian students, I read Eugene Hunn's *Nch'I-Wána, "The Big River": Mid-Columbia Indians and Their Land* along with my students and learned of the malaria epidemics of the early 1830s that had taken 90 percent of the Native populations of the Willamette Valley in Oregon, where I was living and working. Hunn also describes how the annihilation of the Native populations left the landscape so empty of Indians that Oregon settlers were free to impose the names of Portland, Astoria, Eugene, and Salem, while other places in the Northwest, where Native peoples had avoided the malaria epidemics, retained Indian place names: Seattle, Tacoma, Spokane, and Yakima (Hunn 1990, 31). The sanitizing of landscape by clearing it of Indians—to the benefit of white people, historic and contemporary— could not be more starkly evidenced.[1]

Coercive threats to Native people persisted into the twentieth century. Rosebud Reservation continued to be "settled" by white homesteaders during World War I through a *legal* process of tribal land cessions (agreements that are commonly called "treaty-substitutes"). This might seem civilized and fair enough, like any kind of contract or treaty nego- tiation, but it is critical to ask how much the then-recent violence visited on Lakota people in 1890 at the Wounded Knee massacre influenced one party to these agreements. No terrorism is as effective politically, after all, as state terrorism. How much did the Lakotas' awareness that the Bureau of Indian Affairs (BIA) controlled *all* material resources on the reserva- tion influence their "yes" in the "agreements" by which they opened their reservation to homesteaders? How much of contemporary Indian affairs (Indian-white relations) is founded on the historical pacification and de- pendence of Indian peoples (see Biolsi 1992: ch. 1)?

We—non-Indians in this settler society—also know very well the consequences of "Indian affairs" for contemporary Native people: the unemployment rate for enrolled members of Indian tribes on or near reservations was 49 percent in 2001, and "[o]f the 51 percent employed, 33 percent earn[ed] wages below poverty guidelines" (Bureau of Indian Affairs 2001: iii, ii). The poverty rate—which, as is well known, under- counts real poverty—for American Indians and Alaska Natives in 1999, the most recent year for which the Census Bureau has data, was 25.7 percent; the category "Sioux," which includes the people who are the subject of this book, had a poverty rate of 38.9 percent (U.S. Census Bureau 2006: Figure 8). Not surprisingly, the alcohol-related death rate for American Indians is 7.8 times that of whites, the diabetes death rate

1. Of course, there was no historical or empirical reason for me not to have recog- nized similar processes at work on Long Island, New York, where I grew up. The differ- ence between the East and the Northwest for me was the presence of Indian students in my classes at Portland State University who forced me to crack open my partial standpoint to glimpse history from *their* standpoint.

4.4 times, and the age-adjusted death rate 1.57 times (Indian Health Service n.d.). When age of death is plotted, the stunning numbers of Native Americans who die young or during their prime compared to the white population becomes clear (Figure 1). All in all, the measures of socioeconomic distress are appalling (Figure 2).

It would be a critical error, of course, to assume that the misery attending reservation poverty is all that there is to know about the reservation. There is no question that focusing on poverty and oppression without a more expansive view of the reservation would amount to trafficking in the stereotype of the "broken Indian," as Stephanie Fryberg puts it (2002: 25–26). Poverty and misery no more exhaust the reality of the reservation community than do tribal casinos. Yet coverage of the broken reservation Indian is prominent, if episodic. The *New York Times,* for example, recently ran front page articles titled "Through Indian Lands, Drugs' Shadowy Trail" and "Dizzying Rise and Abrupt Fall for a Reservation Drug Dealer" (Kershaw 2006a, 2006b). This kind of coverage is consistent with a larger imagery of reservations as the third world within the first world, but without any consideration of how the first world is implicated in the condition of the third world here or abroad. This kind of imagery of the reservation is commonly resented by Indian people for its negativity and its otherwise biased (as local people see it) — and, I would add, voyeuristic — quality. Indeed, as many Indian

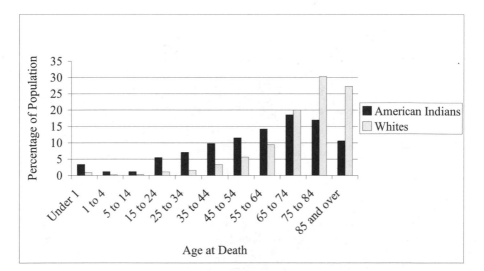

Figure 1. Deaths by age for American Indians and whites. Adapted from Indian Health Service (n.d.), Chart 4.15 and Table 4.14.

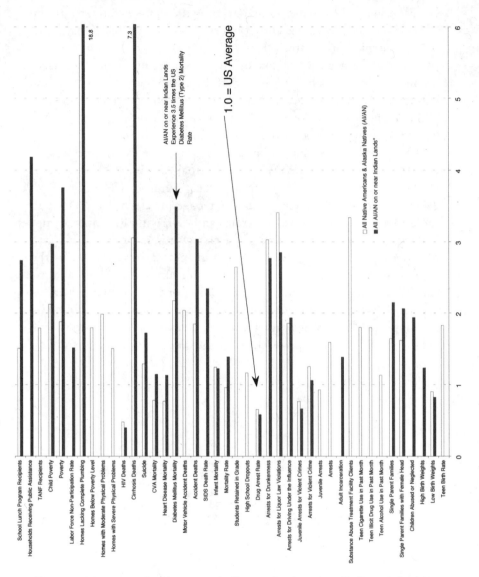

Figure 2. Measures of socioeconomic distress for American Indians and whites. From Henson, Taylor, et al. 2002, Figure 2.

people would insist, the poverty story may deflect attention from other justice issues (such as sovereignty, and thereby misconstrue the situation of Indian people by reducing it to a class position that is blind to the specificities of the colonial situation), as will become clear in this book.

Nevertheless, I ask how the historical and contemporary reality of the Native immiseration just described has been marginalized, made into a morally and politically inert factoid and fodder for mass media spectacle (alongside its mirror-image, fantastic, casino-driven tribal wealth), but not for national obligation. Even if we were to reject the theory that the miseries suffered by Indian people are harms attributable to the fault of white people and to the direct effects of white privilege, we would still be faced with the pressing question of how a self-described democratic society can stand by in the face of such misery among its own fellow citizens. The U.S. government and many of our public intellectuals and citizens speak loudly of human rights, and as David Harvey points out, even the 1948 United Nations Declaration of Human Rights, to which the United States was a signatory, has clear language concerning economic rights, such as the individual's "right to a standard of living adequate for the health and well-being of himself and his family, including food, clothing, housing and medical care and necessary social services, and the right to security in the event of unemployment, sickness, disability, widowhood, old age or other lack of livelihood in circumstances beyond his control" (quoted in Harvey 2000: 90). This right would entail a national *positive obligation for the welfare of others* independent of any demonstrable fault. A no-fault understanding of Indian-white relations, in other words, does not get white people at large off the hook. My question is: how has the collective bad faith, as Sartre no doubt would have put it, of white people toward Native Americans been sustained, even institutionalized? It is the argument of this book that the discourse of federal Indian law—a longstanding body of case and statute law—positively and affirmatively locates thinkable and actionable (morally, politically, and legally) issues of justice for Native peoples *locally*—in the contact zone on and around Indian reservations. Federal Indian law constitutes a regime that produces a very particular geography of race relations and rights struggle. Federal Indian law is a racial politics machine that focuses legal and political attention on local Indian-white interactions, and excludes from view the translocal racial hierarchy in which whites benefit from the historical legacy of the colonization of North America and from the "innocence" produced by their not being called to account for this legacy, or if one adopts the no-fault position, their freedom from responsibility to act affirmatively to address the Native situation. Indian law is a "racial project" (Omi and Winant 1994 [1986]) in that it secures or reproduces the status of white innocence or white nonobligation regarding Native Americans, except for those local whites sacrificed for the larger white absolution.

Whites in general are literally made into innocent bystanders by the particular disputes between local whites and Indians on and around reservations—by the affirmative silences of the discourse of federal Indian law. That is why whites who do not live in Indian country are likely to support the notion of tribal sovereignty once they know or learn something about it. It is important to ask what it means that every U.S. president since George H. W. ("the elder") Bush has publicly affirmed tribal sovereignty. While George W. ("the younger") Bush's 2004 gaffe when he was asked about tribal sovereignty[2] was widely reported, it is important to note that two years earlier he had written the following in a proclamation: "my Administration will continue to honor tribal sovereignty by working on a government-to-government basis with American Indians and Alaska Natives" (Bush 2002). Some members of Congress regularly outdo both themselves and each other in naturalizing the sovereignty of Indian nations. Even the BIA claims to be the guardian of tribal sovereignty. What are we to make of the fact that such representatives of state, class, and racial power would enunciate a principle that was, thirty years ago, heard only from "radicals" such as members of the American Indian Movement?

The main focus of this book will be the role of the discourse of federal Indian law in generating local disputes between Indians and the limited group of whites found on or near reservations. It will also consider how nonlocal whites savor their innocence in these disputes, and how such whites may even view themselves as friends of the Indians in these disputes. The remainder of this introduction will examine how it may be good to think of tribal sovereignty from the standpoint of white privilege.

POLITICAL SOVEREIGNTY

Following Wallace Coffey and Rebecca Tsosie, I will use the term "political sovereignty" to name the "external" understanding of tribal sovereignty held by U.S. presidents, members of Congress, federal judges,

2. "Tribal sovereignty means that. It's sovereign. You're a . . . you're a . . . you've been given sovereignty and you're viewed as a sovereign entity."

and the editors of major American newspapers, and to distinguish it from "cultural sovereignty" as understood (in actuality or potentially) by members of tribal communities (Coffey and Tsosie 2001). The political sovereignty of tribal governments as recognized in established federal Indian law reduces to a neat equation: (1) tribal governments have almost unlimited power to exercise civil and criminal jurisdiction over Indians;[3] (2) tribal governments may exercise no criminal and very little civil or regulatory jurisdiction over non-Indians. The touchstone cases of this equation are two 1978 Supreme Court opinions decided within two months of each other: *Santa Clara Pueblo v. Martinez* and *Oliphant v. Suquamish Indian Tribe*.

The *Martinez* case involved a Santa Clara Pueblo tribal member, Julia Martinez, and her daughter, Audrey, in a dispute with the tribal government. Thurgood Marshall (widely recognized as a friend of tribal sovereignty), writing for the majority, summarized the case:

> Julia Martinez is a full-blooded member of the Santa Clara Pueblo, and resides on the Santa Clara Reservation in Northern New Mexico. In 1941 she married a Navajo Indian with whom she has since had several children, including respondent Audrey Martinez. Two years before this marriage, the Pueblo passed [a] membership ordinance . . . which bars admission of the Martinez children to the tribe because their father is not a Santa Claran. [Footnote omitted.] Although the children were raised on the reservation and continue to reside there now that they are adults, as a result of their exclusion from membership they may not vote in tribal elections or hold . . . office in the tribe; moreover, they have no right to remain on the reservation in the event of their mother's death, or to inherit their mother's home or her . . . interests in [tribal] lands. (*Santa Clara Pueblo v. Martinez*, 436 U.S. 49, 1978, at 52–3)

The ordinance had been adopted by the Pueblo tribal government in order to limit tribal enrollment so as to conserve tribal resources. Julia and Audrey Martinez sued the tribal government, claiming that the membership rule "discriminate[d] on the basis of both sex and ancestry" (51). The Supreme Court found in favor of the tribal government. The Court noted that the Pueblo "ha[d] been in existence for over 600 years" (51), and it quoted the District Court's statement that the ordinance in question "reflect[s] traditional values of patriarchy [!] still significant in tribal life" (54). In the end, the sovereignty of Indian tribes trumped the civil rights of individual Indians:

---

3. The only limit is that federal courts will intervene in tribal government jurisdiction over Indians when petitioned for a writ of habeas corpus.

> As separate sovereigns pre-existing the Constitution, tribes have historically been regarded as unconstrained by those constitutional provisions framed specifically as limitations on federal or state authority. Thus, in *Talton v. Mayes* . . . (1896), this Court held that the Fifth Amendment did not "[operate] upon" "the powers of local self-government enjoyed" by the tribes. . . . In ensuing years the lower federal courts have extended the holding of Talton to other provisions of the Bill of Rights, as well as to the Fourteenth Amendment. (56)

The Court opined that allowing the Martinezes to air their dispute with the tribal government in the federal courts, rather than in a tribal forum, "constitutes an interference with tribal autonomy and self-government" (59). The "commitment to the goal of tribal self-determination" (62) clearly held by Congress, as well as the Court's own "proper respect . . . for tribal sovereignty itself" (60) necessitated a finding in favor of the tribal government, and against the Martinezes.

But this recognition of what the federal courts and Congress call "internal sovereignty" is only half the equation of tribal sovereignty. Two months before the *Martinez* decision, Justice William Rehnquist delivered the Supreme Court majority's opinion in *Oliphant v. Suquamish Indian Tribe* (435 U.S. 191, 1978). Here the question was whether a tribal government may exercise criminal jurisdiction over non-Indians within its territory. The Court insisted that when they were geographically incorporated into the United States, tribes automatically lost aspects of their aboriginal sovereignty "inconsistent with their status" as dependent entities (at 208, quoting the Court of Appeals). The lack of tribal jurisdiction over non-Indians has been judicially extended since 1978 to include severe limits on the civil and regulatory authority of tribes over non-Indians. In the 2001 case of *Atkinson v. Shirley* (532 U.S. 645), for example, Rehnquist, by then Chief Justice, wrote for the majority that the Navajo Nation has no authority to impose a hotel residency tax on a tourist facility owned by a non-Indian on private land in the middle of the Navajo Reservation. Even though the business relies on tribal services—police, ambulance, fire protection, and roads—and on the presence of Navajo people and their culture, which is the raison d'être for the local tourist industry, the Court insisted that the tribe has no authority to interfere in the private business of non-Indian U.S. citizens.

When one considers the gaps in tribal criminal and civil jurisdiction over persons within tribal territory effected by *Oliphant, Atkinson,* and other cases, the governing power of contemporary tribal states seems more like the "heteronomous" (Ruggie 1998: 146) political space of the pre-modern, feudal state—if such can even be called a "state"—characterized by "an intricate puzzle of partial and overlapping sovereignties" (Mattingly 1988 [1955]: 23), than the full territorial jurisdiction associated with the modern state (both at the national level and within the state's subnational divisions) (see Biolsi 2005). From a tribal government standpoint, a rational understanding of tribal sovereignty would recognize that the ability to regulate all persons' actions within a defined tribal territory is a critical component of wise and accountable government. How, for example, is a tribe to develop land use planning without the ability to zone territorially and without reference to the Indian/non-Indian legal status of individuals and businesses, or to institute environmental law without the ability to apply the law uniformly across territorial space? The lack of criminal jurisdiction over non-Indians is regularly cited by tribes as the source of a serious law enforcement gap in Indian country, particularly regarding domestic violence. Many Indian people live with or are married to non-Indians, but tribal police and courts have no criminal authority over non-Indians. While as a matter of law federal jurisdiction applies in theory in the case of a non-Indian assaulting an Indian, federal prosecutors are loath to prosecute what they reportedly regard as nuisance cases.[4] Thus non-Indian domestic batterers are not easy for tribal governments to deal with. In sum, the Supreme Court has been keen to deny tribes any of the basic territorial authority that we all recognize as necessary and legitimate in the case of (nontribal) state or local government.

What is allowed tribal governments in existing federal Indian law is not properly understood as sovereignty: "the case law taken as a whole exhibits only the semblance of sovereignty, creating a set of limits more than powers" (Aleinikoff 2002: 98), and there is some logic other than recognizing the sovereignty of Indian tribes that is at work in the decisions of the Supreme Court and in the actions and rhetoric of the executive and legislative branches. Perhaps it is obvious why federal judges and congresspeople cannot abide tribal governments exercising criminal or civil jurisdiction over non-Indians: they simply do not trust Indians and tribal governments to act fairly when it comes to white people (see Williams 2005). But why is the affirmation of almost absolute tribal control over Indians so ringing in the discourse of Indian law?

---

4. While I was conducting research for this book in 1993, I was told by one tribal law enforcement officer of the federal prosecutor's "six-inch rule." Reportedly, the federal prosecutor would not bring assault charges against any perpetrator who had not wielded a knife with at least a six-inch blade. Even if this was exaggerated, it expresses the frustration of local law enforcement to federal unwillingness to take cases for prosecution.

IMAGINED BOUNDARIES

In order to get at the underlying logic in the political sovereignty of tribes recognized by the federal government, it is necessary to examine the discourse's essentializing of Indian tribes. Let us return to the *Martinez* case. The Court began its opinion, as we saw, by stating that "Santa Clara Pueblo is an Indian tribe that has been in existence for over 600 years." This recognition of historical continuity is certainly reasonable enough: we can agree for political or legal purposes that the Santa Clara Pueblo of six hundred years ago is the same polity as Santa Clara Pueblo of 1978—as, in parallel fashion, we might say that whites of one hundred years ago are ("corporately," as we might say in kinship studies in anthropology) the same race as whites today. But the Court in *Martinez* went beyond historical continuity of the community and asserted by implication that Santa Clara Pueblo was somehow not part of the wider U.S. society, that the modern tribal government had not been established by the BIA, that tribal women (and men) had not been parties to a larger American public sphere engagement with the rights of women, that tribal members somehow could not be civil rights–bearing U.S. citizens at the same time that they are Indians in Indian country. In other words, tribal political sovereignty is best understood as a matter not of imagined Native communities, but rather of *imagined boundaries* between reservation populations and the larger American society. It is important to consider how much is left out of this essentialized picture.

Take the matter of the tribal government to which Julia and Audrey Martinez were left by the Court to take their grievances. Far from a six-hundred-year-old traditional system, the Santa Clara Pueblo Council was an instrumentality of the federal government implemented under the terms of the Indian Reorganization Act (IRA) of 1934. The structure of the modern Santa Clara government was designed by the BIA, which intervened in factional conflict and a legitimation crisis in the Spanish-originated government at the Pueblo in 1935 (Dozier 1966; Arnon and Hill 1979: 302). As a BIA community studies researcher who worked at Santa Clara explained to the BIA central office in 1935, "Owing to serious factional splits in the Pueblo, the Council has been a thoroughly incompetent body for some years, and we can't hope that a new plan will work without much government help and interpretation" (Sergeant 1935a).

While the Santa Clara people had worked on a draft of their constitution, it was heavily edited by BIA central office personnel. Among other changes, the BIA inserted a paragraph itemizing the formidable *state* powers of the Council:

> To enact ordinances, not inconsistent with the constitution and bylaws of the pueblo, for the maintenance of law and order within the pueblo and for the punishment of members, and the exclusion of nonmembers violating any such ordinances, for the raising of revenue and the appropriation of available funds for pueblo purposes, for the regulation of trade, inheritance, land-holding, and private dealings in land within the pueblo, for the guidance of the officers of the pueblo in all their duties, and generally for the protection of the welfare and the pueblo and for the execution of all other powers vested in the pueblo by existing law. (Pueblo of Santa Clara 1935, Art. IV, sec. 5)

This language was disconcerting to the members of the committee that drafted the initial version of the constitution. As the BIA community studies researcher explained, "In making the original draft many times revised in Committee, the powers of the Council were purposely left *undefined;* it was understood by all that exactly here—in the power of the Council—the factional difficulties that have split and rent the Pueblo are centered. . . . The view that the Council had power to regulate, restrict or license trade within its own boundaries, and by its own members was novel and displeasing. . . . [T]o the 'progressive' Indian mind, this clause appeared an infringement of personal liberty" (Sergeant 1935b; emphasis in original).

The constitution also—in provisions apparently inserted by the BIA—defined tribal membership in a way that would have allowed both the Martinez children and Mr. Martinez (a Navajo) to naturalize as Santa Clara Pueblo members.[5] Insertion of these provisions was consistent with

---

5. The constitution provides in Article II:

SECTION 1. *Conditions of membership.* The membership of the Santa Clara pueblo shall consist as follows:

(a) All persons of Indian blood whose names appear on the census roll of the Santa Clara pueblo as of November 1, 1935, provided that within one year from the adoption and approval of this constitution corrections may be made in the said roll by the pueblo council with the approval of the Secretary of the Interior.

(b) All persons born of parents both of whom are members of the Santa Clara pueblo.

(c) All children of mixed marriages between members of the Santa Clara pueblo and nonmembers, provided such children have been recognized and adopted by the council.

(d) All persons naturalized as members of the pueblo.

SECTION 2. *Naturalization.* Indians from other pueblos or reservations who marry a member of the Santa Clara pueblo may become members of the pueblo, with the assent of the council, by naturalization. To do this they must (1) go before the pueblo council and renounce allegiance to their tribe and declare intention of becoming members of the Santa Clara pueblo. They shall swear that from that date on they will not receive any benefits from their people, except through inheritance. (2) A year later they shall go before the pueblo council again, swear allegiance to the pueblo of

presumption of the BIA and the Department of the Interior since 1934 that tribes were vested by "existing law" with the power to determine tribal membership (Solicitor, U.S. Department of the Interior, 1934). But it is noteworthy that when the Pueblo Council in 1939 adopted the membership ordinance at issue in *Santa Clara Pueblo v. Martinez,* there was no amendment of the constitution, a much higher threshold than an act of the tribal council, and one that would have required a majority vote of at least 30 percent of the Pueblo members of voting age as well as approval by the secretary of the interior (Pueblo of Santa Clara 1935, Art. VIII).

Tellingly, for the *Martinez* case, when the Washington draft of the constitution was discussed, "Several members brought up the question of the right of Indians to appeal from the Council's decision to a Court outside the Pueblo—claiming that individual rights would not always be respected in Council decisions. If white folks could appeal to several courts, why not Indians?" (Sergeant 1935b). But the BIA determined as a general rule for IRA constitutions that there would be no separation of powers in tribal government. Judicial power was to reside in the Council that was awarded the power

> to adjudicate all matters coming before it over which it has jurisdiction. In all controversies coming before the pueblo council, the council shall have the right to examine all witnesses and ascertain full details of the controversy, and after the matter shall have been sufficiently commented upon by the interested parties, the council shall retire to a private place to make a decision. (Pueblo of Santa Clara 1935, Art. IV, sec. 2)

The BIA considered separation of powers or checks and balances between government functions—such as the legislative and judicial—to be unnecessary complexities for new tribal governments supposedly just learning during the New Deal how self-government works (see Biolsi 1992: 102–4). In short, the Court directed the Martinezes to air their grievances with the *same body* that had adopted the offending membership ordinance.

All of this BIA work at "tribal organization" under the IRA was part of the "common history" of Indian people and the wider American society that was, to recall Eric Wolf's phrase, "suppressed or omitted . . . for economic, political, or ideological reasons" (Wolf 1982: 19), in this case by the Court. The federal government was *centrally involved* in the

---

Santa Clara and receive membership papers; provided they have kept their promise from the time of their first appearance before the pueblo council.

situation faced by the Martinezes, and the Court's notion that "interference" in a six-hundred-year-old process of self-government must be avoided was simply a legal fiction. Santa Clara Pueblo had a history that was ignored by the boundary-drawing Court: its common history with the United States.

My point is not that *Martinez* was a bad judicial call for Native people or even for Native women (although that question continues to be revisited in the present, along with related questions about the rights of other kinds of tribal minorities, for example, political minorities, sexual minorities, religious minorities, and racial minorities, as well as about freedom of the press).[6] Nor is it my point that it never makes sense to understand Indian communities as relatively autonomous polities with their own—even ancient—histories. Rather, my point is that such *dividing practices and boundary drawing*—making a bright line between internal tribal matters and larger national (U.S.) matters—can cut both ways in terms of the concrete interests of real Indian people. It is certainly the case that this procedure may have its political uses in a strategic essentialism that grows out of and facilitates Native struggles, but, again, we must ask: Why do powerful non-Indian interests support so strongly this kind of line drawing when it comes to tribal authority over Indians? Why do these dividing practices apparently come so easily to the powerful?

NEOLIBERAL GOVERNMENTALITY

We can make sense of this boundary drawing—and its significance for white innocence—by turning to critical studies of governmentality. The concept of governmentality was originally proposed by Michel Foucault to name a form of modern power that works alongside the centralized macropower (Foucault's "sovereignty") of the state and the micropower of discipline located in institutions such as the prison, military, factory, and school (Foucault 1991 [1978]). Since Foucault's original work, studies of governmentality have made important contributions to our critical understanding of modern power by focusing on the nexus where the exercise of power by state actors and representatives of other powerful interests on the one hand, and the techniques by which people make themselves into coherent individuals—subjects—on the other hand, meet

6. On *Martinez,* see MacKinnon 1987 [1983]; Resnik 1989; Christofferson 1991; Valencia-Weber and Zuni 1995; Curry 2001; Skenandore 2002; Aks 2004; Berger 2004; Swentzell 2004; Milczarek-Desai 2005. On racial minorities, see Sturm 1998.

on common ground (Burchell 1996: 20). For present purposes, we can identify three historical forms of governmentality in the United States: liberalism, social government or welfarism, and neoliberalism.

Liberalism was present at the foundation of the United States and persisted throughout the nineteenth century (elements of it continue in the present) and entailed the governing assumption that the powers of the state need to be restrained because there are entities within the nation—the economy, the population with its demographic and health characteristics, and the personal preferences of the irreducibly free individual—that cannot be completely known or adequately regulated by an omniscient and omnipotent state. Rather, good government needs to recognize the internal autonomy of these entities (such as Adam Smith's invisible hand of the market economy) and thus stay its own sovereign hand from injudicious interference. Careful monitoring and corrective action, but not direct control as one might see in a disciplinary institution, are needed. Liberalism was to govern through freedom. This assumption yielded, of course, the widespread nineteenth-century practice of laissez-faire, and state agencies and civic institutions and experts developed crucial statistical and other technologies for creating knowledge about and adjusting the functioning of the relatively autonomous systems under liberal surveillance—and assemblage of knowledge and practices that Foucault called the biopolitical (see Rose 1996; Dean 1999).[7]

Things began to change in the late nineteenth century when state bureaucrats and other social experts began to discover the predictive power of statistical knowledge. First in France, and later in England and the United States, statisticians discovered that it was possible to predict risk and misfortune in national populations (such as those associated with illness, accident, loss of income, advanced age) and that it was possible to spread these risks over the course of a lifetime and over the population as a whole. Thus was born the technology of social insurance

7. This is not at all to suggest that liberalism generalized freedom to everyone. Far from it. As Dean points out, giving relative free rein to certain citizens and processes was premised on a dividing practice in which "people who, for one reason or another, are deemed not to possess or to display the attributes (e.g., autonomy, responsibility) required" of the full citizen were separated off for disciplinary treatment (think of the reservation in the history of Native Americans, which took its place alongside the penitentiary as an institution for retraining) (Dean 1999: 134). Liberalism thus necessitated a coexisting authoritarian governmentality: "[P]ervasive has been the tendency within certain states (Australia, Canada), having ceased to attempt actual genocide, to commit forms of cultural genocide upon indigenous people within their borders in the name of their own well-being, such as is the case of the removal of children from their parents and families. While the bio-political imperative does not account for all that bedevils liberal-democratic states, it is remarkable how much of what is done of an illiberal character is done with the best of bio-political intentions" (132).

by which a small regular tax on the income of all workers could be used to fund provisions for all in their times of need. Unemployment, loss of a spouse's income, loss of income with retirement, illness, other personal and family crises, indeed, poverty itself could be converted into manageable risks and amortized at the level of the population and thus socialized. This new potential biopolitical technique gained widespread favor in the face of the disruptions of the Great Depression, and was at the basis of social security, unemployment, and welfare (Aid to Families with Dependent Children [AFDC]) programs in the United States.

It is important to recognize how deeply social government (Rose 1996; Dean 1999) or welfarism (Rose and Miller 1992; Dean and Hindess 1998) entered into the way that individuals thought about themselves, the state, and society. Governmentality is ultimately a matter of "the fabrication of subjectivities" (Dean 1999: 165), and social government fostered a self-evident, commonsense notion among citizens that they — "we," all of "us" — are both entitled to social guarantees of protection against the risks of modern life in capitalism and, equally important, that "we" are responsible as a society or nation for the welfare of all our fellow citizens. In fact, welfare states are not really based on the technology of insurance (understood as a value-neutral instrument) but on the political commitment of citizens to each other's welfare and to a willingness to *transfer* social surplus in the form of tax-funded benefits from those with the wherewithal to those in need (see Mink 1998: 124). Both social entitlement and social obligation are part of the political subjectivity of the New Deal (and subsequent War on Poverty) citizen produced by social government in the context of economic depression, inequality, and political unrest. Governmentality entails both "technologies of agency" and "technologies of citizenship" (Dean 1999: 167, 168), penetrating deeply into how the individual sees the (social) boundaries of the self and imagines interests, self-worth, and ethical obligations. The subject of social government has both civic and moral dimensions.

It is the transition to neoliberalism — a struggle still very much in play — that is most relevant for understanding the political sovereignty of tribes. Because of complex political and economic forces, including the interests of capital, the consumer movement, the emergence of a widespread interest in self-improvement, and even the left's critique of the welfare state, by the 1970s there emerged a form of governmentality in which individuals were to pursue their "own" "empowerment" (Cruikshank 1993; Rose 1996; Dean 1999; Harvey 2005). One telling mark of this transition is British prime minister Margaret Thatcher's 1987 philosophizing: "[W]ho is society? There is no such thing! There are individual men and women and there are families and no government can do anything except through people and people look to themselves first. It is our duty to look after ourselves." Neoliberalism is thus best understood as a negation—or attempted negation—of social government.[8] Neoliberalism involves the "reform" (the dissolving) of social obligations by a model in which individuals assume responsibility for their own welfare in a competitive marketplace that is ultimately both inescapable and global. Wendy Brown describes it succinctly:

> [N]eo-liberalism normatively constructs and interpellates individuals as rational, calculating creatures whose moral autonomy is measured by their capacity for "self-care"—the ability to provide for their own needs and service their own ambitions. In making the individual fully responsible for her/himself, neo-liberalism equates moral responsibility with rational action; it relieves the discrepancy between economic and moral behavior by configuring morality entirely as a matter of rational deliberation about costs, benefits, and consequences. In so doing, it also carries responsibility for the self to new heights: the rationally calculating individual bears full responsibility for the consequences of his or her action no matter how severe the constraints on this action, e.g., lack of skills, education, and childcare in a period of high unemployment and limited welfare benefits. Correspondingly a "mismanaged life" becomes a new mode of depoliticizing social and economic powers and at the same time reduces political citizenship to an unprecedented degree of passivity and political complacency. The model neo-liberal citizen is one who strategizes for her/himself among various social, political and economic options, not one who strives with others to alter or organize these options. (2003)

We can see neoliberalism's "generalization of an 'enterprise form'" (Burchell 1996: 28–29) in the widespread recognition, at least since the first term of the Clinton administration, that the United States and its citizens need to be globally competitive and cannot expect economic security without accepting responsibility for remaining competitive; or the increasingly common strategy on the part of states and localities to attract business and economic growth by seeing themselves as competing in a national and global market for capital investment—the most extreme cases of this involve enterprise zones; or the passage of the welfare reform act by Congress in 1996, also known as the "Personal Responsibility Act," which erased the entitlement nature of AFDC as

---

8. Neoliberalism also has a more macro-political-economic version involving global free trade, which articulates with, but is not identical to, neoliberalism as a governmentality.

enacted during the New Deal and replaced guaranteed support based on the social insurance model with a model requiring individuals to take affirmative steps toward becoming "job ready" in return for their welfare benefits, which are limited in duration in any event. As this paperback edition goes to press, President George W. Bush has called for an "ownership society" in which the welfare of the individual will be addressed not by entitlements, government, or the U.S. social surplus, but by the appreciation of privately owned assets, humble as they might be in the individual case.

Neoliberalism is thus, as Mitchell Dean puts it, a new form of "responsibilization of individuals, families, households, and communities for their own" welfare. Critically, it is not just individuals and nation-states that are newly responsibilized. So are corporate political units below the level of the national state: states, counties, and cities must act as rational subjects too in the global marketplace, whether that requires cutting back on services and entitlements, limiting or even reducing taxes, or generally making themselves attractive to business. This is most obvious in the institutionalization of "the new federalism" and "federal devolution" (Eisinger 1998).

We are now in a position to understand why judges, congresspeople, and even presidents engage in the dividing practice of recognizing Indian nations and speak affirmatively of tribal sovereignty. Recall that the equation of officially allowed political sovereignty for tribes is quite lopsided, since the actual powers of tribes are limited to jurisdiction over Indians whose U.S. citizenship rights are constrained when they live in Indian country. Tribes are responsible in the Court's view, indeed, almost completely and solely responsible, for the welfare of their own tribal citizens, at least as far as civil rights are concerned. The Court's specific concerns are, of course, with jurisdictional matters and other matters of law, but it is important to see the extent to which the Court's dividing practice of drawing lines between "sovereign" tribes and the rest of us is consistent with a larger prevailing neoliberal common sense about the allocation of civic and personal responsibility. In *Martinez,* the Court subcontracted the responsibility for protection of the civil rights of tribal members to tribal governments. But what are the larger, clear implications of this in the present and in the wider political rationality of neoliberalism? I want to emphasize the logical consistency between, on the one hand, the Court's idea that tribes are sovereign governments and distinct political communities and, on the other hand, the more general and increasingly inescapable assumption that *all places* — nations, states, counties, cities, tribes—must make "their own" economic way in global competition and should not expect taxpayers or others to foot the bill for subsidizing their local economies. One of the ironies of globalization is that the more the world is interconnected economically, the more "local economies" seem to be self-evident and natural responsibilities of the people who live in localities. My point is that the discourse of tribal sovereignty both reflects and helps to concretize the emerging neoliberal hegemony of individual and local responsibility and autonomy.

What is actually being engineered in the judicial and other legal and policy recognitions of tribal sovereignty is the lack of responsibility by those outside the reservation for what happens inside the reservation— even when those outside have been *completely responsible* for what is happening inside. Iris Young describes the "responsibilizing" logic of sovereignty (she is not speaking of American Indian tribal sovereignty, but of national sovereignty in general) this way: sovereignty acts to assign responsibility by "clearly separating a realm of our business from a realm outside that is none of our business, and where those outside must keep out of our business" (2000: 253). While the business of civil rights exercised the Court in *Martinez,* political sovereignty is a general paradigm for responsibilization that goes to *all dimensions* of citizens' welfare. What federal recognition of tribal sovereignty does is to draw a line around tribal peoples and label the interior as none of our business. We might be concerned, as liberals or compassionate conservatives, about reservation poverty and health, but since Indian tribes are their own nations, the best we can offer is some "foreign aid" or what Indian people insist is a matter of specific treaty rights or direct implications of the trust responsibility of the federal government for tribal self-determination and the welfare of Indians. These special accoutrements of an equally special tribal sovereignty are, of course, anything but general obligations of citizens for their fellow citizens' welfare. It is not a historical coincidence that federal assurances of respect for tribal sovereignty and of a commitment to government-to-government relations have become more ringing at a time when the federal expenditures for tribal and Indian programs have fallen behind both concrete needs and the rate of federal spending on the population as a whole (see Figure 3) (see Walke 2000; U.S. Commission on Civil Rights 2003). As I write this introduction, the Bush administration has proposed legislation that would end the U.S. fiduciary obligation and liability for Indian trust land within ten years (U.S. Senate 2006), which sounds to tribal advocates very much like *termination.*

There is no doubt that the separatism of tribal sovereignty has some real, concrete benefits for peoples whose cultures were labeled as savagery and targeted for ethnocide. It is also obvious that the ability of tribes to function as distinct political communities has the potential to address in realistic and effective ways at least some of the specific forms of racial inequality and oppression that American Indian peoples have faced historically and face every day in the present. It is important to recognize that the way the Court and non-Indians in general understand Indian sovereignty—what I have called here political sovereignty—is not necessarily the way Indian people understand what sovereignty means. Most American Indian people who think seriously about these issues see themselves unproblematically as *dual citizens* (see Biolsi 2005) and do not see a contradiction in their simultaneous political autonomy from the United States and entitlement to U.S. funding (under the categories, as we saw above, of Indian treaty rights and U.S. trust responsibility). Furthermore, Tsosie's concept of cultural sovereignty involves much more than Indian tribes simply mimicking aspects of the Western state, but founding principles of tribal self-government in tribal contexts (Tsosie 2002a, 2002b; see also Alfred 1999; Garroutte 2003).

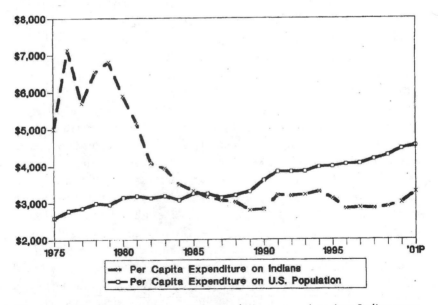

Figure 3. Per capita expenditure, U.S. population versus American Indian population, FY1975–FY2001 (in constant U.S. dollars). Indian per capita expenditures for FY1975 and FY1977 do not include Indian Housing Development. From Walke 2001, Graph 23B, page 237.

It is also important to recognize how indigenous cultural sovereignty gets translated into neoliberal political sovereignty and how the latter fits neatly into a larger neoliberal governmentality and resonates with the current attack on the welfare state and social government. The discursive move at work is the subcontracting of the responsibility of the larger society and of whites in particular for the welfare of Indian people to tribal governments—the responsibilizing of tribal governments for their "own" tribal citizens' welfare. In other words, the logic of sovereignty, as it is expressed by the federal government, is one of desocializing and decontextualizing the real problems faced by Indian people and making those problems local responsibilities (only) of the tribal government and its electorate.

Another way of putting this is that neoliberal assertions of tribal sovereignty have the effect of undermining the social citizenship of American Indians—their guarantees of rights as American citizens under an older, welfarist regime of governmentality. This was brought home to me starkly in two visits I made to Rosebud Reservation. After I graduated from college, I spent a week on the reservation in the summer of 1975, at the height of federal investment in the Great Society programs, progeny of the New Deal. While the unemployment rate was still estimated at about one-third of the workforce, both private enterprise and tribal government employed many people (many of the jobs funded with Office of Economic Opportunity money [see Castile 1998, 2006]), and the reservation even had a thriving industrial park with both tribally and privately owned businesses. I did not return to the reservation until 1984 for my dissertation research. After a term of Reagan budget cuts, the industrial park was deserted, and the unemployment rate was estimated at 85 to 90 percent. In *this* logic of tribal sovereignty (federal defunding), tribal governments increasingly sense—and find imposed on them—the responsibility to generate their own local economic development. Within the governmental regime of neoliberalism, it is almost impossible for tribes or their citizens to suggest that anyone other than themselves—certainly neither states nor Congress—is responsible for local poverty or for doing much about it. This is made all the more a stubborn and taken-for-granted principle by the spectacular success of a handful of extremely lucky tribes that have been able to cash in on Indian gaming; the logic of sovereignty, from a non-Indian point of view, runs like this: "See, if the Pequots can do it, why can't the Lakota?" Or, "Let the Pequots help the Lakota." It is telling that when George W. Bush spoke of the sovereignty of Indian tribes and of a government-to-government relationship, he added that his administration's goal is to make Indian tribes not only "self-governing" but also "self-supporting and self-reliant." He was, of course, only giving expression to a wider rationality of neoliberalism.

Ultimately, I am arguing that the logic of tribal political sovereignty, recognized and publicized by the federal government and judges, lawyers, and politicians who tend to dominate the field of federal Indian law and policy, acts positively to secure white innocence nationally regarding justice for American Indians. White innocence is a very real social fact in the United States. It is not just an ideology or a representation but a *social relation*—a concrete freedom (for some) from legal or political liability for the spectacular racial inequality that is apparent to everyone, every day. Just as we have come to recognize that municipal and school district boundaries play a critical role in the protection of white privilege, the boundaries drawn in the legal and political production of tribal sovereignty do the same. As David Delaney puts it, jurisdictional boundaries are also *boundaries of responsibility* (Delaney 2001 [1995]; see also Frug 1991; Ford 1995 [1994], 2001 [1999]). A concrete and very material white innocence is produced, both in the case of inner-city black neighborhoods and school districts, and in the case of American Indian reservations, through jurisdictional boundaries. This innocence is a function both of literal legal indemnity engineered by jurisdictional lines—the white suburb of Grosse Pointe neither created nor is responsible for correcting the failing all-black schools of Detroit, just as white Americans did not make and cannot be held responsible for reservation poverty—as well as a more general political imaginary undergirded by the prevailing neoliberal notion of distinct, autonomous, self-responsible sovereignties. For American Indians, the non-Indian discourse of tribal sovereignty, while denying tribal governments real sovereignty, insists that they alone have responsibility over and for their own members and, by implication, cannot expect those of us who are not tribal members to do anything more than feel bad about, or at most offer some minimal assistance in addressing, their alarming poverty, their ghastly morbidity and mortality rates, or, indeed, the prospects of their very survival as indigenous peoples. Recognition is cheap, especially when it does not require redistribution.

Berkeley, California
November 2006

REFERENCES

Aks, Judith H. 2004. *Women's Rights in Native North America: Legal Mobilization in the US and Canada.* New York: LFB Scholarly Publishing.

Aleinikoff, T. Alexander. 2002. *Semblances of Sovereignty: The Constitution, the State, and American Citizenship.* Cambridge, Mass.: Harvard University Press.

Alfred, Taiaiake. 1999. *Peace, Power, Righteousness: An Indigenous Manifesto.* New York: Oxford University Press.

Arnon, Nancy S., and W. W. Hill. 1979. "Santa Clara Pueblo." In *Handbook of North American Indians,* vol. 9, *Southwest,* ed. Alfonso Ortiz, 296–307. Washington, D.C.: Smithsonian Institution.

Berger, Bethany R. 2004. "Indian Policy and the Imagined Indian Woman." *Kansas Journal of Law and Public Policy* 14: 103–15.

Biolsi, Thomas. 1992. *Organizing the Lakota: The Political Economy of the New Deal on Pine Ridge and Rosebud Reservations.* Tucson: University of Arizona Press.

———. 2005. "Imagined Geographies: Sovereignty, Indigenous Space, and American Indian Struggle." *American Ethnologist* 32(2): 239–59.

Bobo, Lawrence D., and Mia Tuan. 2006. *Prejudice in Politics: Group Position, Public Opinion, and the Wisconsin Treaty Rights Dispute.* Cambridge, Mass.: Harvard University Press.

Brown, Wendy. 2003. "Neo-liberalism and the End of Liberal Democracy." *Theory and Event* 7(1).

Burchell, Graham. 1996. "Liberal Government and Techniques of the Self." In *Foucault and Political Reason: Liberalism, Neo-Liberalism, and Rationalities of Government,* ed. Andrew Barry, Thomas Osborne, and Nikolas Rose, 19–36. Chicago: University of Chicago Press.

Bureau of Indian Affairs. 2001. *Indian Population and Labor Force Report.* Washington, D.C.: Bureau of Indian Affairs, U.S. Department of the Interior.

Bush, George W. 2002. "Proclamation of National American Indian Heritage Month." http://www.whitehouse.gov/news/releases/2002/11/20021101-7.html (accessed 18 May 2006).

Castile, George Pierre. 1998. *To Show Heart: Native American Self-Determination and Federal Indian Policy, 1960–1975.* Tucson: University of Arizona Press.

———. 2006. *Taking Charge: Native American Self-Determination and Federal Indian Policy, 1975–1993.* Tucson: University of Arizona Press.

Christofferson, Carla. 1991. "Tribal Courts' Failure to Protect Native American Women: A Reevaluation of the Indian Civil Rights Act." *Yale Law Journal* 101: 169–85.

Coffey, Wallace, and Rebecca Tsosie. 2001. "Rethinking the Tribal Sovereignty Doctrine: Cultural Sovereignty and the Collective Future of Indian Nations." *Stanford Law and Policy Review* 12(2): 191–221.

Cruikshank, Barbara. 1999. *The Will to Empower: Democratic Citizens and Other Subjects.* Ithaca, N.Y.: Cornell University Press.

Curry, Lucy A. 2001. "A Closer Look at *Santa Clara Pueblo v. Martinez*: Membership by Sex, by Race, and by Tribal Tradition." *Wisconsin Women's Law Journal* 16: 161–214.

Dean, Mitchell. 1999. *Governmentality: Power and Rule in Modern Society.* Thousand Oaks, Calif.: Sage Publications.

Dean, Mitchell, and Barry Hindess. 1998. "Introduction: Government, Liberalism, Society." In *Governing Australia: Studies in Contemporary Rationalities of Government,* ed. Mitchell Dean and Barry Hindess, 1–19. New York: Cambridge University Press.

Delaney, David. 2001 [1995]. "The Boundaries of Responsibility: Interpretations of Geography in School Desegregation Cases." In *The Legal Geographies Reader,* ed. Nicholas Blomley, David Delaney, and Richard T. Ford, 54–68. Malden, Mass.: Blackwell Publishers.

Dozier, Edward P. 1966. "Factionalism at Santa Clara Pueblo." *Ethnology* 5 (2): 172–85.

Eisinger, Peter. 1998. "City Politics in an Age of Federal Devolution." *Urban Affairs Review* 33(3): 308–25.

Ford, Richard T. 1995 [1994]. "The Boundaries of Race: Political Geography in Legal Analysis." In *Critical Race Theory: The Key Writings That Formed the Movement,* ed. Kimberly Crenshaw et al., 449–64. New York: New York University Press.

———. 2001 [1999]. "Law's Territory (A History of Jurisdictions)." In *The Legal Geographies Reader,* ed. Nicholas Blomley, David Delaney, and Richard T. Ford, 200–217. Malden, Mass.: Blackwell Publishers.

Foucault, Michel. 1991 [1978]. "Governmentality." In *The Foucault Effect: Studies in Governmentality,* ed. Graham Burchell et al., 87–104. Chicago: University of Chicago Press.

Frug, Gerald E. 1991. *City Making: Building Communities without Building Walls.* Princeton, N.J.: Princeton University Press.

Fryberg, Stephanie. 2002. "Really? You Don't Look Like an American Indian: Social Representations and Social Group Identities." Ph.D. diss., Stanford University.

Garroutte, Eva Marie. 2003. *Real Indians: Identity and the Survival of Native America.* Berkeley and Los Angeles: University of California Press.

Harvey, David. 2000. *Spaces of Hope.* Berkeley and Los Angeles: University of California Press.

———. 2005. *A Brief History of Neoliberalism.* New York: Oxford University Press.

Heizer, Robert F. 1993 [1974]. *The Destruction of the California Indians.* Lincoln: University of Nebraska Press.

Henson, Eric, Jonathan Taylor, et al. 2002. *Native America at the New Millennium.* Cambridge, Mass.: Harvard University, John F. Kennedy School of Government, Harvard Project on American Indian Economic Development, http://www.ksg.harvard.edu/hpaied/pubs/pub_004.htm (accessed 18 May 2006).

Hunn, Eugene S., with James Selam and Family. 1990. *Nch'I-Wána, "The Big River": Mid-Columbia Indians and Their Land.* Seattle: University of Washington Press.

Hurtado, Albert L. 1988. *Indian Survival on the California Frontier.* New Haven, Conn.: Yale University Press.

Indian Health Service. n.d. *Trends in Indian Health, 2000–2001.* http://www. ish.gov/NonMedicalPrograms/IHS_Stats/Trends00.asp (accessed 19 February 2006).

Kershaw, Sarah. 2006a. "Dizzying Rise and Abrupt Fall for a Reservation Drug Dealer." *New York Times,* 20 February, sec. A, p.1.

——. 2006b. "Through Indian Lands, Drugs' Shadowy Trail." *New York Times,* 19 February, sec. 1, p. 1.

MacKinnon, Catharine. 1987 [1983]. "Whose Culture? A Case Note on *Martinez v. Santa Clara Pueblo.*" In *Feminism Unmodified,* 63–69. Cambridge, Mass.: Harvard University Press.

Mattingly, Garrett. 1988 [1955]. *Renaissance Diplomacy.* New York: Dover.

Milczarek-Desai, Shefali. 2005. "(Re)Locating Other/Third World Women: An Alternative Approach to *Santa Clara Pueblo v. Martinez*'s Construction of Gender, Culture, and Identity." *UCLA Women's Law Journal* 13: 235–91.

Mink, Gwendolyn. 1998. *Welfare's End.* Ithaca, N.Y.: Cornell University Press.

Omi, Michael, and Howard Winant. 1994 [1986]. *Racial Formation in the United States: From the 1960s to the 1990s.* 2nd ed. New York: Routledge.

Osawa, Sandra Johnson. 1994. *Lighting the Seventh Fire.* Video. Seattle: Upstream Productions.

Pueblo of Santa Clara. 1935. "Constitution and Bylaws." http://thorpe.ou.edu/ IRA/nmsccons.html (accessed 11 May 2006).

Resnik, Judith. 1989. "Dependent Sovereigns: Indian Tribes, States, and the Federal Courts." *University of Chicago Law Review* 56: 671–759.

Rose, Nikolas. 1996. "Governing 'Advanced' Liberal Democracies." In *Foucault and Political Reason: Liberalism, Neo-Liberalism, and Rationalities of Government,* ed. Andrew Barry, Thomas Osborne, and Nikolas Rose, 37–64. Chicago: University of Chicago Press.

Rose, Nikolas, and Peter Miller. 1992. "Political Power beyond the State: Problematics of Government." *British Journal of Sociology* 43(2): 173–205.

Ruggie, John Gerard. 1998. *Constructing the World Polity: Essays on International Institutionalization.* New York: Routledge.

Sartre, Jean-Paul. 2001 [1961]. Preface to *The Wretched of the Earth,* by Frantz Fanon, in *Colonialism and Neocolonialism,* 136–55. New York: Routledge.

Sergeant, Elizabeth S. 1935a. Letter to Joe Jennings (18 November). File 9728-1-1936, United Pueblos, 068; entry 1012, Records of the Indian Organization Division; Record Group 75, Records of the Bureau of Indian Affairs. Washington, D.C.: National Archives.

——. 1935b. Memorandum on the Santa Clara Objections to the Washington Draft of the Constitution and Bylaws. File 9728-1-1936, United Pueblos, 068; entry 1012, Records of the Indian Organization Division; Record Group 75, Records of the Bureau of Indian Affairs. Washington, D.C.: National Archives.

Skenandore, Francine R. 2002. "Comment: Revisiting *Santa Clara Pueblo v. Martinez:* Feminist Perspectives on Tribal Sovereignty." *Wisconsin Women's Law Journal* 17: 347–70.

Solicitor, U.S. Department of the Interior. 1934. "Powers of Indian Tribes (25 October)." 55 I.D. 14. http://thorpe.ou.edu/sol_opinions/p426-450.html (accessed 11 May 2006).

Sturm, Circe. 1998. "Blood Politics, Racial Classification, and Cherokee National Identity: The Trials and Tribulations of the Cherokee Freedmen." *American Indian Quarterly* 22(1–2): 230–58.

Swentzell, Rina. 2004. "Testimony of a Santa Clara Woman." *Kansas Journal of Law and Public Policy* 14: 97–101.

Thornton, Russell. 1987. *American Indian Holocaust and Survival: A Population History since 1492*. Norman: University of Oklahoma Press.

Tsosie, Rebecca. 2002a. "Introduction: Symposium on Cultural Sovereignty." *Arizona State Law Journal* 34(1): 1–14.

———. 2002b. "Reclaiming Native Stories: An Essay on Cultural Appropriation and Cultural Rights." *Arizona State Law Journal* 34(1): 299–358.

U.S. Census Bureau. 2006. "We the People: American Indians and Alaska Native in the United States. Census 2000 Special Reports." http://www.census.gov/prod/2006pubs/censr-28.pdf (accessed 20 February 2006).

U.S. Commission on Civil Rights. 2003. "A Quiet Crisis: Federal Funding and Unmet Needs in Indian Country." http://www.usccr.gov/pubs/na0703/na0731.pdf (accessed 19 May 2006).

U.S. Senate, Committee on Indian Affairs. 2006. "Newly Proposed Provisions for Senate Bill 1439, The Indian Trust Reform Act." http://indian.senate.gov/public/ (accessed 15 November 2006).

Valencia-Weber, Gloria, and Christine P. Zuni. 1995. "Symposium: Women's Rights as International Human Rights: Domestic Violence and Tribal Protection of Indigenous Women in the United States." *St. John's Law Review* 69: 69–135.

Walke, Roger. 2000. "Indian-Related Federal Spending Trends, FY1975–FY2001." Congressional Research Service (1 March). In Senate Report 106–251 (2nd sess.), Report of the Committee on the Budget.

Williams, Robert A., Jr. 2005. *Like a Loaded Weapon: The Rehnquist Court, Indian Rights, and the Legal History of Racism in America*. Minneapolis: University of Minnesota Press.

Wolf, Eric R. 1982. *Europe and the People without History*. Berkeley and Los Angeles: University of California Press.

Young, Iris M. 2000. "Hybrid Democracy: Iroquois Federalism and the Post-colonial Project." In *Political Theory and the Rights of Indigenous Peoples*, ed. Duncan Ivison et al., 237–58. New York: Cambridge University Press.

Deadliest Enemies

Introduction

"Deadliest Enemies"
and the Discourse of Indian Law

"Because of local ill feeling, the people of the States where [Indian tribes] are found are often their deadliest enemies." Thus did the Supreme Court, in its 1886 *United States* v. *Kagama* opinion, enunciate what can be called the deadliest enemies hypothesis for identifying the central political conflict—and problem of justice—in Indian-white relations in the United States.[1] The assumption that the deadliest enemies of Indian tribes are local non-Indians in and around Indian country is an old story in the narratives of federal Indian law in the United States. Indeed, it has its origins in the 1830s "Cherokee cases," which did much to found federal case law regarding Indian people, where it was clear that the Georgia state legislature was no friend of the Cherokee.[2] In the interests of justice, the hypothesis goes, it is up to the federal government to protect Indian tribes from "local ill feeling" through execution of its "trust" or "fiduciary" responsibility over its "dependent" Indians. Law, in other words, is to stand above and ameliorate the inevitable racial oppression of Indian people on the ground.

The deadliest enemies hypothesis continues to be an important assumption in the narratives of federal Indian law. As the Court of Appeals for the Ninth Circuit put it in *Oliphant* v. *Schlie* in 1976, "It may not be as true as it once was that... '[b]ecause of local ill feeling, the

1. 118 U.S. 375, 384.
2. *Cherokee Nation* v. *Georgia*, 30 U.S. (5 Pet.) 1 (1831); *Worcester* v. *Georgia*, 31 U.S. (6 Pet.) 515 (1832).

people of the states where they are found are often their deadliest enemies.'.... But antagonism between reservation Indians and the *surrounding populations* does persist. History, broken promises, cultural differences and neglect all contribute to it. Reluctance on the part of the States to accord to Indians rights guaranteed to them by treaties still exists."[3] This hypothesis is found not only in the court opinions but also in the scholarship of federal Indian law:

> Indians are a politically impotent minority. It is to Congress's credit that it has generally sought to deal honorably with them.... State and private interests a have much less creditable record....[4]

> [T]he [Supreme] Court has made practical judgments that soften the harshness of colonization: it has centralized power in Congress, not in the state legislatures (where local passions would be more prejudicial to Indians).[5]

Even scholarly critics of federal Indian law seem to accept the deadliest enemies hypothesis. Robert A. Williams, for example, has written a compelling critique of the "White Man's Indian Law"[6] and gives the lie to the assumption that it is Indian law written by Congress and interpreted by judges that has historically protected Indian tribes and Indian people, as suggested in *Kagama*. It is *Indian* resistance and the native vision of law and peace that informed the original treaty negotiation, Williams argues, that has protected indigenous nations. The orthodox assumption that the legal opinions of "dead white males," such as Marshall, protect Indians critically misconstrues history: "We are talking, remember, about the legal system of one of the modern world's most efficient colonizing powers."[7] Far from protecting Indian people, Indian law in fact confronted them with a "genocidal and ethnocidal threat." What is noteworthy about Williams's critique for present purposes is that although he questions the presumption of Indian law protecting Indian people, he leaves the deadliest enemies hypothesis unexamined: "History teaches Indian peoples that in a federal system of government, the white racial power organized through state governments represents the gravest and most persistent threat to Indian rights and cultural survival on the continent."[8]

3. 544 F.2d 1007, 1013 (9th Cir. 1976) (footnote omitted, emphasis added).
4. Collins 1979:529.
5. Frickey 1990:1205.
6. Robert Williams 1996:981.
7. Ibid., 986.
8. Ibid., 987.

The deadliest enemies hypothesis is not only a recurrent narrative in legal circles: the hypothesis is commonly recited by "lay" people both in South Dakota and beyond. Consider, for example, the following. Until 1997 a mural titled "The Spirit of the People," painted in 1910 by Edwin Howard Blashfield, hung in the South Dakota governor's office in the capitol in Pierre.[9] Here is the commentary of one of my Lakota informants on the mural and its significance:

> Have you ever seen that one in the executive office?... [I]t's a picture... done by this Edwin Blashfield.... He was commissioned in 1909 when they were building the capitol.... There's...two settlers there. One has a rifle, one has a six shooter.... And they're standing there, and they've felled a field of Indians, and they're standing above them. There's only one Indian alive and he's got his hand upreached.... And there's a beautiful white lady up above them. She represents South Dakota and all that is good, and then there's an angel with her, you know, kind of like giving God's hand to all this. ... And the wagon train in the back. And there's a dark hooded lady or person...who is being run off, and she's...as dark as the Indians.... What this is, is they're chasing off evil, see, and, you know, it's a manifest destiny. You know, God gave his hand to do all that.... To me, you know, it's a litmus test. I mean, us as Indian people know that [attitude] is current....[10]

The idea that the Blashfield mural was the tip of a deeper white racist iceberg is not at all an unusual point of view among Lakota people. Many Indian people resented the mural's prominent place in the governor's office until it was walled over in 1997, and it is not uncommon to hear Indian people speak about the "frontier mentality" of whites in the state. In December 1999, after a series of deaths of Indian men in South Dakota, the United States Civil Rights Commission visited Rapid City and took testimony from a long line of Indian witnesses. The deaths—most unexplained, and one "explained" but unpunished—are assumed by many Lakota people to be hate crimes, and these incidents, as well as the commission hearing, occasioned broad commentary on race relations in general throughout the state. One well-known Lakota woman summed up the opinion of many Indian people in her statement to the commission on "the racist activity of this state."[11] A prominent American Indian

9. The mural was sealed and covered over with drywall and an Indian star quilt after an Indian grandmother convinced the governor that the mural "was hurting feelings" ("Star Quilt to Cover Controversial Mural," *Rapid City Journal*, 22 October 1997).

10. Passages from informant interviews conducted by the author, such as this one, will not receive attribution in this book in order to protect the privacy of my informants. The interviews were conducted between 1991 and 1993.

11. "Statement to the U. S. Civil Rights Commission," *New Lakota Times*, 13–20 December 1999.

Movement activist also articulated the feelings of many Indian people when he told a rally in Rapid City, "we live in a racist state, like in the Deep South."[12] The South Dakota Advisory Committee to the Civil Rights Commission summarized the hearing in its 2000 report: "There is a longstanding and pervasive belief among many Native Americans that racial discrimination permeates all aspects of life in South Dakota and that prejudice and bigotry play out on many levels, including the workplace, schools, businesses, and public accommodations."[13]

Many non-Indian people agree that there is deep-seated racial tension, even if they do not see the problem as rooted in white racism, or white racism alone. An editorial penned by a Lakota woman in a local Rosebud Reservation newspaper must have expressed the reasoning of many people, both Indian and white, about South Dakota race relations: "The 'problem' with Indians and whites goes back centuries. It's part of the landscape, present in the very fabric of our social conscience. It comes from both sides, white and Indian."[14] It is not difficult to imagine both Indian and white heads nodding in agreement with a *Washington Post* editorial carried by a local Rosebud Reservation newspaper: "Indians and whites... have never really stopped fighting in South Dakota since Gen. George A. Custer made his last stand at Little Bighorn." The racial tensions in South Dakota, the columnist observed, "reflect a vast cultural divide and a gulf of suspicion and mistrust between Indians and whites in a state that historically was one of the bloodiest battlegrounds between the races during the great westward expansion."[15]

The racial divide thus appears to those caught up in it as not only self-evident, both also primordial and perennial. It is the stuff of historic murals, "part of the landscape," and is something deeply embedded in the social "fabric" of South Dakota. This local narrative interlaces seamlessly with the federal Indian law discourse, which also naturalizes local Indian-white hostility. The question posed in this book is: how did race relations come to be so naturalized—to seem so inevitably and inescapably conflictual—in South Dakota? I do not mean to say that we should be surprised that conflict and struggle, hate crimes, and both openly and coded racist behavior and speech, are to be found in situations of colonialism and racial inequality, for that would obviously be

12. "[AIM Activist] Calls State 'Killing Field,'" *Indian Country Today*, 4–11 October 1999.
13. U.S. Commission on Civil Rights 2000: chap. 3, p. 3.
14. "It Was No Slip of the Computer Key," *Sincangu Sun Times*, 1–15 October 1999.
15. "Indian, White Fighting Has Never Really Stopped," *Sicangu Sun Times*, 1–15 November 1999.

absurd. South Dakota whites are no more racially innocent than any other whites in America. But why should we expect racial conflict necessarily to trump all other potential conflicts—for example, those based on region, class, and gender—and to rule out solidarity and alliances *across* race lines on the basis of these other divisions? Why *deadliest* enemies? Even in twentieth-century European colonialism, the boundary between who benefits and who pays in the "contact zone"[16] was never either clear or natural, although there were continuous attempts to clarify and naturalize it. Some fractions of "the colonizers" were always prone to take seriously how much more they had in common with "the colonized" than with the colonial elites (both in terms of interests and in terms of culture), even when "the colonized" were supposedly of a "different race."[17]

In the case of Indian-white relations in North America, Richard White has named this transracial territory of shared culture and interests the "middle ground."[18] And it is worth noting that the middle ground has commonly been a "marrying ground."[19] In 1934, for example, 149 of the 1,575 married couples (9 percent) on Rosebud Reservation were composed of white men married to Lakota women, and 68 (4 percent) were composed of white women married to Lakota men.[20] The numbers are even higher today, and one source estimates that nationally almost 60 percent of Indian people are presently married to non-Indians.[21] Indeed, many older Lakota people are concerned because their grandchildren do not possess the "one-fourth (1/4) or more Sioux Indian blood" required for tribal enrollment.[22] All this marrying and mixing is significant not only because of the cross-racial commonalities built on the basis of love and family,[23] but also because "mixedblood" children necessarily undermine clear "racial" boundaries on either side of which people can "naturally" affiliate.[24] Indeed, "miscegenation" was long

16. Pratt 1992.
17. See Stoler 1989a; Stoler 1989b.
18. White 1991.
19. Nash 1999:13; Godbeer 1999.
20. Indian Census Rolls, Roll 383, Microfilm Publication M595, National Archives and Records Administration, Washington, D. C.
21. Thornton 1998:30.
22. Constitution and By-Laws of the Rosebud Sioux Tribe, art. II, sec. 1(c).
23. See Hodes 1999.
24. On the undermining of the Lakota-white race line, see Biolsi 1992:170–71; Biolsi 1995:40–42; on other cases regarding Native Americans and non-Indians, see Dippie 1982: chap. 15; Harmon 1995; on the Black-white race line, see Jordan 1974:86; Williamson 1980:73–75; Harrison 1998:622; Zack 1993:61, 163–64; on European colonial race lines, see Stoler 1989a; Stoler 1989b.

touted and administratively encouraged as the solution to "the Indian problem" because it would *erase* the Indian-white race line.[25]

In short, clearly demarcated racial division and "naturally opposed" racial interests, where they do appear as in South Dakota, are political accomplishments—always subject to undermining and breakdown—not social facts. Such apparently "natural" racial affiliation requires careful explanation. Even in the most stark situations of formal colonial racism—indeed, even under racial slavery[26]—a clear "dichotomy of colonizer and colonized" is never automatic; it requires political work.[27] This book will focus on that political work. It will question the deadliest enemies hypothesis and examine how the work of demarcating political interests along racial lines has been done by the law itself. Rather than mediating "ill feelings" between Indian and non-Indian people in and around Indian country, the discourse of Indian law has done much to *produce* racial politics and racial tensions there.

THE DISCOURSE OF INDIAN LAW

"Orientalism," writes Edward Said, is the Western colonial apparatus "for dominating, restructuring, and having authority over the Orient." Through Orientalism, Europe came "to manage—and even produce—the Orient."[28] This book will argue that Indian law is a discourse that dominates, restructures, and has authority over Indian-white relations in the United States. And like Orientalism, Indian law produces "race relations" of a particular kind—and decidedly not other kinds.

Indian law has a long history as an identifiable body of legal knowledge in the United States and continues to be an important area of federal law. Its origins are preconstitutional, rooted in medieval European law,[29] but federal Indian law was born with the creation of the new republic. The United States commenced treaty-making with Indian tribes in 1778, and, by the time the Constitution was ratified in 1788, treaties had been concluded with the Delaware, Six Nations, Wyandot, Cherokee, Choctaw, Chickasaw, and Shawnee.[30] Indians are specifically mentioned in the Constitution under the Commerce

25. See Jordan 1974: chap. 12; Biolsi 1995:40–41.
26. Higginbotham 1978:26–28; Roediger 1991:24–25.
27. Stoler 1989a:136.
28. Said 1979:3.
29. Robert Williams 1990.
30. See Kappler 1903.

Clause.[31] Congress enacted the first Indian Trade and Intercourse Act in 1790.[32] By 1832, the "Marshall trilogy" of Supreme Court cases on Indian law had been handed down, founding a long line of federal case law that continues to this day. In 1834 Congress formally defined Indian country as a legal zone, within the exterior boundaries of the United States, in which special laws apply.[33] By at least as early as 1846, "Indian" had become a specific legal status that an individual on American soil could have—or be denied—as an obligatory matter of federal law.[34] The Senate had ratified 348[35] Indian treaties by the time it stopped making treaties with tribes in 1871, but Congress continued to ratify negotiated "agreements" with tribes. These treaties and agreements constitute a substantial body of statute law that continues to have profound effect on Indian/non-Indian relations. Entire volumes of the United States Code (Title 25, "Indians," as well as a substantial chunk of Title 18, "Crimes and Criminal Procedures") and the Code of Federal Regulations (Title 25, "Indians") pertain to Indian people, and there is so much case law on Indian matters that "Indians" is one of the topical keys used to index cases in the published court case reporters found in law and college libraries all over the United States.

All of this law, of course, goes along with a literal industry of specialization in the law profession. Several law schools have specialized Indian law programs, including the University of Arizona and the University of New Mexico. At least five current textbooks are devoted to Indian law,[36] as well as growing literature in the form of law journal articles, newsletters, and even a law journal (*American Indian Law Review*, University of Oklahoma) and court case reporter (*Indian Law Reporter*, American Indian Lawyer Training Program).

But—and this is an important fact for the argument of this book—Indian law is read and practiced not only by professional attorneys. "Legal consciousness," as Sally Merry has made clear, or "legal culture," as

31. "The Congress shall have the power ... [t]o regulate commerce with foreign nations, and among the several States, and with the Indian tribes" (U.S. Constitution, art. I, sec. 8, subsec. 3).

32. 1 Stat. 137.

33. 4 Stat. 729. Indian country had its origins in the Royal Proclamation of 1763 (Shortt and Doughty, eds., 1918:163). On Indian country, see also Deloria and Lytle 1984a: chap. 3.

34. *United States* v. *Rogers*, 45 U.S. (4 How.) 567 (1846).

35. Prucha 1994:103.

36. Strickland 1982; Canby 1998; Clinton, Newton, and Price 1991; Conference of Western Attorneys General 1998; Getches, Wilkinson, and Williams 1993.

Barbara Yngvesson has shown, exists—necessarily, if differentially—among all of us, not just those professionally trained as lawyers,[37] and Elizabeth Colson has discerned a prevalent *knowledge* of the law among American Indian people.[38] Many Indian people on Rosebud Reservation in South Dakota know a great deal, and have strong reasoned opinions, about Indian law as it pertains to them; court cases, federal statutes, and Indian rights under law are commonly discussed in tribal council and other meetings and in local newspapers. "Sovereignty" and "jurisdiction" are household words among Lakota families in South Dakota. And it is not only Indian people. Many *non*-Indians who live in and around Indian country in South Dakota also know a great deal about, and intelligently comment on, Indian law as it pertains to them and their rights. Thus Indian law, as well as the rights it involves, is a distinct topic in the "public sphere" on and around Rosebud Reservation—a conversation sustained not only by judges, lawyers, litigants, and defendants but also by politicians, activists, journalists, and "everyday people." Of course, this dialogue over rights is not precisely a public sphere as that phrase was used by Jurgen Habermas to refer to an arena of free discussion unconstrained by power or inequality.[39] Obviously judges, legislators, and lawyers have a certain authority in the "conversation" under examination here. But, there *is* a public discussion, however unequal it may be, and it is the *public* nature of law that is of interest in this book.[40]

What precisely does it mean to call this dialogue, which both is "about" and sustains Indian law, a discourse? For the purposes of this book I mean four interrelated things by the term "discourse."[41] First, and most obviously, Indian law as a body of knowledge exhibits certain "discursive regularities" among all the parties to it—in terms of common assumptions and definition of objects and problematics.[42] Discourse, as James Ferguson puts it, is a "world of acceptable statements and utterances."[43] This world of acceptable statements and utterances

37. See Merry 1985, 1986; Yngvesson 1989; Merry 1990; Yngvesson 1994 [1988]; Merry 1995.

38. Colson 1974:3.

39. See Calhoun 1992.

40. Alternatively we might think of the actors here as engaged members of an "interpretive community" (Fish 1980), although not in the sense that this term is usually used in speaking of the law. In the Rosebud Reservation case, the interpretive community goes beyond the bar.

41. My reliance upon James Fergusson (1990) and Arturo Escobar (1995) will be apparent in what follows.

42. Foucault 1972.

43. Ferguson 1990:18.

is shared by all the participants in the discourse, even though they may disagree with one another other about fundamental matters. As will be seen, there are fundamental disharmonies in the discourse of Indian law, but below the level of argument is an infrastructure of common assumptions that makes engaged argument possible—even between what appear to be, and, of course, are, fundamental opponents.

Second, Indian law as a discourse has decidedly hegemonic effects. As Alan Hunt and Gary Wickham describe it, "What the concept captures is that people live and experience within discourse in the sense that discourses impose frameworks which structure what can be experienced or the meaning that experience can encompass, and thereby influence what can be said, thought and done. Each discourse allows certain things to be said, thought and done and impedes or prevents other things from being said, thought and done. . . . Discourses have real effects; they are not just the way that social issues get talked and thought about. They structure the possibility of what gets included and excluded and of what gets done or remains undone."[44] Discourses "produce what is possible to think, speak and do" in practical terms. And when a discourse is animated by a central *contest,* as is the case with Indian law, the discourse "sets up what it is that is argued over and fought about."[45]

This is not to say that discourse is an inescapable "prison house."[46] Ruth Frankenberg reminds us that discourse involves thinking and acting subjects in both "entrapment" and "conscious engagement with" elements of discourse itself.[47] While the hegemonic properties of discourse are real enough, "penetrations," as Paul Willis calls them, are always possible.[48] Penetrations may even be common, based on the concretely different experience of the subaltern relative to that of the dominant authors of discourse.[49] What Raymond Williams had to say of the related concept of hegemony applies also to discourse: it is "continually resisted, limited, altered, challenged by pressures not at all its own."[50]

44. Hunt and Wickham 1994:8.
45. Ibid., 9. See also Gordon 1984:111.
46. See Everett 1997 for a useful critique of the limitations of poststructural analysis of discourse.
47. Frankenberg 1993:140.
48. Willis 1977:126.
49. James Scott, for example, argues that critical alternatives to dominant worldviews are the *usual* state of things among the subaltern, even if they are not foolish enough to articulate these within earshot of those in power (1985, 1990).
50. Raymond Williams 1977:112.

Third, as alluded to in the quotation from Said above, discourses "can *create* not only knowledge but also the very reality they appear to describe."[51] Discourse, in other words, is not merely a matter of *representations* of—understood as "pictures" of—reality, or merely inert "speech," "text," or "rhetoric." Discourse includes these elements, but it is also *productive* of extradiscursive social reality, which in turn reinforces discourse: there is a kind of feedback between discourse and its "external" objects.[52] Said's concrete example of how this works is worth quoting in full:

> If one reads a book claiming that lions are fierce and then encounters a fierce lion . . . , the chances are that one will be encouraged to read more books by that same author, and believe them. . . . A book on how to handle a fierce lion might then cause a series of books to be produced on such subjects as the fierceness of lions, the origins of fierceness, and so forth. [A]s the focus of the text centers more narrowly on the subject—no longer lions but their fierceness—we might expect that the ways by which it is recommended that a lion's fierceness be handled will actually increase its fierceness, force it to be fierce since that is what it is, and that is what in essence we know or can only know about it.[53]

Discourse, in other words, by definition produces a "real product," not simply an illusory picture of the real, and a product that reinforces the truth and power of discourse.[54] These circuits between conceptual models of reality and the reality "out there" need to be included in our concept of discourse.

This book, then, will examine Indian-white relations as if these were "fierce lions" produced by discourse—not a natural object that precedes discourse. The focus on Indian law as a discourse will, thus, not be simply on legal texts and reasoning but on a complex circuitry involving texts, statements, practices, social arrangements, and local knowledges. This discursive formation has had a remarkable degree of temporal coherence—staying power—particularly regarding its central problematic. A wide range of differently situated actors have participated in and reproduced this discursive formation. The discourse of Indian law is not located in any one institution but rather is dispersed among a wide range of institutional settings. In this sense, no one is "in control," although different actors have decidedly different degrees of

51. Said 1979:94.
52. See, especially, Foucault 1980.
53. Said 1979:94.
54. Foucault 1980:48.

power within the discourse. The discourse has clear structuring effects over both practical thought and action, and it is productive of concrete racial interests and race relations. The central energizer of the discourse—what drives its reproduction and its racial productivity—is its principle problematic, the central unresolved question to which it perennially returns and to which we now turn.

CONTRADICTION IN FEDERAL INDIAN LAW

One of the central themes of this book is the contradiction and indeterminacy that lie at the heart of the discourse of federal Indian law—as well as the consequences of this for Indian-white "race" relations. It may well be that law in general is fraught with contradiction and indeterminacy, as scholars in critical legal studies have argued.[55] The issue here, however, concerns the *exceptional* degree of contradiction and indeterminacy in Indian law. As Philip Frickey has put it, Indian law "is characterized by doctrinal incoherence"—"[m]ore than any other field of public law."[56]

It is commonly recognized among Indian law scholars that contradiction was present at the creation of law by the colonizers for native peoples in North America. Perhaps the most obvious manifestation of contradiction was the move by which "the rights of man" were denied to native peoples. It certainly should not go without notice, for instance, that the Declaration of Independence contains a racist binary in counterpoising "all men . . . created equal" and "endowed with . . . inalienable rights" against, later in the text, the "merciless Indian Savages" of our frontiers who would be denied the rights of men—even after American expansion encompassed them within our frontiers. And there are early American legal texts that are even more explicit regarding the racial (and, therefore, legal) impediments of Indian people in the republic. In *Johnson* v. *McIntosh* (1823),[57] the first case of the Marshall trilogy (including *Cherokee Nation* v. *Georgia* [1831][58] and *Worcester* v. *Georgia* [1832])[59] that founded the basic and enduring principles of United States Indian case law, Chief Justice John Marshall

55. See, for example, Klare 1978:336; Kennedy 1979:211–15; Kairys 1982; Gordon 1984. For a recent criticism of the critical interpretation, see Solum 1997.

56. Frickey 1997:1754.

57. 21 U.S. (8 Wheat.) 543.

58. 30 U.S. (5 Pet.) 1.

59. 31 U.S. (6 Pet.) 515.

found it necessary to recognize the legal validity of the doctrine of discovery. This was the presumption of the European "right to take possession [of North America], notwithstanding the occupancy of the natives, who were heathens."[60] Indians would thus be put beyond the private property protections of the Fifth Amendment.[61] Although Marshall implicitly criticized the conceit of this theory of European dominion over Indian peoples based on an assumed cultural or racial superiority over Indian peoples, he also clearly articulated the inescapable fact that the doctrine of discovery was "the law of the land." Marshall recognized that denying native peoples the right to own the land on which they lived was "opposed to natural right," but he elevated this legal fiction, contradictory as it was, to a foundational truth "indispensable to that system under which the country has been settled."[62]

Other symptoms of this underlying contradiction of "human beings excluded from personhood"[63] are not difficult to discern in the course of American legal history. When Congress made ex-slaves—indeed, "all persons born in the United States"—citizens in the 1866 Civil Rights Act, it excluded "Indians not taxed."[64] And when it appeared that the Fourteenth Amendment (making "all persons born or naturalized in the United States" citizens guaranteed due process and equal protection of the laws in their states) might have—inadvertently?—made Indians into citizens,[65] the Supreme Court clarified the issue in *Elk* v. *Wilkins* (1884) by holding that an Indian was not a citizen, even when he had "severed his tribal relation."[66] Indian people would thus be excluded from equality before the law within this nation. It was far from an idle or merely "academic" question when a legal treatise asked in 1888: "is an Indian a person?"[67]

---

60. 21 U. S. (8 Wheat.) at 576.

61. "No person shall . . . be deprived of . . . property, without due process of law; nor shall private property be taken for public use without just compensation" (ratified 1791).

62. 21 U. S. (8 Wheat.) at 590; see Robert Williams 1990 for a survey of "the discourse of conquest."

63. Wald 1995:39. This process, of course, did not just apply to Indians. See Gotanda 1991 on race and the Constitution. See Mehta 1996 on "liberal strategies of exclusion" in general.

64. 14 Stat. 27.

65. The Fourteenth Amendment was ratified in 1868.

66. 112 U. S. 94, 95 (1884).

67. Weil 1975 [1888]:74. Although Weil was forced to answer the question in the affirmative, Priscilla Wald has quite correctly pointed out that *Cherokee* v. *Georgia* "named the Cherokees into a legal status . . . of nonpersonhood" (Wald 1995:35). On the inscription of racist difference in the law (involving Indian peoples), see Lee 1974; Robert Williams 1986, 1990; G. Edward White 1991; Deloria 1992; Asch 1993a; Harris 1993;

If Indian peoples were to be excluded from the Enlightenment's purportedly universal "natural rights," how *were* they to fit into the modern scheme of things? This was the question that the Marshall trilogy sought to answer. But the attempt to resolve the contradiction of explicit racial estates in a democracy founded on the equality of persons before the law only shifted the terrain of the contradiction. Indian nations, Marshall wrote, were "distinct, independent political communities," and "[t]he very term 'nation,' so generally applied to them, means 'a people distinct from others.' "[68] Thus, one might not expect political representation for Indians as citizens within the United States anymore than one would expect political representation in Congress for Englishmen. This was hardly a denial of the humanity of Indian people but rather a recognition of their *alien* humanity.[69] But—and here the contradiction again emerges—although they were nations distinct from the United States, Indian nations were not to take their place among "the community of nations" or "family of nations."[70] They were not *foreign* nations—that is, independent of the United States—but were "more correctly . . . denominated domestic dependent nations. . . . [T]hey are in a state of pupilage. Their relation to the United States resembles that of a ward to his guardian," Chief Justice Marshall wrote.[71]

Thus was articulated the central tension animating the history of law and policy pertaining to American Indians in the United States—a conflict between Indian people construed as members of distinct (sovereign) nations, and as people *within* the United States. Put differently, it is a conflict between treaty rights (seeing tribes and their citizens as legally *different* from other Americans and to whom different rules apply) and constitutional rights (seeing Indians as essentially the *same* as other Americans—if still "savage," "uncivilized," or "primitive"—and to whom the same rules should, and eventually must, apply). As legal scholar Frank Pommersheim puts it, the Marshall trilogy was—as,

Macklem 1993; Wald 1993, 1995: chap. 1. Deloria and Lytle point out that the assumption of guardianship over Indian peoples by the United States is not founded on any constitutional source but is based purely on the fictional representation of Indian peoples as somehow primitive or backward (Deloria and Lytle 1984a:42; see also Wilkins 1997:80). A racist discourse of "otherness" is thus foundational in U. S. Indian law.

68. 31 U. S. (6 Pet.) at 559.

69. Compare this with the attempted "resolution" of the contradiction with respect to African Americans through the positing of their essential *non*-humanity as justification for their exclusion from civil rights (Fields 1990).

70. The phrase is from Justice William Johnson's concurring opinion in *Cherokee* v. *Georgia* (30 U. S. [5 Pet.] at 27).

71. 30 U. S. (5 Pet.) at 17.

indeed, is Indian law in general—"majestically ambiguous."[72] The contradiction originates historically in Marshall's attempt to reconcile the conflicting social forces at odds over what to do about the aboriginal inhabitants within the new republic. Marshall hoped to "forge a compromise that would permit the United States to view itself as a nation under the rule of law while continuing its quest to control the continent."[73] In hindsight the Marshall trilogy, in all its contradiction, seems to have been composed by a "conqueror with a conscience."[74]

Ultimately the contradiction in federal Indian law is between preserving special laws for Indian nations—even *international* law—and eradicating all special provisions for Indians and doing away with *Indian* law as a distinct area of law as Indians become progressively assimilated into the nation. Indian law thus has the seeds of its dissolution within its own discursive terms; it is fundamentally laden with contradiction. For the purposes of this book, the contradictory[75] moments of Indian law are best summarized as a tension between *uniqueness* and *uniformity*.[76]

The tension between uniqueness and uniformity, since its emergence, has played itself out in an identifiable historical sequence, commonly understood by students of Indian law and policy as an oscillation or cycling between the two opposed principles, or more precisely, as the swinging of an imaginary Indian policy pendulum between periods of "assimilation" and "separatism."[77] During each "period," one moment of the Indian law dialectic gains dominance through political and judicial ascendancy. Thus, the last century of Indian policy in the United States is commonly divided into the following rough sequence: the "civilization" period, 1880–1934 (uniformity/assimilation); the Indian New Deal, 1934–1950 (uniqueness/separatism); the "termination" period, 1950–1968 (uniformity/assimilation); and the "self-determination" period, 1968–the present (uniqueness/separatism). None of these periods

72. Pommersheim 1995:50.
73. Norgren 1996:6; see also Shattuck and Norgren 1991.
74. Pommersheim 1995:9.
75. For a concise summary of contradiction in federal Indian law, see the opening section of Wilkins 1999; see also Clinton 1975:951, 952; 1976:576; Deloria and Lytle 1984a:33; Wilkinson 1987; Frickey 1990; Furber 1991; Shattuck and Norgren 1991; Gillingham 1993; Wilkins 1993; Prucha 1994; Pommersheim 1995:8–9, 39, 50; Wilkins 1995; Frickey 1997; Wilkins 1997.
76. Frickey 1990:1201. Closely related is the tension between separatism and assimilation as principles of policy toward Indians (Wilkinson 1987:13).
77. This is not by any means to say that the pendulum swings automatically. For analyses of the social forces involved, see Bee 1992; Nagel 1997: chap. 8.

has been politically monolithic, and the contending position remains a principled minority standpoint and textual reading in each historical period. Thus, the central contradiction in Indian law has both a binary form and a cyclical historical trajectory. The inability of debates about Indian law and policy to break out of either the binary or the cycle—as will be described in this book—is one of the characteristics of the remarkably closed discourse of Indian law.

For the purposes of this book, we pick up the historical cycle with a period during which assimilation and uniformity assumed political and interpretative ascendancy. During the "civilization" period, the assimilation of Indians through "pupilage" and "wardship" was the central assumption in both law and policy. "Civilization" was the goal and the measure of Indian policy in a wide range of institutional sites, including the Bureau of Indian Affairs (BIA), Congress, the federal courts, education, social work, ethnology, philanthropy, and missionary work.

But civilization was not a seamless worldview. Internal debates considered the pace of civilization and the best ways to promote it and measure it. Critics attempted to call it fundamentally into question, usually from positions of relative weakness, outside the institutions of power. These critics, of course, included Indian people themselves, as well as some non-Indians. The textual basis for this countervailing position was the hundreds of treaties and agreements that United States had signed with Indian tribes; the Marshall trilogy itself recognized the extra- and preconstitutional rights of Indians. When conditions in the larger political-economic context changed drastically in the 1930s and a strategic opening presented itself, a radically different vision of Indian law and policy quickly emerged and rapidly colonized the dispersed loci of power in Indian affairs in the United States.

The "Indian New Deal" rejected the assimilationist policy and uniformist legality of the civilization period and reorganized Indian affairs in the United States on the basis, not of wardship, but of "self-government" and cultural pluralism. The New Deal was, of course, no less colonial than was civilization, and it was grounded in the same discursive formation—Indian law as described above. Its premises, goals, measurements, and social imaginaries, however, were profoundly different from those of the earlier period; this in itself is an important part of the dynamic of the discourse of Indian law.

The New Deal was followed by a return to an assimilationist approach, not in the precise terms of civilization—which no longer resonated with prevailing American values—but as "equal rights," or as we might now say (albeit with some irony), a "color-blind" framework. The termination period was characterized by the goal of terminating the special legal status of Indian people and Indian tribes and assimilating them into the nation. Termination had a compelling textual basis: the constitutional guarantees of equality in which "treaties" with *American citizens* and other "special rights" for Indians appeared anomalous. How could the law recognize a nation within a nation?

Termination was followed by a turn in the history of federal Indian law and policy commonly known as the "self-determination" period, the period in which we now find ourselves. It is premised on a return to the principles of Indian sovereignty inscribed in the Marshall Trilogy and the Indian treaties and agreements, and like the New Deal, recognizes the right of Indian people and Indian nations to a "measured separatism."[78]

CONTESTED RIGHTS AND RACE RELATIONS

What is critical for this study is that law—both statutes and case law—produced during all of these periods continues to be on the books in the present. Law that was meant to do away with tribes and reservations and civilize or otherwise assimilate Indians remains in effect, as does law meant to protect and make permanent Indian treaty rights and the sovereignty of native nations. This is by no means a usual circumstance in American law, despite the contradiction and indeterminacy that critical legal scholars have persuasively found at its heart. The significance of the present state of contradiction in Indian law can best be appreciated if we contemplate what things would be like if the laws of slavery *and* the Thirteenth through Fifteenth Amendments to the Constitution[79] were equally on the books, or if both *Plessy* v. *Ferguson,* which upheld "separate but equal," and *Brown* v. *Board of Education,* which overturned it, were equally "good law" in the present.

In what follows, I will argue that uniformity and uniqueness represent not just contradictory moments in the Indian law discourse but bases of profoundly conflicting rights-claims for Indian and non-Indian people in and around Indian country. Rights conceived and organized in terms of the "uniqueness" moment in federal Indian law are fundamen-

---

78. Wilkinson 1987:4.
79. These amendments outlawed slavery, made former slaves citizens, and guaranteed civil rights against racial discrimination, respectively.

tally inconsistent with rights organized in terms of the "uniformity" moment, but each of these frameworks is readily available to interested parties because of the inherently contradiction-laden nature of Indian law, and because of the continuing effectivity of fundamentally opposed bodies of law "on the books." Every law in Indian affairs, every basis for the assertion of the rights of people in Indian country—as it turns out because of the law, the rights of Indian people *versus* the rights of non-Indians—is always already problematized because of other legally and politically compelling, but contradictory, law.

The "interested parties" described here who make use of and live with this contradiction are the Sicangu Lakota (or Rosebud Sioux) people and the non-Indians (almost all of whom are white) living on and around Rosebud Reservation in south-central South Dakota. The Sicangu Lakota settled in the area in conformity with their rights under the Fort Laramie Treaty of 1868, and they reserved Rosebud Reservation specifically by their consent to the Great Sioux Agreement, or Crook Treaty, in 1889. White settlers began to enter what they called "the Rosebud Country" in 1904, as provided for in a series of laws enacted by Congress to do away with the reservation and absorb the Lakota people into the state of South Dakota and the nation. Because of a complex history to be examined in this book, by the 1970s Indian and white people were making profoundly inconsistent rights-claims on the basis of critically contradictory laws. In fact, the conflicting rights-claims came to dominate Indian-white relations in south-central South Dakota, and the judicial and political contests came to make these two groups into deadliest enemies—at least politically speaking.

From the standpoint of race relations, the critical fact of federal Indian law is its indeterminacy regarding the basic rights of Indian and non-Indian people. Because of the contradiction in the law, litigation, judicial close calls, and judicial reversals continually well up in and around Indian country. In defense of their rights, litigants bring into court equally valid but profoundly contradictory sets of law, made—either by legislatures or courts—in different historical periods. Then begins a highly technicalized law-game[80]—technical in the sense of removal from the substantive matters of Indian and non-Indian rights involved.

80. I mean no disrespect for what lawyers and judges do in Indian law by calling it a game—indeed, on the contrary. All discourses are word-games in the sense of relying to some degree on conventional rules, self-referentiality, and necessarily arbitrary premises. But in Indian law it is the closeness of the calls, and the consistently high level of indeterminacy regarding the basic rights of people in Indian country that is noteworthy.

The basic rule of the game is that the players must assume that the laws are *not* in conflict—even though the substance of the law is clearly contradictory as far as Indian and non-Indian rights are concerned. The rule of the game is that there is a judicial answer that reconciles the simultaneous effectiveness of both sets of law and that also "settles" the particular conflict at hand. The players must assume that those who made the apparently conflicting laws *intended* them both to have legal effect in the present. The game is to assume that Indian law is coherent. The judicial choice between the laws—laws assumed to be equally "good" law—inevitably becomes a highly close call. All Indian law cases are, legally speaking, *hard* cases. A reasoned choice in such cases cannot be based on the substance of Indian law regarding the rights of people in Indian country. This is because both sides have substantive legal arguments that are equally correct and equally capable (or incapable) of trumping the other side in terms of rights-claims. Treaty rights *exist,* just as surely as do the rights of non-Indians that are in conflict with treaties. The judicial choice thus requires narrowing the legal question to a highly abstract, minute, and often obviously arbitrary, even fictional, matter. This technicalized question serves as a trip-wire for giving priority to one set of laws in the conflict. The answer to this narrow question, far removed from the substance of the Indian law, rests on very specific facts and the interpretive proclivities of the judge. Slightly different fact situations, or a judge with a slightly different interpretive framework, could easily produce precisely opposite judicial results.

Concrete rights for real people, thus, remain insecure even after cases are "settled." Litigation resolves concrete disputes only in a "thin and unsatisfying" manner.[81] The losers will always be unsatisfied with the call—which they will see as based on a *technicality*—and will argue that it is an arbitrary decision far removed from what the law "plainly" says. They will believe the judge to be "wrong," and will believe they have the law on *their side*—and their attorneys will agree. But litigation over race-based rights-claims is necessarily a zero-sum political game, in which wins for Indian people represent losses for whites, and vice versa. As the South Dakota attorney general said of Indian law litigation in 1975, "there is no such thing as a friendly lawsuit. It always creates hard feelings."[82] Indian law, thus, does not ameliorate local ill feeling or protect

81. Frickey 1997:1780.
82. "[Attorney General] Tells Solons Problems Faced by State on Indian Jurisdiction Issue," *Argus Leader,* 7 February 1975, 4.

Indian people from attacks by the people of the states. Rather, it is an incitement[83] to litigation, political struggle, and racial "hard feelings."

ROSEBUD RESERVATION AND THIS BOOK

As of 1997 the Census Bureau estimates that 7,734 Indian people live on Rosebud Reservation, along with 1,510 whites.[84] The Rosebud Sioux Tribe administers the reservation along with the state of South Dakota and its subdivisions (Todd County, and the cities of Mission and St. Francis), and the United States government (which has a presence because the reservation is legally Indian country). During the last quarter of the twentieth century, the tribe and its members have been locked in a series of court cases and political struggles with the state of South Dakota and its white citizens over how the political space of Rosebud Reservation/Todd County will be organized and even over the boundaries of the reservation itself. The history of this litigation and political struggle is the primary material of this book.

Chapter 1 examines the early history of Rosebud Reservation, from its establishment in 1889 through the New Deal period. Chapter 2 focuses on a struggle in the mid-1970s over the boundaries of Rosebud Reservation, a struggle that reached the Supreme Court before it was "settled." Chapter 3 concerns a dispute in the 1980s over the City of Mission Liquor Store, a municipal enterprise that operated in the middle of Rosebud Reservation until it was shut down by the Rosebud Sioux Tribe in 1984. Chapter 4 describes a conflict between the tribe and the state over jurisdiction on highways running through the reservation. Only after the matter had gone to the United States Court of Appeals was it "clear" that the state had no authority to exercise jurisdiction over Indian people on highways within the reservation. Chapter 5 examines the assertion of tribal civil jurisdiction over non-Indians living on the reservation, and their resistance to that jurisdiction as a violation of their constitutional rights as United States citizens. Finally, Chapter 6 returns to the central argument of the book and demonstrates how these jurisdictional disputes—generated out of the central contradiction in the Indian law discourse—produce Indian-white relations of a particular kind.

83. Foucault 1980.
84. Rosebud Reservation is here defined only as Todd County, although as will be shortly seen, that is a problematic assumption.

CHAPTER I

A Short History of Rosebud Reservation

In 1868 a group of Lakota chiefs signed a treaty at Fort Laramie that, among other things, established the Great Sioux Reservation, including all of the western half of present-day South Dakota as the "permanent home" of the Lakota. The treaty also provided that no future land cessions would be valid without the approval of three-fourths of the men.[1] By 1877, all the Lakota (except for Sitting Bull's band, which had fled to Canada) had settled on the Great Sioux, and the Rosebud Agency was established the following year for the Sicangu Lakota. In 1889 the United States negotiated—in conformity with the three-fourths rule— the Great Sioux Agreement, which established Rosebud and other reservations (Cheyenne River, Crow Creek, Lower Brûlé, Pine Ridge, and Standing Rock; see Map 1), provided for the allotment of these reservation lands to individuals, and "restored" eleven million acres outside the separate reservations to the public domain for non-Indian homesteading.[2] Although Congress ceased making treaties with Indians in 1871, agreements such as the Great Sioux Agreement were ratified by Congress and have come to be known in Indian law as treaty substitutes and have essentially the same legal force as treaties. Indeed, the Lakota sometimes call the Great Sioux Agreement the Crook Treaty, after one

1. 15 Stat. 635. On the negotiation of the treaty, see Institute for the Development of Indian Law 1974, 1975; Catherine Price 1996:77–83.
2. 25 Stat. 888. On the negotiation of the Great Sioux Agreement, see U. S. Congress, Senate 1890; Biolsi 1992:39–42.

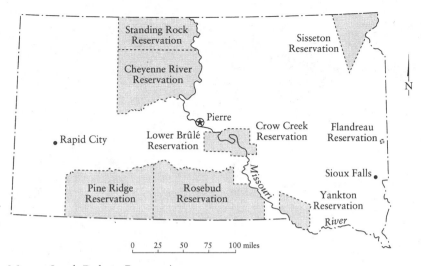

Map 1. South Dakota Reservations

of the government negotiators. Rosebud Reservation was designated as a "permanent reservation" for the Sicangu by this agreement.

But the Great Sioux Agreement, besides being a treaty, was also a manifestation of the federal policy to make such agreements with tribes obsolete—by civilizing Indians through the institution of private property, as envisioned in the General Allotment Act (or Dawes Act) of 1887.[3] The aim was to supersede "tribal relations" by empropertying Indians as individuals. By the magic of enlightened self-interest, the architects of Indian civilization argued, Indians would become farmers and discipline themselves in matters of self-support, "industry," judicious use of time and resources, and other modern habits of character. But as is well known to students of this history, allotment was not only desirable for the purpose of civilizing Indians. After Indians were allotted (at a specified acreage per individual allottee), vast tracts of "surplus" reservation land remained that could be thrown open to homesteading by the general population. This interested potential farmers from both the United States and Europe, speculators who saw an opportunity to invest in farmlands that would appreciate in value with the expanding urban demand for foodstuffs, and railroads and other concerns—large and small—that would make profits from the settlement of the West. The happy marriage of civilizing the Indians and opening the

3. 24 Stat. 388.

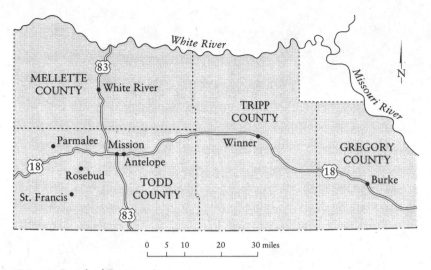

Map 2. Rosebud Reservation

western lands to non-Indians saw its best expression in the idea that settling non-Indians next to Indians actually aided Indian civilization by
providing white teachers, models, and object lessons for Indian
"pupils." It also benefited Indians because non-Indian improvements—
from fences and roads, through towns, to railroads—increased the market value of all the surrounding territory, including Indian allotments; it
was in everyone's interests to see the development of the country. Given
all this, those responsible for Indian civilization would be remiss in their
responsibilities if they did not find ways to settle non-Indians among Indian people.[4]

Allotment of Rosebud Reservation began in 1893. Under the terms
of the Great Sioux Agreement, a head of family received 320 acres, each
single person over the age of eighteen and each orphan under eighteen
received 160 acres, and each minor received 80 acres. These formulas
were later amended to provide for a division of allotments between
husbands and wives and to double the acreage allotted to children. The
first allotments were made in the eastern part of the reservation, Gregory County, "the most desirable portion" for farmers, with the highest
average rainfall (see Map 2). The original allotment work was completed by 1905, but children born to Lakota people continued to be allotted until all unallotted land had been either allotted or ceded for

4. Otis 1973; Prucha, ed., 1978; Hoxie 1984; Prucha 1984a; Biolsi 1995.

homesteading. By 1917 approximately 8,600 allotments had been made. Allotments initially had trust status, which meant that title was held by the United States in trust for the allottee, and the land was not taxable, or subject to sale, mortgage, or lease without the consent of the Secretary of the Interior.[5]

THE "SURPLUS LAND" OPENINGS

One of the clearest—hardly tacit because it was regularly enunciated—assumptions that underlay the civilization policy and its implementation in South Dakota was the proposition that Indian reservations were temporary and would eventually disappear. The policy arguments among those interested one way or another in Indian affairs was over the *timing* of reservation disappearance, not its inevitability. The assumption of reservation disappearance was commonly expressed in South Dakota boosterism, in which Indian reservations and "progress" were seen as mutually exclusive, the latter requiring the erasure of the former. The state commissioner of immigration, for example, said of the 1890 opening of "surplus lands" on the Great Sioux Reservation to homesteading that it transferred "a magnificent domain, red-peopled and virgin, from the way of barbarism to the domain of enlightened civilization": "[N]o other incident can be so potent for [South Dakota's] welfare in the future until the day shall come when the last tepee on her soil shall be struck, the last tent folded, and the last Indians shall silently steal away beyond her confines forever. There is no longer a Chinese wall across the state from north to south, stopping human enterprise and delaying the march of civilization at the Missouri river."[6]

But it was not only the boosters who assumed that the reservations must and would eventually disappear. Even those who ostensibly had the interests of Indian people in mind—the Indians' "guardians"—believed the reservations would disappear. Federal Indian policy during

5. Agent to Commissioner of Indian Affairs, 19 April 1893, Special Cases File 147, Rosebud, Record Group 75, National Archives and Records Administration, Washington, D. C.; 25 Stat. 888; Allotting Agent to Commissioner of Indian Affairs, 23 October 1893, Special Cases File 147, Rosebud, Record Group 75, National Archives, Washington, D. C.; 30 Stat. 1362; Allotting Agent to Commissioner of Indian Affairs, 29 May 1905, Special Cases File 147, Rosebud, Record Group 75, National Archives, Washington, D. C.; 34 Stat. 1230; Statistical Report, 1935, Rosebud, Superintendents' Annual Narrative and Statistical Reports, Microfilm Publication M1011, National Archives, Washington, D. C.
6. Commissioner of Immigration 1890:56.

this period was premised on the legal doctrine of wardship or pupilage enunciated in *United States* v. *Kagama*.[7] Wardship and pupilage, the raison d'être of the Bureau of Indian Affairs (BIA) and the reservation system, by definition implied that one day the "education" of the "pupil" would end—that all Indians would become citizens subject to the same laws to which all other citizens are subject and would take their place alongside their non-Indian neighbors as full and productive members of American society. The disappearance of the reservations would take place partly through more openings of "surplus" reservation lands to non-Indians as the 1889 Great Sioux Agreement had done, and partly through the issuance of deeds to allottees as they became "competent" and the trust restrictions over their allotments were removed and they became United States citizens. We turn first to the opening of surplus lands.

Pressure to open land remaining after allotment began early on Rosebud Reservation.[8] Indeed, would-be homesteaders had invalidly staked claims within the reservation during the 1890s, believing incorrectly that they were to the east of the reservation boundary. By 1901, residents of Gregory County, which straddled the reservation's eastern boundary, had pressured the South Dakota congressional delegation to persuade the Department of the Interior to seek the opening of that part of the county lying inside the reservation. A BIA inspector was detailed to negotiate for the opening, and in 1901 he reached agreement with the Sicangu. They consented to "cede, surrender, grant, and convey to the United States all their claim, right title, and interest in and to" 416,000 acres of unallotted tribal land in Gregory County for the sum of $1,040,000. The agreement was signed by 1,031 men—more than three-fourths, in conformity with the 1868 treaty. A bill was prepared by the BIA effectuating the cession, and it was presented to Congress. Both chambers balked, however, at the prospect of paying for the cession and giving the land free to homesteaders. Instead, Congress proposed merely acting as the "trustee" in collecting payment from the homesteaders and conveying it to the tribe as received.[9]

The BIA dispatched its inspector to Rosebud again to explain the new policy of Congress, but this time Lakota consent to the cession was

7. 118 U.S. 375 (1886). See Wilkins 1997: chap. 3 on the invention of the doctrine of wardship by the Supreme Court.
8. For a detailed history of the openings, see Hughes and Tobin 1973.
9. 33 Stat. 254; U.S. Congress, Senate 1901; Hughes and Tobin 1973; Lucas 1984 [1913].

not legally necessary. In the landmark 1903 *Lone Wolf* v. *Hitchcock* case,[10] the Supreme Court held that Congress had "plenary" power over Indian affairs and could, in the light of its own wisdom as guardian, abrogate treaty provisions unilaterally. This was explained to the Lakota by the inspector, although they were clearly offended by the proposition that their approval was not required. The BIA sought tribal consent as a show of the government's good faith, however, and the inspector was able to secure the signatures of 737 men (48 more than half, but 296 short of three-fourths) on an agreement by which the United States would act as sales agent. Congress enacted the Gregory County Act in 1904. The original 1901 agreement for a direct sale to the United States was appended as a preamble to the bill, and reference to *cession* by "said Indians" was included in the operative language, but the act affirmatively stated that the United States was not purchasing the land, a passage that would become crucial during the 1970s: "[N]othing in this Act . . . shall in any manner bind the United States to purchase any portion of the land herein described . . . [11] or to guarantee to find purchasers for said lands . . . , it being the intention of this Act that the United States shall act as trustee for said Indians to dispose of said land and to expend and pay over the proceeds received from the sale thereof only as received. . . ."[12]

In another passage that would come to have significance during the 1970s, Congress provided for the protection of treaty rights by declaring that "nothing in this agreement shall be construed to deprive the said Indians . . . of any benefits to which they are entitled under existing treaties or agreements, not inconsistent with the provisions of this agreement."[13] This kind of treaty-rights protection is now commonly known in Indian law as a saving clause.

It was immediately apparent that there would be many more applicants than the 2,412 available homesteads, so the General Land Office organized a lottery in 1904. The lottery drew 106,308 registrants, and entry began in the same year. "The prairie was soon dotted with

10. 188 US. 553.

11. Except for sections purchased by the United States for transfer to the state of South Dakota for common schools, in conformity with the 1889 enabling act for statehood.

12. 33 Stat. 258; *Lone Wolf* v. *Hitchcock*, 187 U.S. 553; *Minutes of a Council Held at Rosebud Agency, So. Dak.*, Roll 26, James McLaughlin Papers, Assumption Abbey Archives, Richardton, N.D.; McLaughlin to Secretary of the Interior, 31 August 1903, Roll 26, McLaughlin Papers; Hughes and Tobin 1973.

13. 33 Stat. 257.

homesteaders' shacks," and there were even "sooners" who camped out on townsite lots before the official opening. The area's economy quickly developed, and by 1907 a line of the Chicago and North Western Railway from Sioux City, Iowa, had crossed the newly opened portion of Rosebud Reservation to Gregory and was poised for the anticipated next opening to the West.[14]

Pressure to open the reservation to homesteading was hardly diminished by the opening of Gregory County lands; in fact, two towns in Tripp County—Colome and Lamro—were founded on Indian allotments even before that county was opened. Continued pressure by the South Dakota congressional delegation on the Department of the Interior resulted in the BIA inspector returning to the reservation to negotiate the opening of surplus lands in Tripp County (and a sliver of land in what would become Lyman County) in 1906. An agreement with the Sicangu—again, not required under the terms of *Lone Wolf* but desirable for purposes of getting the bill through Congress—was reached on the 838,000 acres of unallotted land, signed by 42 more than half of the 1,368 men. On the basis of the agreement, Congress enacted the Tripp County Act in 1907. The operative language provided that the Secretary of the Interior would "sell or dispose" of the unallotted lands, and the same clause exempting the government from purchase found in the Gregory County Act was included in the 1907 legislation. The act also included the same saving clause inserted into the Gregory County Act.[15]

The Chicago, Milwaukee and St. Paul Railway distributed a booster brochure titled "Opening of the Rosebud Indian Lands" which extolled the economy of South Dakota and the lands of Tripp County and explained to land-seekers how to register for the homestead lottery and how to get to the registration points from Chicago, Minneapolis, and Sioux City by railroad.[16] The lottery drew 114,769 registrants for the 4,000 available homesteads, and entry began in 1909. By 1913, Winner, the county seat, was the western terminus of the Chicago and North Western, and had three banks, seven hotels, five general stores, two hardware stores, and two men's clothing stores. As one homesteader

14. Green 1940:167–70; Casey and Douglas 1948:315; Schell 1975:254; Chambers 1984 [1913]; Jackson 1984 [1913]:19.
15. 34 Stat. 1230.
16. Chicago, Milwaukee and St. Paul Railway, 1908, Opening of the Rosebud Indian Lands, Lakota Archives and Historical Research Center, Sinte Gleska University, Rosebud, S.D.

said of the opening, "The Rosebud had been opened up and swallowed by the advancing wave of people westward."[17]

The "ink had not yet dried" on the proclamation opening Tripp County when a South Dakota senator began agitating for an additional opening.[18] In 1909 the BIA inspector once again visited the Sicangu, not to get their consent, which was not needed, but to "take up with the Indians . . . the matter of opening" surplus lands in Mellette County.[19] Although a formal agreement was not signed, the inspector reported that there was strong support among the Sicangu for the opening. Congress enacted the Mellette County Act in 1910, with the same "sell and dispose" clause, the same limitation of the role of the United States to trustee, and the same saving clause as in the Tripp County Act. In 1911 the 466,562 acres available for settlement in Mellette County were opened to homesteading.[20]

FEE PATENTING AND CHECKERBOARDING

The other mechanism by which the reservations would disappear was the process of civilizing individual Indians, by which each allottee would eventually, as he or she became "competent," be declared a citizen and have the trust restrictions removed from her or his allotment. When this happened, the allottee would, in theory, no longer be a ward, would be subject to state law as any other citizen, and her or his land would, legally speaking, no longer be different from any other citizen's land. The reservation—or at least that particular piece of it—would have literally disappeared. This was the process of assimilation envisioned in the General Allotment Act, and in order to facilitate it, Congress in 1906 passed the Burke Act,[21] which, among other things, authorized the Secretary of the Interior to issue a patent-in-fee simple for an allotment—that is, to

17. Edith E. Kohl, *The Land of the Burnt Thigh* (1938), quoted in Green 1940:176; *Proceedings of a Council Held at Rosebud Agency*, S.D., Roll 27, McLaughlin Papers; McLaughlin to secretary of the Interior, 12 February 1907, Roll 27, McLaughlin Papers; 34 Stat. 1230; Hughes and Tobin 1973; Schell 1975:254; Chambers 1984 [1913]; *Gregory Times—Advocate* 1984 [1913]; Jackson 1984 [1913].

18. Hughes and Tobin 1973:111.

19. Instructions to Inspector, 2 April 1909, quoted in Brief for Appellant-Plaintiff, filed May 1974, *Rosebud Sioux Tribe* v. *Kneip* (8th Cir., 74-1211) file, Tobin Law Office, Winner, S.D. The proposal included lands in the eastern part of what would become Todd County, but this provision was dropped from the act because of Indian resistance to the opening of Todd.

20. McLaughlin to Secretary of the Interior, 22 April 1909, Roll 29, McLaughlin Papers; 36 Stat. 448; Jackson 1984 [1913].

21. 34 Stat. 182.

TABLE I.   POPULATION OF TODD COUNTY,
BY RACE

	1910	1920	1930	1940	1950	1960	1970	1980	1990
White	231	871	3,121	2,653	2,090	1,936	1,995	1,588	1,431
Indian	1,933	1,912	2,776	3,058	2,646	2,725	4,600	5,688	6,883
Total	2,164	2,783	5,897	5,711	4,736	4,661	6,595	7,276	8,314

SOURCE: U. S. Department of Commerce, Census of Population, various years.

remove its trust status and convey clear title to the allottee—when the allottee was deemed "competent and capable of managing his or her affairs." Fee patenting made the allottee a citizen and made the allotment
fully private property; the owner had full power to sell, mortgage, or
rent the land, as well as the obligation to pay property taxes. The act also
authorized the secretary to sell or issue a fee patent for lands of deceased
allottees (which had become hopelessly fractionated by complex heirship), and the following year Congress authorized the supervised sale of
the trust land of "any noncompetent Indian" at the discretion of the secretary.[22] These mechanisms would, in theory, solve the problem of outlying allotments in the opened counties, as well as ultimately solve "the
Indian problem" in South Dakota by fee patenting the remaining undiminished reservation land (in this case, Todd County) and converting the
remaining ward Indians into citizens of the state of South Dakota (and,
of course, the United States).

Through a combination of sales by the BIA to non-Indians of allotments in heirship status or held by "noncompetent" allottees, and the
loss of fee-patented allotments to non-Indians by sale, defaulted mort-
gages, and tax sales,[23] Todd County/Rosebud Reservation quickly became "checkerboarded" with non-Indian lands, and the non-Indian
population quickly rose (see table 1) Although Todd County was an
"unorganized" county, it was a subdivision of the state of South
Dakota, where taxable land existed and where state citizens—both non-
Indians and, arguably, fee-patented Indians—were subject to state jurisdiction.[24] In 1913, Mission was platted by a non-Indian as a townsite

22. 34 Stat. 1018.
23. On fee patenting see Schmeckebier 1972 [1927]; McDonnell 1980; *A Report on
the Bureau of Indian Affairs Fee Patenting and Canceling Policies, 1900–1942*, 1981, Institute for Indian Studies, University of South Dakota, Vermillion; Hoxie 1984; Prucha
1984a; McDonnell 1991; Biolsi 1992: chap. 1, Biolsi 1995.
24. Todd County was originally attached to Lyman County for administrative and judicial purposes. In 1929 Todd was attached to Tripp County. It was organized with its
own board of county commissioners in 1981.

on a fee-patented allotment. The Mission Townsite Company was organized in 1920, and Mission incorporated as a town under South Dakota law in 1932.[25] The scene was set for jurisdictional confusion over the rights of Indians and non-Indians.

THE EVOLUTION OF INDIAN COUNTRY

THE EARLY PERIOD

From the beginning, it was clear that South Dakota did not have lawful jurisdiction over Indians in Indian country. The 1889 state constitution, pursuant to the federal act that enabled statehood,[26] has a disclaimer providing that "Indian lands shall remain under the absolute jurisdiction and control of the Congress of the United States," and that the people of South Dakota "forever disclaim all right and title to...all lands lying within [South Dakota] owned or held by any Indian or Indian tribes."[27] Furthermore, in the quasi-biblical *Worcester* v. *Georgia* decision of 1832, Justice Marshall held that an Indian nation on a reservation is "a distinct community...in which the laws of [a state] can have no force."[28] The federal government also explicitly had jurisdiction over interracial crimes in Indian country under the Indian Country Crimes Act (which was part of the 1834 Indian Trade and Intercourse Act),[29] and over major crimes committed by Indians against Indians under authority of the Major Crimes Act of 1885.[30] Although South Dakota originally had jurisdiction over crimes committed by non-Indians against non-Indians on reservations,[31] the state legislature ceded that jurisdiction in 1901 because of insufficient revenue, and Congress accepted it for major crimes in 1903.[32] "Indian Country" at the time was a clearly delineated geographic region, in which the federal

25. *A Record of the Organization and Incorporation of Mission Townsite Company,* 4 May 1920, City of Mission Office, Mission, S.D.; Order and Judgment of Acquittal, Criminal Case 3131, 9 July 1948, Appended as Supplementary Exhibit 37, Affidavit in Support of the Defendants' Motion to Set Aside the Judgement, filed October 1983, *United States* v. *Mission* (8th Cir., 82-2516) file, City of Mission Office; "A History of the Town of Mission," *Todd County Tribune,* 15 July 1965.

26. 25 Stat. 676.

27. South Dakota Constitution, art. 22; see also art. 26.

28. 31 U.S. (6 Pet.) 515, 561.

29. 4 Stat. 733.

30. 23 Stat. 385.

31. The jurisidiction was established by the U.S. Supreme Court in *U.S.* v. *McBratney* (104 U.S. 621 [1882]) and *Draper* v. *U.S.* (164 U.S. 240 [1896]).

32. South Dakota Session Laws, 1901, chap. 106; U.S. Congress, House of Representatives 1975; 32 Stat. 793.

government had authority and the state of South Dakota did not. It must have seemed as if it was *not part of* the state.

Matters quickly became complicated, however, because of the openings and fee-patenting, and by the 1920s, two jurisdictional contradictions had arisen. One was more potential than actual at the time and concerned the opened counties; the other was quite concrete and concerned Mission and Todd County. We turn first to the matter of the opened counties.

By 1913 the Rosebud Country was sufficiently settled (see table 2) that a booster could confidently write the following lyric epitaph to the Lakota: "the wilderness goeth away, the white man tilleth the soil.... The Indian quietly, peacefully, paid for his land, slowly went his way. The Hebrews came to drive away a heathen enemy; the settlers of the Rosebud Country came to supersede an ancient foe."[33] Of course, in describing what he saw as a "wondrous transformation," this author was neglecting to mention all the Indian allottees who continued to live on Indian trust land in the opened counties and who were still under the jurisdiction of the federal government—little pieces of Indian country surviving in the "Rosebud Country," as the newly opened area had come to be called by the white settlers. At the time Gregory County contained 452 allotments and 500 Indians, Tripp County 2,600 allotments and 500 Indians, and Mellette County 4,230 allotments and 1,400 Indians. This was clearly a messy fact that did not square very well with the assumption that the opened counties had been "ceded" or were no longer "part of the reservation." The Rosebud Agency of the BIA continued to treat these people as reservation Indians, and the BIA maintained operations and buildings in the opened counties. Tribal constitutions adopted in 1916, 1920, and 1924 included provisions for the representation of Indian communities in the opened counties, and the constitutions did not differentiate these communities from communities on the undiminished reservation (Todd County). The assumption among those who thought these things out, of course, was that this contradiction—continued Indian communities and trust land treated *as part of the reservation* in the opened counties that were supposedly no longer part of the reservation—would resolve itself in time as the trust lands disappeared through fee patenting or other mechanisms of converting trust into deeded land.[34]

33. Miller 1984 [1913]:2.
34. Constitution and Bylaws of the Rosebud Tribal Council, 1916, copy in author's possession; Constitution of the Rosebud General Council, 1920, and Revised Constitution

TABLE 2. POPULATION OF THE OPENED
RESERVATION COUNTIES, BY RACE[1]

Year	Gregory County[2]		Mellette County		Tripp County	
1910	White:	12,761	White:	122	White:	7,833
	Indian:	300	Indian:	1,578	Indian:	490
	Total:	13,061	Total:	1,700	Total:	8,323
1920	White:	12,388	White:	2,679	White:	11,631
	Indian:	312	Indian:	1,171	Indian:	339
	Total:	12,700	Total:	3,850	Total:	11,970
1930	White:	11,002	White:	3,809	White:	12,231
	Indian:	415	Indian:	1,471	Indian:	473
	Total:	11,420	Total:	5,293	Total:	12,712
1940	White:	9,240	White:	2,833	White:	9,501
	Indian:	314	Indian:	1,269	Indian:	430
	Total:	10,552	Total:	4,107	Total:	9,937
1950	White:	8,459	White:	2,504	White:	8,915
	Indian:	97	Indian:	537	Indian:	222
	Total:	8,556	Total:	3,046	Total:	9,139
1960	White:	7,123	White:	1,868	White:	8,279
	Indian:	276	Indian:	796	Indian:	482
	Total:	7,399	Total:	2,664	Total:	8,761
1970	White:	6,383	White:	1,591	White:	7,668
	Indian:	318	Indian:	822	Indian:	501
	Total:	6,710	Total:	2,420	Total:	8,171
1980	White:	5,768	White:	1,364	White:	6,687
	Indian:	236	Indian:	872	Indian:	569
	Total:	6,015	Total:	2,249	Total:	7,268
1990	White:	5,065	White:	1,133	White:	6,245
	Indian:	284	Indian:	999	Indian:	670
	Total:	5,359	Total:	2,137	Total:	6,924

SOURCE: U. S. Department of Commerce, *Census of Population*, various years.
1. Total may include individuals other than white or Indian.
2. Data for Gregory County include the eastern section of the county, which was never part of Rosebud Reservation.

The degree of haziness in the prevailing understanding of what was, and was not, part of the reservation is well illustrated by two maps published by the Interior Department as part of the *Annual Report of the Commission of Indian Affairs*. A 1914 map showed Todd County shaded as reservation land, and the remainder of the 1889 Rosebud

and By-Laws of the Rosebud General Council, 1924, File 101910–1922–054, Rosebud, Central Classified Files, Record Group 75, National Archives, Washington, D. C.; Brief for Appellant-Plaintiff, filed May 1974, *Rosebud Sioux Tribe* v. *Kneip* (8th Cir., 74-1211) file, Tobin Law Office; Caton 1984 [1913].

Reservation merely outlined and keyed as "opened." A 1923 BIA map again showed Todd County shaded as reservation land but depicted the remainder of the 1889 reservation crosshatched and keyed as "former" reservation land. Clearly, the BIA continued to have responsibility for this "former" or "opened" reservation area, but the legal status of this area was not specifiable—nor was it a practical question that required resolution—at the time. It is likely that the rural Indian communities in the opened counties were of little jurisdictional interest to the county governments, and when Indian people came into towns such as Winner, they were subjected to local jurisdiction without concern on anyone's part. Certainly neither the BIA nor the Rosebud Tribal Council thought that the towns of Winner or Gregory were "part of" the reservation.[35]

The real jurisdictional problem during this early period concerned the undiminished portion of Rosebud Reservation in Todd County, which was heavily checkerboarded. Non-Indian communities forming on the undiminished reservation, such as the town of Mission, had good reason to seek some kind of general jurisdiction over "all persons" within their territorial limits in order to maintain the general order when the BIA would or could not do so. Thus the South Dakota legislature enacted a law in 1929 providing for jurisdiction in Indian country concurrent with that of the United States over "any person committing any offense under the laws of the state of South Dakota." Congress was advised of this law by the governor and asked to modify federal law to grant South Dakota concurrent jurisdiction, but since Congress never acted, the effect of the South Dakota law was, as the state attorney general put it, "nugatory": "Anything the State legislature may do in the matter can in no way affect the exclusive jurisdiction of the Federal Courts." This state statute, however, remained on the books and was included in the 1939 revision of the state code.[36]

But fee patenting had opened another possibility for the assertion of state jurisdiction within the reservation. Although the state might not legally have jurisdiction over Indians in Indian country—as was clear enough in the state constitution—the question was whether deeded land within the exterior boundaries of the diminished reservation was Indian country and whether fee-patented Indians were, legally speaking, Indi-

35. U. S. Department of the Interior, *Annual Report of the Commissioner of Indian Affairs*, 1914; U. S. Department of the Interior, *Annual Report of the Secretary of the Interior*, 1923.

36. South Dakota Session Laws, 1929, chap. 158; *Biennial Report of Attorney General*, 1939–40:507; South Dakota Code, 1939, chap. 34.0502.

ans. The United States District Court entertained the geographic question in *United States* v. *Black Spotted Horse* (1922).[37] The defendant, a
member of the Rosebud Sioux Tribe, had been charged in federal court
with murder, but his attorney argued that since the offense had taken
place on fee-patented land which the federal government had "parted
with its title to," the alleged crime was not subject to federal jurisdiction. The court rejected this argument, insisting that federal jurisdiction
remained on any reservation, notwithstanding the issuance of a patent
in fee. While recognizing that "the Indian title is being rapidly extinguished [in the West], and . . . we may reasonably expect in the near future, such progress as to leave few, if any, Indian reservations in existence," Rosebud Reservation had yet to be "abolished" by Congress,
and fee patents did not affect federal jurisdiction over Indians (and, implicitly, the exemption of Indians from state jurisdiction). Thus did the
federal court deny that checkerboarding had any impact on the Indian
country status of the land in question.[38]

THE INDIAN NEW DEAL

But there was not to be a final withering away of the reservations, trust
land, or the special legal status of Indians or tribes. In one of the more
remarkable shifts in the history of federal Indian policy, President
Franklin Roosevelt appointed John Collier commissioner of Indian Affairs in 1933, and Congress enacted the Indian Reorganization Act (IRA)
in 1934.[39] The IRA halted the allotment of Indian lands, provided for
the restoration of alienated lands to trust status, and authorized reservation Indian people to establish tribal governments operating under federally recognized constitutions with the force of law. It was, as historian
Francis Paul Prucha puts it, the "antithesis" of the General Allotment
Act and its vision of the disappearance of reservations.[40] After the passage of the IRA and its application to Rosebud Reservation, the trust status of reservation land became permanent (and fee patenting, although
not legally prohibited, would no longer be pursued administratively),
and fractionated heirship lands would be returned to tribal ownership,
not sold to non-Indians. The reservation land base, in short, would be ex-
panded and permanently protected as Indian country. What this meant is

37. 282 F. 349.
38. Ibid., 351.
39. 48 Stat. 984. See Biolsi 1992 on the IRA among the Lakota.
40. Prucha 1984b:263.

that the earlier process of the disappearance of the reservation, which had proceeded substantially during many years of fee patenting and checkerboarding, was frozen in time before it could be completed under the auspices of the now defunct civilization policy. What is more, a tribal constitution was ratified by the voters on Rosebud Reservation in 1935, and the Rosebud Sioux Tribal Council was established in 1936. Thus was set in place a permanent tribal government and a permanent reservation with Indian country status, eventualities few people, Indian or non-Indian, South Dakotan or Washingtonian, could have imagined when fee patents were issued during the early part of the twentieth century. This tribal government would eventually come to demand *territorial* jurisdiction within the reservation. Whatever "solution" to checkerboarding could now be envisioned, it would not amount to doing away with reservations, Indian country, or Indian tribes as legal entities.[41]

Because after the IRA Indian title was no longer being "rapidly extinguished" and the reservations would not disappear in the "near future"—the solution to checkerboarding that the district court had envisioned in 1922—the Court of Appeals for the Eighth Circuit reconsidered the effect of fee patenting on jurisdiction within the reservation in its 1943 *Kills Plenty* v. *United States* opinion. The case involved Rosebud Sioux tribal members charged in federal court with theft of an automobile in Mission. The defendants demurred in the district court on the ground that Indian title had been extinguished on land in the townsite of Mission, even though it was within the exterior boundaries of Rosebud Reservation. The demurrer was overruled and they were convicted. The appeals court found that federal jurisdiction covered Indian country in South Dakota "regardless of the ownership of the lands upon which the crimes were committed."[42]

A revision of the United States Code by Congress in 1948 also made clear that Indian country jurisdiction was not affected by fee patenting or by the penetration of state highways within reservation boundaries. The statute defined Indian country to comprise, inter alia, "all land within the limits of any Indian reservation under the jurisdiction of the United States Government, notwithstanding the issuance of any patent, and, including rights-of-way running through the reservation."[43]

41. Biolsi 1992.
42. 133 F.2d 292, 293.
43. 62 Stat. 757. The 1948 revision also returned to the state jurisdiction over crimes committed on South Dakota reservations by non-Indians against non-Indians. The state accepted this relinquishment of jurisdiction in 1951 (62 Stat. 758; *State ex. rel. Olson* v.

Of course, both *Kills Plenty* and the 1948 act were—in practice—problematic. Just as the white booster who had claimed that "the Indian went away" was ignoring the continued existence of trust land in the opened counties, so both the *Kills Plenty* court and Congress were pretending that whites had not moved into the reservations in significant numbers. It is instructive to note that whites constituted fifty-three percent of the Todd County/Rosebud Reservation population in 1930, forty-six percent in 1940, and forty-four percent in 1950.

The IRA would also—eventually, during the 1970s—have implications for the opened counties. The existing pieces of outlying trust land did not disappear through fee patenting, and the IRA even provided for returning to tribal ownership any remaining surplus lands not sold to homesteaders. Furthermore, the Rosebud IRA constitution of 1935, like the earlier tribal constitutions, provided for the representation of Indian communities in the opened counties and specifically stated that the jurisdiction of the tribal council extended to the reservation boundaries established by the 1889 Great Sioux Act—that is, "the reservation" was to include the "opened" counties. This assertion would be the basis of serious conflict during the 1970s.[44]

CONCLUSION

Thus, by the end of the New Deal, the scene had been set for serious jurisdictional conflict, both within Todd County and within the larger confines of the 1889 reservation. Two legal fictions had been instituted by the operation of federal law. First, Todd County was imagined in law to be a reservation—Indian country—as if the presence of thousands of non-Indian citizens, their property, and their businesses and communities had no bearing on the reality of Indian country. Second, the opened counties were imagined to be no longer reservation, as if the presence of hundreds of Indian people living on thousands of acres of trust land and who saw themselves as Rosebud Sioux had no bearing on matters.

Although the latter fiction would not cause problems until the 1970s, the first fiction had immediate repercussions for local people. How did the residents of Todd County live with the insistence that all of the county—including the city of Mission—was in Indian country? They

---

Shoemaker 39 N. W.2d 524 [S. D. S. Ct., 1949]; South Dakota Session Laws, 1951, chap. 187.

44. Constitution and By-Laws of the Rosebud Sioux Tribe, 1935, art. I, art. III, sec. 2.

simply ignored that troublesome (legal) fact. Neither the *Black Spotted Horse* (1922) and *Kills Plenty* (1943) decisions, nor the 1948 congressional definition of Indian country, had any effect on what the Todd County sheriff and the city of Mission had been doing from the beginning: *exercising* criminal jurisdiction over Indians. Mission and Todd County exercised criminal jurisdiction over Indians on the undiminished Rosebud Reservation from at least as early as 1921, as is clear from state circuit court records examined by the author.[45] It is not clear whether they were simply ignorant of, or chose to ignore, federal law. Even the South Dakota attorney general was oblivious to *Black Spotted Horse* when he held in 1940 that the state had jurisdiction over Indians when the crime was committed on fee-patented land.[46] He also opined that a fee-patented Indian assumes "the full rights and responsibilities of citizenship and is subject, like any other person, to the laws of the state wherein he resides."[47] Indian people might have had some question about the assertion of state jurisdiction within the reservation, but Indian defendants seldom had sufficient legal counsel. And in terms of policy, no doubt many assumed—the IRA notwithstanding—that it was only a matter of time before trust land, Indians, and reservations disappeared as legal entities and solved whatever jurisdictional questions existed in Todd County,[48] in the same way that these erasures would solve any question remaining about Indian trust lands in the opened counties. Both Mission and Todd County continued, when it suited their purposes, to assert jurisdiction over Indian people in Mission, on highways, and over fee-patented Indians anywhere on the reservation.

One 1957 issue of the *Todd County Tribune* gives an example of what state law was being enforced on Indians in its list of convictions of tribal members in Mission Municipal Court (held under a justice of the peace):

1. Stealing a blanket from a truck—10 days in jail, $10.00 fine, $5.70 court costs.

2. Disturbing the peace—10 days in jail, suspended if $10.00 fine and $5.70 court costs paid.

45. Todd County court records are stored in the Lyman County Courthouse, Kennebec, for the period to 1929, and in the Tripp County Courthouse, Winner, from 1929 to the present.

46. *Biennial Report of Attorney General,* 1939–40:483.

47. Ibid., 212.

48. Of course, it remains an interesting historical question, albeit difficult to answer with the sources available, as to whether Lakota people also assumed that the reservation and Indians would "disappear."

3. Intoxication—$10.00 fine and $5.70 court costs.

4. Intoxication and disturbing the peace—10 days in jail, $10.00 fine, $5.70 court costs.

More serious cases, such as driving under the influence, were initiated in the municipal court but were ultimately heard in the state circuit court in Winner. None of these convictions, of course, were lawful, but this illegality is one way local non-Indians dealt with the conflict between the law pertaining to Indian country and the reality of life in South Dakota.[49]

49. "In Municipal Court," *Todd County Tribune*, 13 June 1957. The rationale— erroneous as a matter of federal law—behind these assertions of state jurisdiction over Indians on the reservation may have been based on the 1929 assumption by the state of concurrent jurisdiction—which even the state attorney general had said was ineffective. It may have been based on the attorney general's 1940 opinion that fee-patented Indians were subject to state law (*Biennial Report of Attorney General, 1939–40:480*). It also may have been based on a 1951 state statute that accepted jurisdiction held by South Dakota before it was ceded to the United States in 1901 and 1903, and relinquished by the United States back to South Dakota in the 1948 revision of the United States Code. This jurisdiction, of course, did not grant any jurisdiction over Indians, but the statute added: "In the absence of treaty or statute of the United States, the state of South Dakota shall have jurisdiction to arrest, prosecute, convict, and punish any person committing any offense under the laws of the state of South Dakota on any Indian Reservation or in the Indian country" (South Dakota Session Laws, 1951, chap. 187). This last provision caused at least some local state officials to assume that they had jurisdiction over Indians in Indian country. The sheriff of Shannon County on Pine Ridge Reservation, for example, argued that the 1951 law was the basis of state jurisdiction over tribal members on the reservation (*High Pine*, 99 N.W.2d 40 [S. D. S. Ct., 1959]). Some may also have erroneously believed that Public Law 280 (see pp. 104–5) had automatically transferred jurisdiction to the states. The reasoning of local officials and judges also may have been based on the opinions of the South Dakota attorney general. In addition to his opinions on state jurisdiction over fee-patented Indians and fee land mentioned in the text, he also opined in 1951 that the state had jurisdiction over crimes that are not the "exclusive jurisdiction" of the federal government; the question of exclusivity is a complex one not likely to be brought up in circuit court or seen by judges, state's attorneys, justices of the peace or officials as bars to jurisdiction, prosecution and conviction in minor cases (*Biennial Report of Attorney General, 1951–52:299*). State judges and local officials would have had copies of, and would likely have been familiar with, state codes and reports of the attorney general. They would have been less likely to place credence in (or even to have been aware of)) federal appeals court holdings, such as *Kills Plenty*, or other challenges to state jurisdiction unless the case had been made into an issue by an attorney defending an Indian client; local attorneys were no more likely to have been well acquainted with federal decisions. Indeed, an individual who had been active in state law enforcement during the 1950s told me that local officials assumed that the state had concurrent jurisdiction over all crimes that were not covered by the Major Crimes Act.

The first judicial test of these local assertions of state jurisdiction over Indians in Indian country was the South Dakota Supreme Court case of *Petition of High Pine*, which interpreted the effects of what some claimed was the state's 1951 assumption of jurisdiction in Indian country, and treated the question of state jurisdiction under Public Law 280. An Oglala Sioux tribal member had been arrested within Pine Ridge Reservation for public intoxication and sentenced by the justice of the peace to ten days in jail. He filed a

It would not be long, however, before Indian people became aware—
acutely aware—of their rights under federal law, and that awareness
would foreground the contradiction of a town like Mission in the midst
of Indian country. It greatly exacerbated racial tensions between Indian
and non-Indian people. We will examine this in chapter 3, but we turn
first to the contradiction of little patches of Indian country in the
opened counties.

---

petition for a writ of *habeas corpus,* questioning the jurisdiction of the justice of the
peace. The state circuit court held that the justice did not have jurisdiction, and the sheriff appealed to the state supreme court. He claimed that the 1951 act of the South Dakota
legislature was the basis of the state's jurisdiction. The state supreme court noted, however, that congressional reports accompanying Public Law 280 made it clear that in 1953
South Dakota *did not* have jurisdiction in Indian country. The intent of the state legislature in 1951, the court concluded, was not to extend jurisdiction over Indians but to remove any uncertainty about the resumption of jurisdiction over non-Indians ceded by
South Dakota to the United States in 1901 (99 N. W.2d 38). There is no evidence that this
decision had any effect on the arrest and conviction of Indians on Rosebud Reservation.

CHAPTER 2

Rosebud Sioux Tribe v. Kneip

Reservation Boundaries and Legal Rights

In April 1972, two young attorneys from South Dakota Legal Aid[1] attended a Rosebud Sioux Tribal Council meeting. They proposed that the tribe seek a declaratory judgment in federal court that the reservation had not been diminished by the county-opening acts; that Rosebud Reservation contained all the land within the original 1889 boundaries; and that Mellette, Tripp, and parts of Gregory and Lyman counties were still within Rosebud Reservation. The attorneys explained the precedents and legal reasoning for such a suit, and they pointed out that a favorable ruling would require the Bureau of Indian Affairs (BIA) to extend police protection and tribal court coverage into the outlying communities. It would exempt tribal members from the state sales tax and from state criminal jurisdiction in the opened counties. It would also expand the effect of BIA traders' licenses: merchants in the opened counties who dealt with Indians would be required to have BIA licenses. An unfavorable holding, on the other hand, would simply leave things as they were.[2] Thus, the council members were advised that they had everything to gain and nothing to lose in a suit. The

1. South Dakota Legal Aid, funded by the federal Office of Equal Opportunity, set up offices in Rosebud in February 1964 ("Rosebud News," *Todd County Tribune*, 10 February 1966).

2. "Tribal Council Okays Legal Action So Federal Court Can Set Boundary," *Todd County Tribune*, 4 May 1972.

council adopted a resolution directing the attorneys to seek a declaratory judgment.[3]

Rosebud Sioux Tribe v. *Kneip*[4] had a profound impact on political relations between Indian and non-Indian people. Prior to *Kneip,* most Lakota people had few dealings with whites in the opened counties. To be sure, Lakota families resided in the opened counties, and many Lakota families both on the reservation and in the opened counties went to Winner and White River to shop. But there was no *political* content to race relations.[5] Indeed, most Lakota people were no doubt largely oblivious to whites in the opened counties and did not come in contact with them except for occasional business dealings—and vice versa. Certainly, prior to 1972 the Rosebud Sioux Tribal Council never discussed non-Indians in the opened counties, and the county and city governments in the opened counties never discussed "the reservation" or "Indian tribes." From the point of view of the county and city governments, Indian tribes were no more than "miscellaneous bumps on the horizon,"[6] and much the same could be said about the tribal view of the opened counties.

Kneip transformed—by directly politicizing—relations between Indians and whites across south-central South Dakota. It did not take long for Lakota people to realize that the suit could mean a revolution in treaty rights, in particular their restoration: if the Rosebud Sioux Reservation was restored to its original bounds as laid out in the 1889 agreement, Indian people would be free from the jurisdiction of South Dakota and its subdivisions throughout the opened counties. And as the ideology of *sovereignty* emerged, the implications of restoring the 1889 reservation boundaries took on even more political significance. Not only would the state of South Dakota, the counties, and such cities as Winner and White River not have authority over Indians, but the Rose-

---

3. Resolution 72-51, 26 April 1972, Rosebud Sioux Tribal Office, Rosebud, S.D.

4. Richard Kneip was the governor of South Dakota from 1971 to 1979.

5. Other litigation during the 1970s took a different route to politicizing Indian-white relations. In 1971 South Dakota Legal Aid filed a class action suit against the city of Winner, claiming "invidious discrimination" on the part of the city for failing to construct and maintain adequate streets, lights and utilities in "Indian town" (*Fire* v. *Winner,* Civ 71–22W, D. S.D., 1972, John Simpson Law Office, Winner, S.D.). In 1975 Indian citizens in Todd County won the right to vote for the county commissioners who provided services to them. See *Little Thunder* v. *South Dakota,* 518 F.2d 1253 (8th Cir., 1975). This suit was also brought by Legal Aid. These kinds of civil rights cases were eclipsed, however, by the *Kneip* case and others based on treaty rights, not civil rights. For an important early statement of the distinction, see Deloria 1985 [1974].

6. Wilkinson 1987:23.

bud Sioux Tribe could claim authority over all those thousands of non-Indians living, farming, ranching, and operating businesses in the opened counties. Taking the tribe's argument seriously meant a radical reorganization of legal rights—who had authority over whom, and who could claim what rights in which political and judicial forums.

Non-Indians living in the opened counties quickly became aware of the possibility that they might be "put back into" Rosebud Reservation, and many feared the prospect. There was, to begin with, the concern that the state subdivisions would no longer have jurisdiction over Indians. As one of my white informants recalled, "what they were afraid of was . . . that they wouldn't have control over Indians, that suddenly if two Indian fellows get in a fist fight on Main Street of Winner that the . . . city police couldn't arrest them." Beyond criminal jurisdiction, civil matters were a prominent concern: businesses worried that they could not enforce contracts, collect on defaulted loans or bad checks, or repossess liened property.

Some non-Indians had grave concerns about tribal jurisdiction over whites. A white resident of Winner recalled his fears: "[T]he tribe could go into . . . Winner and say to the lawyer, 'You're doing business on the reservation. Your license will cost you one dollar a year.' Second year, 'five thousand,' or, second year, 'Give us your 1040, and we will assess a rate.' They also talked about the possibility of the tribe having [criminal] jurisdiction over . . . non-Indians . . . if those original [reservation boundaries] could be re-established. . . . And of lot of this scared me." Another white informant recalled the fear

> that "they'll tax us: . . ."; the operative word there is "they," meaning the tribe, and there was an absolute distrust of the tribe's ability to govern. . . . I was taken aback on a couple of occasions by . . . the depth of the passion, because, "by God," they "weren't going to be an Indian reservation, I homesteaded this land, and God damn it. . . . " [One group] was almost to the point of hysteria about "we could be just like Todd County, and there won't be any law and order." . . . It was the tribe taking over. That's what they saw. They saw it as the tribe taking over.

Indeed, an attorney from Gregory wrote to the governor in 1974:

> Last night I watched on TV a program entitled "The Winds of Change." I was appalled by the approach of most of the Indians questioned in the documentary, that the tribal governments in and around Indian reservations could have some jurisdiction over non-Indians. The people on this program suggested that Indian tribes are asserting the power to impose taxes on non-Indians as well as the power to subject them to the tribal jails and tribal court

systems. Such assertions are getting very close to home and affect me personally as the Rosebud Sioux Tribe is claiming that Gregory and Tripp Counties are under their jurisdiction.

The correspondent asked that the governor take a stand on the matter of tribal jurisdiction over non-Indians, particularly in Gregory and Tripp counties.[7]

Some non-Indians—and Indians—even believed that a finding in favor of the tribe in the *Kneip* case would return homesteaded land to the tribe. While this was not correct legally speaking, it was apparently articulated by some Indian people and was a source of concern to white people in the opened counties. One tribal member was reported to have walked into a bank in Winner and told the manager that "she would be living in his home inside of two years."[8]

In their answer to the complaint filed by the Rosebud Sioux Tribe in *Kneip,* the governor and state attorney general articulated what must have been the commonsense understanding of most whites in the opened counties regarding *their* rights: "[N]o white person would have settled within, homesteaded, and applied and accepted a patent to land in the disputed area, were he to believe, or were he told at the time of so acting that his patented land remained within the boundaries of the Rosebud Sioux Indian Reservation, under the control of the Congress of the United States, any of its authorized agents, and any authorized tribal council or other governing body of the Rosebud Sioux Tribe."[9]

This situation, marked by profoundly contradictory (racially based) rights-claims, was a direct result of the freezing in time of the allotment process noted in the previous chapter. Reviewing the history of allotments, the Supreme Court observed recently in another South Dakota case that "[a]lthough formally repudiated with the passage of the Indian Reorganization Act in 1934 . . . , the policy favoring assimilation of Indian tribes through the allotment of reservation land left behind a lasting legacy. The conflict between the modern-day approach to tribal self-determination and the assimilation impetus of the allotment era has

7. Attorney to Kneip, 16 September 1974, Law Enforcement on Reservations File, Box 179, Richard Kneip Papers, Richardson Archives, University of South Dakota, Vermillion.

8. As reported by a United States senator from South Dakota (Opening Statement, Rapid City Meeting on Jurisdiction, 30 November 1974, Indian Materials File, Box 287, Richard Kneip Papers, Richardson Archives, University of South Dakota, Vermillion).

9. Answer of Defendants, 16 October 1972, in Appendix, Vol. 1, *Rosebud Sioux Tribe v. Kneip* file, Tobin Law Office, Winner, S. D.

engendered"[10] a series of "jurisdictional quandaries."[11] These quandaries drove litigation that eventually reached the Supreme Court. An attorney representing the state described the consequences of the *Kneip* case for South Dakota race relations as "tearing the guts out of our state."[12]

CONTEMPORARY RESERVATION BOUNDARIES

In January 1972 the United States Court of Appeals for the Eighth Circuit in St. Louis handed down its decision in *City of New Town* v. *United States*.[13] The city had sought a declaratory judgment that a 1910 act opening a portion of the Fort Berthold Reservation in North Dakota to settlement[14]—the part in which the city of New Town is located—had removed that land from the reservation. The complaint was filed in response to a 1970 opinion of the Department of the Interior solicitor stating that the opened sections of the reservation were still part of the reservation and that, therefore, the city as a subdivision of the state of North Dakota did not have criminal or civil jurisdiction over Indians within city limits. The United States District Court found that the 1910 act had not altered reservation boundaries, although it had opened part of the reservation to settlement, and that the city of New Town was in Indian country.

The court of appeals grounded its interpretation of the 1910 statute on three principles of United States Supreme Court precedent. First, once a reservation is established, all of its lands remain part of the reservation unless removed by Congress. Second, "the purpose to abrogate treaty rights of Indians is not to be lightly imputed [by the court] to Congress."[15] And finally, "[t]he opening of an Indian reservation for settlement by homesteading is not inconsistent with its continued existence as a reservation," as the Supreme Court opined in *Seymour* v. *Superintendent*, in finding that a 1906 act of Congress opening the Colville

10. *South Dakota* v. *Yankton Sioux Tribe*, 522 U. S. 329, 339–40.

11. Ibid., 333.

12. "Rosebud Boundary Case Heard in Supreme Court," *Todd County Tribune*, 20 January 1977.

13. 454 F.2d 121.

14. 36 Stat. 455.

15. 454 F.2d at 125. The opinion cites the ruling of the United States Supreme Court in *Menominee Tribe* v. *United States* (391 U. S. 404 [1968]), in which the Court took a restrained view of the effects of congressional termination of Menominee Reservation upon other Menominee treaty-based rights (hunting and fishing rights).

Reservation in Washington to homesteading had not had the effect of "wiping out" the Indian-country status of the land.[16] To reach its finding, the court of appeals reasoned that "[t]he right to have the reservation boundaries undiminished carries with it many important subsidiary rights, among them the right for unemancipated Indians to be subject only to federal and tribal jurisdiction. The 1910 Act specifically recognized that the opening of the reservation for homesteading was not intended to deprive the Indians of any rights not inconsistent with the Act, and as *Seymour* established, homesteading is not inconsistent with the maintenance of the original reservation boundaries. The 1910 Act clearly by its own terms does not purport to alter the reservation boundaries."[17] The *New Town* decision had a clear and direct bearing on Rosebud Country. Shortly after the opinion was handed down, the BIA superintendent at Rosebud wrote to the BIA area office asking, in light of *New Town* and other cases, "what portions of the original Rosebud Reservation remain...as the 'undiminished Portion' of the present Rosebud Reservation?"[18] The Department of the Interior field solicitor responded to the inquiry in April 1972 and applied the three principles enunciated in *New Town* to the acts opening Gregory, Tripp (and a sliver of Lyman), and Mellette counties. The 1904 Gregory County Act made no mention of diminishment nor did it provide that the land would be made part of the public domain. The same was true of the 1907 Tripp County Act. The 1910 Mellette County Act was more complicated: it included the phrase "on the diminished reservation" to refer to Todd County, but it also situated Mellette County "on said reservation." Furthermore, the Mellette County Act was passed by Congress only two days before the Fort Berthold Act examined in *New Town*: "The Fort Berthold decision," the Interior Department's field solicitor reasoned, "clearly indicates the intent of Congress at such time in history." In other words, Rosebud Reservation still consisted of all the territory laid out in the 1889 Great Sioux Agreement, notwithstanding the opening of tracts in several counties to homesteading—at least in the opinion of the Interior Department's field solicitor.[19]

By June 1972—when the *Kneip* suit was filed—the United States District Court for the District of South Dakota had decided *Condon* v. *Erickson* (1972), a case that raised another critical question about reserva-

16. 368 U.S. 351 (1962).
17. 454 F.2d 126.
18. Superintendent to Area Director, 23 February 1972, Rosebud Sioux Tribal Office.
19. Field Solicitor to Area Director, 6 April 1972, Rosebud Sioux Tribal Office.

tion boundaries. The case involved a tribal member who was convicted in state court of rape in Eagle Butte, within a section of Cheyenne River Reservation opened to homesteading by Congress in 1908. The tribal member filed a petition for a writ of *habeas corpus* with the district court.[20] Although the language of the 1908 act seemed to imply that the reservation had been diminished, under *New Town* mere implication was not sufficient. Cheyenne River Reservation, the court reasoned, had been established by a treaty-substitute—the 1889 Great Sioux Agreement—as a "permanent reservation," and the 1908 act specifically provided that nothing in the act would deprive the Indians "of any benefits to which they are entitled under existing treaties or agreements not inconsistent with the provisions of this Act." Since one of the benefits that tribal members received under the 1889 agreement was freedom from state jurisdiction on the reservation, it was not reasonable to assume that this treaty right was abrogated simply by Congress's opening the reservation to non-Indian homesteading. The court granted the appellant's petition for a writ of *habeas corpus*. Prospects must have looked very good from Rosebud, where the opening acts had been very similar to the 1908 Cheyenne River opening act.[21]

THE DISTRICT COURT CASE

The Rosebud Sioux Tribe's complaint against the state and the four counties[22] argued that "[a]ll of the Rosebud Reservation, as described in the Sioux Treaty of 1889 is still 'Indian Country' as defined by the laws of the United States, and none of the three homestead Acts, allowing non-Indian homesteads within the Rosebud Sioux Indian Reservation, reduced the size of the Rosebud Sioux Indian Reservation."[23] The tribe went on to detail its claims more specifically:

> Within the areas of "Indian Country" of the Rosebud Sioux Indian Reservation, the Plaintiff has exclusive criminal jurisdiction, excepting those crimes

20. The petition for a writ of *habeas corpus* had been denied by the South Dakota Supreme Court (*Condon v. Erickson,* 182 N. W.2d. 304 [1970]) and by the United States District Court. On appeal, however, the Court of Appeals for the Eighth Circuit ordered the district court to reconsider the writ on the question of jurisdiction (*Condon v. Erickson,* 459 F.2d. 663 [1972]).

21. *Condon v. Erickson,* 344 F. Supp. 777, 779.

22. The suit involved four counties rather than three, because part of the land opened by the 1907 Tripp County act now lies in Lyman County.

23. Complaint, filed 30 June 1972, *Rosebud Sioux Tribe* v. *Kneip* (D. SD.), No. 001337, 19720630, National Indian Law Library, Boulder, Colo.

defined in [the Major Crimes Act], over all Indians to the exclusion of the jurisdiction of the Defendants. . . .

. . .

[W]ithin the areas of "Indian Country" of the Rosebud Sioux Indian Reservation, the Plaintiff has exclusive jurisdiction over all civil matters affecting Indians to the exclusion of the jurisdiction of the defendants.[24]

The central legal question in the case was discerning the "intent of Congress" regarding reservation boundaries in opening the counties to homesteading in 1904, 1907, and 1910. The question came down to this because of the central premise in Indian law that Congress has *plenary power* over Indian affairs. The plenary power doctrine has two components: (1) Congress can abrogate treaty rights or make other decisions affecting the rights of a tribe without consulting the tribe because tribes and their members are wards; and (2) Indian affairs in the United States are a *political* matter, not a *judicial* one: the courts have no business investigating the propriety of congressional decisions in Indian matters, and must assume that Congress acts with utmost good faith toward its wards.[25]

But how was the court to decide what Congress "intended?" The tribe argued in its brief that the court should concentrate on the language and internal logic of the acts themselves, in comparison with the language of other surplus lands acts that had been construed by other courts. The congressional acts at issue in *Kneip* were essentially the same as those considered by the federal courts in *Seymour, New Town,* and *Condon;* those decisions had held that the acts did not diminish the reservations involved. Among other things, the statutes analyzed in *Seymour, New Town,* and *Condon* included the same provision contained the three Rosebud acts—"identical clauses" that made it "indisputable that the United States was acting only as the trustee of the Indians for the disposition of some of their lands. . . . Since this was explicitly a trust relationship, beneficial title to all the opened lands remained in the tribes, until and unless the entrymen perfected their entries, or until and unless some other disposition was made." An agreement that would have involved a cession of Gregory County lands by the tribe to the

24. Amended Complaint, filed 25 August 1972, *Rosebud Sioux Tribe* v. *Kneip,* Civil Case 72-3030 (D. S D), Federal Records Center, Denver, Colo.
25. The plenary power doctrine was laid out most clearly in *Lone Wolf* v. *Hitchcock,* 187 U. S. 553 (1903), but for a concise statement regarding its role in reservation boundary cases, see *South Dakota* v. *Yankton Sioux Tribe,* 522 U.S. 329 (1998). For critical analyses of the doctrine, see Williams 1988 and Wilkins 1997.

government had been negotiated in 1901, but Congress, the tribe noted, never ratified that agreement. Rather, the 1904 Gregory County Act represented a new legislative policy, under which lands were not purchased from tribes; rather, reservations were opened to home-steading, with the government acting as broker. The opened lands were never placed in the public domain; they simply moved, homestead-by-homestead, from tribal ownership to each settler, as he or she perfected the individual claim and completed payments. Reservation boundaries had never been altered, and land had never been ceded by the tribe to the United States.[26]

The three Rosebud acts as well as the statues at issue in *New Town* and *Condon* also contained clauses guaranteeing and preserving Indian rights not expressly inconsistent with the statutes themselves. The tribe argued that "Congress is certainly capable of making its intent clear to disestablish a reservation and restore it to the public domain." In the absence of such language, however, the rights-preservation provision compelled an assumption that Congress had not intended to disestab-lish a reservation, an action that would have constituted a clear viola-tion of Indian rights guaranteed in earlier statutes (in the Rosebud case, the 1889 Great Sioux Agreement).[27]

Although the governor and state attorney general as defendants had filed an answer to the tribe's complaint, they did not file a brief in the case, probably because there were votes at stake. The governor and at-torney general were Democrats, and, by 1972 a substantial number of Indian voters in the state had started to switch allegiance from the Re-publican to the Democratic party. Mounting a robust defense in the *Kneip* case risked alienating Democratic Indian voters; failing to sup-port the defense strongly would only alienate the white (largely Repub-lican) voters in the four counties. In a state where a few thousand votes can decide an election, a Democratic incumbent could not afford to ig-nore his Indian constituents.

On the local level, however, the non-Indians in the four counties in-volved had a great deal to lose if the tribe prevailed in the suit. Several concerned citizens in Winner felt that the defense could not be left in the hands of the Democratic governor's and attorney general's offices, and they organized a committee to work on the defense of the four counties. The committee met with the county commissioners, explaining that the

26. Plaintiff's Brief, filed 22 December 1972, *Rosebud Sioux Tribe* v. *Kneip* (Civil Case 72-4055), No. 001337, 19720818, National Indian Law Library.
27. Ibid.

case would likely reach the Supreme Court, and the commissioners agreed to pay for legal counsel based on the assessed valuation of each county. The committee retained an attorney, made some suggestions regarding legal strategy (concentrating on legislative history), and the attorney for the counties hired a law student in Washington to work on research. As one informant put it, "we were fighting for our lives, we felt, business-wise. We didn't want to become a [city like] Mission."

The attorney for the four counties filed a lengthy reply to the tribe's brief, arguing that analyzing the intent of Congress in the acts needed to go beyond the texts of the acts themselves into reconstructing the historical context in which they were enacted. The counties conceded that recent federal decisions had construed similar acts as having not diminished other reservations, but they pointed out that "none of these decisions has been made in light of either an adequate legislative history of the particular act under consideration or the historical origin of the acts in general." The brief suggested that the language of the acts was not clear in and of itself on the question of diminishment. Linguistic constructions suggesting both continued reservation status ("on, in, within") and diminishment ("former, heretofore") could be found in the acts in question and in subsequent acts. In the context of the legislative history, however (and particularly the committee reports and the remarks on the floor of Congress), the congressional intent became clear: the legislators obviously believed that they were diminishing the reservation.[28]

The counties insisted, in opposition to the tribe, that there had not been a fundamental change in how Congress opened surplus reservation lands: from 1904 onward, as had been true earlier, opening involved cession, extinguishing Indian title by restoring lands to the public domain and thus diminishing the reservations. What had changed was only the method of paying tribes for the lands. Congress had begun to resist the idea of the government paying outright for Indian lands, but the goal was the same as it had been before: "to remove and separate the [lands] from the [reservation] in such a manner that they would never again be considered to be either within the exterior boundaries of the reservation or subject to whatever powers the Rosebud Sioux Tribe might lawfully exercise therein." There was clearly a continuity of policy reflected in the language and provisions of the acts, the statements by federal officials, the personnel who negotiated the agreements, and

28. Brief for the Four Counties, *Rosebud Sioux Tribe v. Kneip* (Civil Case 72-4055), 18A-3, Tobin Law Office.

so on. Reports accompanying the bills referred to the acts as changing the size and shape of the reservation. For example, a Senate report stated that the Gregory County bill would leave Rosebud Reservation "compact and in a square tract and a reservation about equal in size to the Pine Ridge Reservation."[29]

The counties also argued that the boundary changes being urged by the tribe would imperil non-Indians residing in the four counties. A finding in favor of the tribe would, in fact, be "much to the detriment of the non-Indian settlers and their descendants, who will nearly sixty years later suddenly find themselves within the exterior boundaries of a reservation and subject to tribal jurisdiction."[30]

The tribe's reply brief challenged the counties' argument that the acts must be interpreted against the background of historical context reconstructed with archival and other extrinsic materials: "before a Court can look behind a statute to find its meaning there must be some doubt as to its meaning on the face of the statute." There was no doubt as to the meaning of the act when one examined the saving clause and the provision limiting the role of the United States to that of trustee. And in any event, the historical material presented by the other side evidenced not an intent to eradicate the reservation per se, but a "desire for land"; thus, the legislative history was indeterminant regarding the question of jurisdiction.[31]

The fears of county officials in Tripp, Mellette, and Gregory that they might be "put back into" the reservation were not unfounded. In 1973 the Court of Appeals for the Eighth Circuit handed down its decision in the *Condon* appeal, sustaining the district court's holding that Cheyenne River Reservation had not been diminished. Declining to go beyond the text of the act into its history, the court wrote "[w]e cannot say that the 1908 Act on its face affected the exterior boundaries of the reservation, although it is a close question." The language of the act was nearly "identical to other contemporaneous acts held not to have changed the boundaries" of reservations.[32] However, the act's language was sufficiently distinct—in its use of the terms "diminished" and "public domain"—to give the court pause. In the final analysis, however, the court held that when the meaning of the language is in doubt, an act should be

29. Ibid.
30. Ibid.
31. Plaintiff's Reply Brief, filed 14 August 1973, *Rosebud Sioux Tribe* v. *Kneip* (Civil Case 72-4055), No. 001337, 19730427, National Indian Law Library.
32. *Condon* v. *Erickson*, 478 F.2d 684, 687 (1973).

construed so as to favor federal jurisdiction (that is, to favor the tribe, not the state), "unless Congress has *expressly or by clear implication* diminished the boundaries."[33] A staff report prepared by the South Dakota Task Force on Indian-State Government Relations[34] in September 1973 extrapolated from *Condon* that it was "reasonable to assume that all of the areas within the original boundaries of the Pine Ridge, Rosebud, and Lower Brûlé Reservations will be found to still be Indian country."[35]

Another important reservation boundary question that was decided while *Kneip* was pending in district court concerned Sisseton-Wahpeton Reservation (formerly Lake Traverse Reservation). The Eighth Circuit's *Feather* v. *Erickson* involved *habeas corpus* proceedings on behalf of twenty-two Sisseton-Wahpeton tribal members incarcerated in the state penitentiary. This decision struck down the decisions of the South Dakota Supreme Court[36] and the United States District Court[37] on the Sisseton-Wahpeton boundaries. Surplus land on the reservation was opened to homesteading by an act of Congress in 1891, ratifying an agreement by which the tribe agreed to "cede, sell, relinquish, and convey" the surplus lands to the United States.[38] The court of appeals reasoned[39] that in 1891 Congress was well aware of what language to use in an act in order to terminate a reservation, and it had not clearly done so in the case of the Sisseton-Wahpeton Reservation. Nor did the legislative history or subsequent legislation demonstrate an intent to terminate the reservation. In short, "Congress established the Lake Traverse reservation as a 'permanent' reservation in 1867. Since that time Congress has not through clear expression or by innuendo shown an intention to disestablish."[40] The court of appeals' holding that the state had no jurisdiction over the alleged crimes of the twenty-two tribal members forced their release from the penitentiary.[41] Clearly, the

33. Ibid., 689 (emphasis in original).

34. The task force was authorized by the legislature and was appointed by the governor in 1973 to study potential solutions to jurisdictional problems and propose legislative remedies.

35. Staff Report on Taxation, September 1973, Taxation—Sales Tax File, Subject Files, Task Force on Indian-State Government Relations, Location 540, South Dakota State Historical Society, Pierre.

36. *Application of DeMarrias,* 91 N. W.2d 480 (1958); *State* v. *DeMarrias,* 107 N. W.2d 255 (1961).

37. *DeMarrias* v. *South Dakota,* 206 F. Supp. 549 (1962).

38. *Feather* v. *Erickson,* 489 F.2d 99, 100 (1973).

39. In line with *Mattz* v. *Arnett,* 412 U. S. 481 (1973).

40. 489 F.2d at 102.

41. Task Force Attorney to Chairman of House Taxation Committee, 20 February 1974, Indian Material File, Box 287, Kneip Papers.

county commissioners and non-Indians in Gregory, Lyman, Mellette, and Tripp counties had good reason for concern.

The district court reached its decision in the *Kneip* case in February 1974 and wrote a detailed and highly technical memorandum in support of its holding.[42] Significantly, the court did not limit itself to comparing the language of the Rosebud acts with the language of other surplus land acts considered by other courts, as had been urged by the tribe. Rather, following the logic of the defendants' brief and citing as authority the ruling in *Feather* by the court of appeals (which had in turn cited the Supreme Court in *Mattz* v. *Arnett*),[43] the district court assumed that the "surrounding circumstances and legislative history" were appropriate material for consideration beyond the text and internal evidence of the act itself.[44] The court noted that one of the reports on the bills shed light on the intent of Congress by referring to the reservation that would remain after the cession as a square tract: a "quick glance at the map" the court argued, "will show that Gregory County must be *removed* to provide a 'square tract.'"[45] "It is difficult to read the House and Senate debates and reports," the court insisted, "without coming to the conclusion that the 1904 Act was an attempt to 'do away' with the Rosebud Reservation in Gregory County. That purpose simply seems to be an assumption upon which all actions were taken and statements premised."[46] True, it was not possible to find "an express discussion of state versus federal jurisdiction over the lands in question. However, the whole tenor of the discussion in Congress convinces this Court that the purpose was to 'do away' with the reservation in this area."[47] It was also the case, the court reasoned, that the Lakota believed that the act removed Gregory County from the reservation. In discussions in 1906, for example, a Lakota spokesman named High Pipe referred to Tripp County as the *eastern* part of the reservation.

The 1907 Tripp County Act and the 1910 Mellette County Act represented a continuation of the policy behind the Gregory County Act. The same kinds of documentary and internal evidence are apparent as in the case of the Gregory County Act. The court found persuasive evidence in a House report accompanying the Mellette County Act, which

42. *Rosebud Sioux Tribe* v. *Kneip*, 375 F. Supp. 1065.
43. 412 U.S. 481 (1973).
44. 375 F. Supp. at 1067.
45. Ibid., 1071.
46. Ibid., 1072.
47. Ibid., 1074.

explained that if passed the act would leave a reservation remaining of one million acres—Todd County: "There is little question from reading this House Report that the House of Representatives contemplated a diminished reservation by not only the 1910 Act, but the acts passed in 1904 and 1907 as well."[48]

The court recognized the profound interests at stake in the question before it: the decision would have "great political, social, cultural and economic effects" for a large portion of the state of South Dakota. This served as a basis for a holding of laches, or justifiable expectations, as urged by the governor, attorney general, and counties: "From the time these acts were passed," the court concluded, "these counties have been treated as outside the Rosebud Sioux Reservation by the settlers, their descendants, the State of South Dakota and the federal courts."[49]

In the final analysis, however, the court held that the clear intent of Congress *at the time of the acts* was dispositive, notwithstanding subsequent changes in federal Indian policy, federal Indian law, and notions of social justice: "There can be little doubt but that the members of Congress coveted the Indian lands. This Court must determine the intent of Congress as it existed at the turn of the century. Time and again the Indians were given reservations, only to have the settlers' need for land mandate a redefining of the reservation boundaries. While this Court does not necessarily agree with the mores or methods employed at that time, there is little doubt that the congressmen were engaged in the process with the 'doing away' of the reservations. This Court's only function is to determine Congressional intent, not to rewrite history."[50]

THE *KNEIP* APPEAL

The district court's holding was met with disbelief by the Rosebud Sioux Tribal Council. At a meeting in February 1974, one member of the council wondered aloud "how much the Judge was paid to make this decision." Resolutions were adopted calling upon the Justice Department, the Secretary of the Interior, and the Interior Department's solicitor to intervene and join in an "all-out effort" to appeal the district court decision.[51] New counsel, the Washington firm handling the Sioux Nation Black Hills claim, was retained for the appeal.

48. Ibid., 1079.
49. Ibid., 1084.
50. Ibid., 1084.
51. Minutes, 26 February 1974, Rosebud Sioux Tribal Office.

Although Indian people on Rosebud Reservation were concerned about the loss of Indian country status, by the summer of 1974 non-Indian people throughout South Dakota were growing concerned about the possibility of "newly restored" reservations (see table 3).[52] The Court of Appeals for the Eighth Circuit had reversed federal court decisions regarding the boundaries of Cheyenne River and Sisseton-Wahpeton, holding in 1973 that these reservations had never been diminished (*Condon* v. *Erickson*[53] and *Feather* v. *Erickson*[54]), and even the South Dakota Supreme Court now held that Standing Rock Reservation had not been diminished (*State* v. *Molash*).[55] Residents of the four opened Rosebud counties were understandably worried about what might happen in the court of appeals or in the Supreme Court. The extent of concerns among non-Indians was made clear to me by a white resident who recalled seeing a South Dakota highway map released by the Standard Oil Company while the *Kneip* case was pending. The map showed Indian country, printed in *red*, extending from Pine Ridge Reservation "clear to the Missouri River"—the opened Rosebud counties shown as *on* the reservation: "There was a lot of talk and fuss about that." My informant said that if he had lived in Tripp County he would have sued Standard Oil "for showing me as on that reservation."

One concern of non-Indian citizens was that the tribes would attempt to assert jurisdiction over non-Indians in the newly restored reservations.[56] A new Rosebud Sioux tribal administration was pushing a broader notion of tribal self-government: a government, in the strictest sense of the word, with territorial jurisdiction over all persons within its territory like that of any other government. The Rosebud Sioux tribal code was amended in 1974 to assert jurisdiction "over all offenses when committed by any person" and "over all suits wherein the defendant is a resident" within the original reservation boundaries. The code also provided for the forcible removal of any nonmember who "commits a crime under the Federal or tribal laws" or who "is deemed by the Rosebud Sioux Tribal Court...a person of undesirable character."[57] These provisions became effective in August 1974 and were

52. Kneip to Correspondents, 27 August 1974, Indian Affairs File, Box 11, Kneip Papers.

53. 478 F.2d 684 (1973).

54. 489 F.2d 99 (1973).

55. 199 N.W.2d 591 (1973).

56. Kneip to President, 10 September 1974, Indian Affairs File, Box 11, Kneip Papers.

57. Excerpts from Rosebud Sioux Code of Justice, Appendix A, Reply Brief, January 1977, *Rosebud Sioux Tribe* v. *Kneip* file (United States Supreme Court), Tobin Law Office.

TABLE 3. SOUTH DAKOTA RESERVATION BOUNDARY CASES

Year	Case	Holding
	Cheyenne River Reservation	
1911	*U. S.* v. *Laplant* U. S. Dist. Ct. 200 F. 92	Reservation diminished
1925	*State* v. *Sauter* S. D. S. Ct. 205 N. W. 25	Reservation diminished
1963	*State* v. *Lafferty* S. D. S. Ct. 125 N. W.2d 171	Reservation diminished
1965	*State* v. *Barnes* S. D. S. Ct. 137 N. W.2d 683	Reservation diminished
1972	*Condon* v. *Erickson* U. S. Dist. Ct. 344 F. Supp. 777	Reservation not diminished
1973	*Condon* v. *Erickson* U. S. Ct. App. 479 F.2d 684	Reservation not diminished
1977	*Stankey* v. *Waddell* S. D. S. Ct. 256 N. W.2d 117	Reservation diminished
1978	*U. S.* v. *A Juvenile* U. S. Dist. Ct. 453 F. Supp. 1171	Reservation diminished
1979	*U. S.* v. *Dupris* U. S. Ct. App. 612 F.2d 319	Reservation not diminished
1980	*State* v. *Janis* S. D. S. Ct. 317 N. W.2d 133	Reservation diminished
1984	*Solem* v. *Bartlett* U. S. S. Ct. 465 U. S. 463	Reservation not diminished
	Pine Ridge Reservation	
1957	*Putnam* v. *U. S.* U. S. Ct. App. 248 F.2d 292	Reservation not diminished
1959	*Hollow Horn Bear* v. *Jameson* S. D. S. Ct. 95 N. W.2d 181	Reservation diminished
1966	*Swift* v. *Erickson* S. D. S. Ct. 141 N. W.2d 1	Reservation diminished

TABLE 3. *(continued)*

Year	Case	Holding
	Pine Ridge Reservation	
1974	*Cook* v. *S. D.* S. D. S. Ct. 215 N. W.2d 832	Reservation diminished
1975	*Cook* v. *Parkinson* U. S. Dist. Ct. 396 F. Supp. 473	Reservation diminished
1975	*Cook* v. *Parkinson* U. S. Ct. App. 525 F.2d 120	Reservation diminished
	Rosebud Reservation	
1974	*Rosebud Sioux Tribe* v. *Kneip* U. S. Dist. Ct. 375 F. Supp. 1065	Reservation diminished
1975	*Rosebud Sioux Tribe* v. *Kneip* U. S. Ct. App. 521 F.2d 87	Reservation diminished
1975	*State* v. *White Horse* S. D. S. Ct. 89 S. D. 196	Reservation diminished
1977	*Rosebud Sioux Tribe* v. *Kneip* U. S. Sup. Ct. 430 U. S. 584	Reservation diminished
	Sisseton-Wahpeton Reservation	
1958	*App. of DeMarrias* S. D. S. Ct. 91 N. W.2d 480	Reservation diminished
1961	*State* v. *DeMarrias* S. D. S. Ct. 107 N. W. 2d 255	Reservation diminished
1962	*DeMarrias* v. *S. D.* U. S. Dist. Ct. 206 F. Supp. 549	Reservation diminished
1973	*DeCoteau* v. *Dist. Cnty. Ct.* S. D. S. Ct. 211 N. W.2d 843	Reservation diminished
1973	*Feather* v. *Erickson* U. S. Ct. App. 489 F.2d 99	Reservation not diminished
1975	*DeCoteau* v. *Dist. Cnty Ct.* U. S. S. Ct. 420 U. S. 425	Reservation diminished

(continued)

TABLE 3. *(continued)*

Year	Case	Holding
	Standing Rock Reservation	
1972	*State* v. *Molash* S. D. S. Ct. 199 N. W.2d 591	Reservation diminished
1976	*U. S.* v. *Long Elk* U. S. Dist. Ct. 410 F. Supp. 1174	Reservation diminished
1977	*U. S.* v. *Long Elk* U. S. Ct. App. 565 F.2d 1032	Reservation not diminished
	Yankton Reservation	
1964	*Wood* v. *Jameson* S. D. S. Ct. 130 N. W.2d 45	Reservation diminished
1973	*State* v. *Williamson* S. D. S. Ct. 211 N. W.2d 182	Reservation diminished
1984	*State* v. *Thompson* S. D. S. Ct. 355 N. W. 2d 349	Reservation diminished
1995	*Yankton Sioux Tribe* v. *Southern Missouri Waste* *Management Dist.* U. S. Dist. Ct. 890 F. Supp. 878	Reservation not diminished
1996	*Yankton Sioux Tribe* v. *Southern Missouri Waste* *Management Dist.* U. S. Ct. App. 99 F.3d 1439	Reservation not diminished
1997	*State* v. *Greger* S. D. S. Ct. 559 N. W.2d 854	Reservation diminished
1998	*Yankton Sioux Tribe* v. *Gaffey* U. S. Dist. Ct. 14 F. Supp. 2d 1135	Reservation not diminished
1998	*South Dakota* v. *Yankton* *Sioux Tribe* U. S. S. Ct. 522 U. S. 329	Reservation diminished
1999	*Yankton Sioux Tribe* v. *Gaffey* U. S. Ct. App. 188 F.3d 1010	Reservation diminished

reported on the front page of the *Winner Advocate*—below an article explaining the tribe's appeal of the *Kneip* case in the Eighth Circuit.[58] The extent to which tribes had jurisdiction over the actions of non-Indians remained unsettled until the Supreme Court's 1978 *Oliphant* v. *Suquamish* decision (see pp. 148–52); given these uncertainties, non-Indians had cause to be concerned about what these assertions of tribal jurisdiction would mean for them.[59]

Non-Indians were also worried about tribal civil and regulatory authority. When the Rosebud Sioux Tribal Council adopted a liquor ordinance and attempted to enforce it on the grounds of the Mission Golf Club in 1972, the *Winner Advocate* reported the action on the front page in language that must have alarmed non-Indian residents of Winner.[60] Clearly, non-Indians in the opened counties were concerned about tribal jurisdiction over them—what they saw as violation of their basic civil rights. One Gregory correspondent advised the governor in 1974: "I can't see myself as a citizen of the United States have [sic] to pay taxes to a foreign nation within a nation. Our forefathers came to America to get away from the strictness of the British rule and now the same thing is happening here in South Dakota where the Tribe thinks we are going to pay taxes to them. . . . I just can't believe that this can be happening. . . . The ranchers and farmers and people who live in these towns paid for their land, etc., and have worked the fields and in their homes, and now if somebody wants they can come along and tax us, take our home or burn them, and we have nothing to say about the whole matter. This is very sickening."[61]

Another concern was that the BIA police and tribal courts would be unable to provide adequate law enforcement over Indian people in areas removed from state jurisdiction and restored to Indian country status.[62] The Eighth Circuit's 1973 *Feather* decision had restored Sisseton-

58. "Non-Indians Now Subject to Tribal Law; Appeals Court to Hear Indian Jurisdiction Case," *Winner Advocate,* 11 September 1974.

59. Why non-Indians should have been any more concerned about tribal jurisdiction over them they were about city, county, state, or federal jurisdiction over them is another question, which will be addressed in chapter 5.

60. "Tribe Seeks to Control Liquor on the Reservation," *Winner Advocate,* 30 August 1972.

61. Gregory Correspondent to Kneip, 25 September 1974, Law Enforcement on Reservations file, box 179, Kneip Papers.

62. Attorney to Kneip, 16 September 1974, Law Enforcement on Reservations file, box 179, Kneip Papers; The White House to Kneip, 19 September 1974, Law Enforcement on Reservations file, box 179, Kneip Papers; Assistant Attorney General to Congressman, 18 October 1974, Law Enforcement on Reservations file, box 179, Kneip Papers.

Wahpeton reservation and resulted in the release of Indian inmates from the state penitentiary. The concern of non-Indians about law and order was heightened by "civil disturbances" in these restored reservation areas (in particular, protests and incidents led by the American Indian Movement [AIM] and other groups). For residents of Tripp County, developments in the city of Mission—located in the middle of Rosebud Reservation—were a example of what could happen if the county was restored to Rosebud Reservation. In June 1974 the *Winner Advocate* ran the headline "AIM Leader Involved in Fracas at Mission," describing how AIM had caused serious bodily injury to two county law enforcement officers at the Mission Golf Club. The article pointed out that because Mission was on the reservation, the local authorities were "powerless to do anything."[63] As the governor (encouraged by the South Dakota Department of Public Safety)[64] put it in a telegram to the U. S. president: "This is to advise you of an increasingly serious and volatile situation developing on and around South Dakota's Indian reservations. Legal restraints created by federal law and federal court decisions severely restrict the ability of local and state law enforcement to deal with growing lawlessness in reservation areas. Fearful citizens threaten to take the law into their own hands unless they can be assured of law enforcement protection which can only be provided by federal authorities."[65] The Department of Public Safety was concerned that the Federal Bureau of Investigation and the United States marshals, who had criminal jurisdiction over Indians in the newly restored reservation areas and in Indian country generally, had indicated an "unwillingness to assume a paramilitary posture in future civil disorder situations,"[66] a posture that some residents of South Dakota believed was a necessary response in the wake of AIM's 1973 occupation of Wounded Knee.

In October 1974, Civil Liberties for South Dakota Citizens (CLSDC), a lobbying group, was formed in the town of Martin (in Bennett County, which was in the midst of a series of cases over the diminishment of Pine Ridge Reservation). Its founding was provoked by concerns that "law and order have broken down" on the reservations, such

63. *Winner Advocate,* 26 June 1974.
64. Secretary of the Department of Public Safety to Governor, 20 August 1974, Law Enforcement on Reservations file, box 179, Kneip Papers.
65. Governor to President, 22 August 1974, Indian Affairs file, box 11, Kneip Papers.
66. Department of Public Safety Draft of Governor to President, 20 August 1974, Law Enforcement on Reservations file, box 179, Kneip Papers.

as incidents of arson, in which ranchers' haystacks were set on fire.[67] Although the boundary question was not seen as the sole root of the problem, it was a central issue.[68] The ultimate purpose of the group was "to promote the uniform protection of constitutional liberties and property rights of all South Dakota citizens, regardless of race, creed, color or religion and to promote uniform and equal application of civil and criminal laws to all citizens in South Dakota."[69] CLSDC's president was quoted: "The day may come when both Indians and non-Indians can take the shells out of their guns,"[70] a reference to the apparent need for law-abiding citizens to protect themselves, given the perceived failures of law-enforcement in Indian country. CLSDC held a meeting of concerned citizens in Winner in December 1974, attended by 250, no doubt worried about, among other things, the pending appeals court decision in the *Kneip* case.[71] A Tripp County chapter of the organization was organized,[72] along with twenty-two other county chapters. CLSDC claimed more than two thousand members by February 1975, when it adopted a resolution at its state-wide meeting calling on the president and Congress to exclude opened reservation areas from the statutory definition of "Indian country"—a legislative resolution of the *Kneip* controversy.[73]

The boundary issue was also aired at a meeting in Rapid City in November 1974, convened by one of South Dakota's United States senators who chaired the Subcommittee for Indian Affairs. In addition to speaking of the general problems of assertion of tribal jurisdiction over non-Indians and of insufficient law enforcement on the reservations, he addressed the concerns of non-Indians in opened counties: "if one understands that non-Indians who have lived on lands they believed in good faith to be under state jurisdiction, who now find themselves under tribal and federal jurisdiction, which is totally strange and inadequate to

67. "Law Situation on Reservations Aired at Rapid City Meeting," *Winner Advocate,* 23 October 1974.

68. United States Commission on Civil Rights 1978, 124–25.

69. "Civil Liberties Group to Meet in Winner," *Todd County Tribune,* 12 December 1974.

70. "66 'Civil Liberties for SD Citizens' Formed," *Todd County Tribune,* 7 November 1974.

71. "Civil Liberties Meeting Draws Large Crowd," *Winner Advocate,* 18 December 1974.

72. "Civil Liberties Group to Meet," *Winner Advocate,* 22 January 1975.

73. CLSDC also sought a congressional limitation of tribal jurisdiction so that it extended only over Indian people ("Civil Liberties Group Adopts Resolutions at State Meeting," *Winner Advocate* 12 February 1975).

their needs, it is easier to understand the apprehensions under which they now live."[74] Approximately six hundred people (including Indians) attended a meeting called by the senator in Winner in January 1975. He assured the crowd that contrary to the misconception held by some, a finding in favor of the tribe by the court of appeals would not mean that "the land will go back to the Indians." Title to land and property would not be affected by the holding. An attorney from Gregory County spoke for many, however, when asked about recent tribal assertions of jurisdiction over non-Indians and the authority of the tribe to remove non-Indians from the reservation. A holding by the appeals court that the opened counties were still part of the reservation clearly had implications for non-Indians. The senator told the crowd: "I will try my best not to let any drastic change happen that will affect this area."[75]

In the midst of the *Kneip* appeal, the Supreme Court handed down its decision in *DeCoteau* v. *District County Court,* reversing the Eighth Circuit's holding in *Feather* that the Sisseton-Wahpeton Reservation had not been terminated: the reservation had, indeed, had its boundaries erased. The decision had clear implications for the *Kneip* case. The Court held unambiguously that historical reconstruction beyond the text of the act can be factored into the analysis of the intent of Congress. The decision examined the "familiar forces" of history that "work[ed] upon" the land base of Sisseton-Wahpeton Reservation soon after it had been established by treaty: "A nearby and growing population of white farmers, merchants and railroad men began urging authorities in Washington to open the reservation to general settlement."[76] As an example, the Court quoted from a letter to the secretary of the interior from a South Dakota banker asking that the reservation be opened for development.

The Court also considered the language of the act, however: what the act *said* and what it *did* as a legal instrument. The act originated in a treaty-substitute, which had been signed by a majority of the adult male members of the tribe and ratified by an 1891 act of Congress, by which the tribe agreed to "cede, sell, relinquish and convey to the United States all their claim, right, title and interest" in the unallotted lands. This language was, the Court insisted, "precisely suited" to cede the

74. Opening Statement, Rapid City Meeting on Jurisdiction, 30 November 1974, Indian Materials file, box 287, Kneip Papers.

75. "Indian-State Jurisdiction Problems Aired at Meeting," *Winner Advocate,* 8 January 1975.

76. 420 U.S. 425, 431.

land to the government and restore it to the public domain and for that reason differed from that in the acts that had been analyzed by the Court in *Mattz*[77] and *Seymour*[78] to determine that surplus land acts had not diminished other reservations. The act at issue in *Mattz* had not been based on any negotiations with the tribe but had merely declared the reservation lands "subject to settlement, entry, and purchase" under the homestead laws and authorized allotment to tribal members. "[T]he 1891 Act before us," the Court noted, "is a very different instrument. It is not a unilateral action by Congress but the ratification of a previously negotiated agreement, to which a tribal majority consented. The 1891 Act does not merely open lands to settlement; it also appropriates and vests in the tribe a sum certain... in payment for the express cession and relinquishment of 'all' of the tribe's 'claim, right, title and interest' in the unallotted lands. The statute in *Mattz*, by contrast, benefitted the tribe only indirectly, by establishing a fund dependent upon uncertain future sales of its land to settlers [that is, the government acted as trustee, not purchaser]." The statute at issue in *Seymour* was also unilateral, and like *Mattz*, it "merely opened the reservation land to settlement and provided that the uncertain future proceeds of settler purchases should be applied to the Indians' benefit."[79] In short, the explicit language of the Sisseton-Wahpeton act, its legislative history, and the "surrounding circumstances," all pointed to the fact that the reservation had been terminated.[80]

The Court of Appeals for the Eighth Circuit considered briefs from the *Kneip* parties on the relevance of the Supreme Court's *DeCoteau* opinion[81] and affirmed the district court *Kneip* decision in July 1975. The court of appeals was convinced by the four counties of the appropriateness of going beyond the language of the act to engage in historical reconstruction to arrive at congressional intent: "We have reviewed with care the pressure for opening, the legislative histories of the Acts, their content, provisions, and contemporaneous construction, as well as their subsequent treatment and interpretation. Against this background it is clear beyond reasonable question that the Acts were passed with the

77. 412 U.S. 481 (1973).
78. 368 U.S. 351 (1962).
79. 420 U.S. at 448.
80. Ibid., 445.
81. Memorandum of the United States, filed April 1975, *Rosebud Sioux Tribe* v. *Kneip* file, Tobin Law Office (The United States had intervened on behalf of the Rosebud Sioux Tribe as amicus curiae); Supplemental Brief for Appellee, filed April 1975, *Rosebud Sioux Tribe* v. *Kneip* file, Tobin Law Office.

intent of doing away with the Reservation in those portions affected by the opening of the lands for entry and settlement. The boundaries were thus necessarily altered."[82] The court cited *DeCoteau* as authority for consulting "all materials reasonably pertinent to the legislation," including "those bearing upon the historical context...such as the social forces then at work in the area and particularly the demands of our westward moving society."[83] The tribe was simply incorrect in its assumption that there must be "express language" of diminishment for a surplus land act to have that effect. "Precise verbal formulae of extinguishment or alteration of boundaries...are not a *sine qua non* of disestablishment," and congressional intent "may be variously expressed."[84] Although there was much documentary evidence that the congressional intent—and, indeed, the intent of the Sicangu—had been to diminish the reservation, the court could find no historical evidence to support the tribe's contention that the openings were intended to leave the reservation boundaries intact: "Such an intention is utterly foreign to the entire tenor of the contemporary materials before us. The land was being thrown open for farming. The settlers were emigrating in great numbers to the new land in the West, buying their farms and planting their crops. The Indian reservations were being eroded, not preserved."[85]

THE SUPREME COURT CASE

The tribe petitioned the Supreme Court for a writ of *certiorari* in October 1975.[86] After the Supreme Court granted *certiorari*, the litigants—the United States, ten states, and numerous Indian tribes and advocacy organizations—filed briefs. Essentially the same arguments that had exercised the lower courts—textual language versus historical context—were rehearsed in the Supreme Court case. The four counties did, however, make explicit for the Court the dangers that a holding for the tribe would pose to non-Indians. First, the counties argued, the loss of state jurisdiction would create grave problems for law and order. South

82. *Rosebud Sioux Tribe* v. *Kneip*, 521 F.2d 87, 113–14.
83. Ibid., 91. Indeed, the Court's first "historical" citation is to *My Friend the Indian*, written by James McLaughlin, who was the government negotiator in the three county openings.
84. 521 F.2d at 90.
85. Ibid., 102.
86. Petition for a Writ of Certiorari, filed 11 October 1975, *Rosebud Sioux Tribe* v. *Kneip* (No. 75-562) file, Tobin Law Office.

Dakota, and especially Rosebud Reservation, was plagued with serious AIM-related criminal incidents that the tribal and federal enforcement and judicial systems were unable to address. When one considered, the counties argued, the related loss of the inherent power of state and local government to regulate drivers' licenses, license plates, motor vehicle safety inspections, and other related regulatory provisions; misdemeanors and repeated offenses such as driving while intoxicated, which are not felonies or even crimes under the Federal statutes in an area where for all practical purposes neither the tribe nor the federal government had ever provided adequate law enforcement protection for either tribal members or non-members, the effect of a reversal of the lower court's decision could not be underestimated. If the state lost jurisdiction in the four-county area, who—what governmental entity—would be in a position to maintain order? The threat that Winner could become like Mission—without any control over Indians—was clearly conjured up for the court.[87]

The counties also expressed concern about the civil-rights implications of extending tribal jurisdiction over non-Indians: "Within the past two years, the Rosebud Sioux Tribe has enacted two important ordinances. The first ordinance asserts *complete* civil and criminal jurisdiction over *all* persons within the original boundaries of the Reservation. The second ordinance asserts the right to *remove* any person deemed 'socially undesirable.' Although the tribal court has not issued any orders to date under the second ordinance, it does routinely issue and attempt to act on arrest warrants for non-members, felonies and misdemeanors alike, pursuant to the first ordinance."[88] It was one thing that the tribe was attempting within Todd County—within what everyone agreed was Rosebud Reservation—to "subject non-members to general tribal jurisdiction, special trader's licenses, taxes for the right to do business on the reservation, special statutes regulating intoxicants, professional competency certifications for the right to practice law or medicine or any other profession in a tribal hospital [or] court of law." At least there, where it was understood by all concerned that the area was

87. Reply Brief for Respondents in Opposition, filed May 1976, *Rosebud Sioux Tribe v. Kneip* (No. 75-562) file, Tobin Law Office; Brief for the Tribe, filed August 1976, *Rosebud Sioux Tribe v. Kneip* (No. 75-562) file, Tobin Law Office; Brief for Respondents, October 1976, filed *Rosebud Sioux Tribe v. Kneip* (No. 75-562), 001337, 19761030, National Indian Law Library.
88. Reply Brief for Respondents in Opposition, filed May 1976, *Rosebud Sioux Tribe v. Kneip* (No. 75-562) file, Tobin Law Office. Indeed, at the time the tribal court had issued a criminal arrest warrant for a high-ranking state of South Dakota official.

Indian country, "citizens..., both members of the [tribe]...and non-members, have elected to live within the boundaries of a reservation. They have knowingly decided to subject their lives and property to the many special Federal and tribal laws on such reservations. This choice presumably has been made with the realization as to the consequences of the choice." The opened counties, however, were another matter, because the citizens there had assumed from the beginning that they were not living and working on a reservation. To allow tribal jurisdiction over non-Indians (and Indians, for that matter) in the opened areas now, the counties argued, would be "a drastic step, after 65 years of history in which the State of South Dakota and its local government units have exercised jurisdiction and general governmental powers over this area."[89]

The Supreme Court handed down its decision in April 1977, sustaining the holding of the appeals court.[90] Justice William Rehnquist, who delivered the opinion of the majority, wrote that the historical context of the enactment of the statutes made clear what the intent of Congress was, as it responded to the "familiar forces" analyzed in *DeCoteau*[91] — to diminish reservations and make lands available to homesteaders. The Court also took seriously the subsequent jurisdictional history of the area: neither Congress nor the Interior Department had challenged the exercise of state jurisdiction in the opened counties. With respect to civil rights, non-Indians had "justifiable expectations" that they were not living on a reservation.[92] Furthermore, the 1910 Mellette County Act provided for Indian allottees "on the tract to be ceded" to "relinquish sale and select allotments in the lieu thereof on the diminished reservation." Here was an indication on the *face* of the act—in its plain. language—that congressional intent involved cession and reservation diminishment.[93]

In his dissenting opinion, Justice Thurgood Marshall decried attempts to reconstruct congressional intent and urged the Court to focus on what the language of the acts did—to look at the acts as legal instruments. He accused the majority of effacing the critical distinction between a "DeCoteau-type purchase," in which land was purchased by the United States under an agreement with the tribe, and a "Mattz-type

89. Ibid.
90. 430 U. S. 584 (1977).
91. Ibid., 590.
92. Ibid., 605.
93. Ibid., 613.

'opening,'" in which lands on the reservation were made available to non-Indian homesteaders with the government merely acting as sales agent for the tribe. In the *Kneip* decision, the Court "obliterates this distinction," Marshall wrote, "and by holding against the Tribe when the evidence concerning congressional intent is palpably ambiguous, erodes the general principles of interpreting Indian statutes" (that statutory ambiguities are to be resolved in favor of the tribe involved).[94] At base, there was no express language in the three acts disestablishing the reservation status of the affected counties. In fact, the Court had ignored the express language in all three acts which stated that "nothing in this agreement shall be construed to deprive the...Indians...of any benefits to which they are entitled under existing treaties or agreements, not inconsistent with the provisions of this agreement."[95] Certainly, having a reservation as large as that set out in the 1889 act was a benefit that the opening acts did not expressly override.

The majority, Marshall complained, based its opinion on the legislative history of the acts, but that history was "extraordinarily sparse."[96] There was little or no pertinent congressional debate on the proposed acts. In fact, Congress seemed to have completely ignored the boundary question in the three acts:

> The issue was of no great importance in the early 1900's as it was commonly assumed that all reservations would be abolished when the trust period on allotted lands expired. There was no pressure to accelerate this timetable, so long as settlers could acquire unused land. Accordingly, Congress simply did not focus on the boundary question. Its indifference is perhaps best manifested by the fact that in legislation concerning the Reservation enacted immediately subsequent to the Rosebud Acts, Congress at times referred to the opened counties as part of the Reservation and at times referred to them as no longer part of the Reservation [footnote omitted]. For the Court to find in this confusion and indifference a "clear" congressional intent to disestablish the reservation is incomprehensible.[97]

Many tribal members and advocates as well found the decision legally incomprehensible. By contrast, one of the attorneys who worked on the counties' briefs was quoted in *The Winner Advocate:* "The decision renews faith in the judicial system at a time when many people were becoming disillusioned with federal decisions in this area of the

94. Ibid., 618.
95. Ibid., 623
96. Ibid., 626.
97. Ibid., 629–30.

law."[98] The South Dakota Attorney General was quoted in the *Todd County Tribune*: "I couldn't be more pleased." The *Tribune* also reported: "Reservation area ranchers, business people and employed people, for the most part, expressed surprise with the ruling since some felt the high court would rule in favor of the Tribe. Others, later on Tuesday, said the Supreme Court really couldn't go any other way and be fair."[99] The attorney who represented the four counties counseled: "An all-out effort should now be made by responsible people living within this area to heal the wounds that this conflict has caused to the extent that we may all live as one people instead of continuing the distinction, if there is one, between Indian and non-Indian."[100] The call for living "as one people," however, was wishful thinking. The wounds would not be easily healed, and "the distinction between Indian and non-Indian" would not be easily erased.

LEGAL CONTRADICTION AND RIGHTS-CLAIMS

The *Kneip* case grew out of a contradiction in federal Indian law and the inconsistent rights-claims it underwrites. Congress had opened the reservation to homesteading in the early twentieth century under the assumption that it was only a matter of time before the reservations would be terminated and that Indians would relinquish any special legal status and become full United States citizens. Of course, this eventuality never came to pass; in fact, Congress reversed course radically in 1934 and provided for permanent reservation land bases with Indian country status, permanent special legal status for Indian people, and permanent tribal entities with rights of self-government. The withering away of the reservations, which for a time was a real-enough historical process facilitated by earlier congresses, was essentially frozen in time in 1934, and residents of localities like the Rosebud Country were forced to live with the consequences. They did live with them and apparently without great difficulty for decades. The agreed-upon reading of the contradiction (accepted even by Indian leaders) was that three-quarters of Rosebud Reservation had been terminated and that Indian people had no special (treaty) rights in those areas, nor did the Rosebud Sioux Tribe have any business in the ter-

98. "Court Rules against Rosebud Tribe," *Winner Advocate*, 6 April 1977.
99. "Supreme Court Upholds Lower Court Decision in Boundary Case," *Todd County Tribune*, 7 April 1977.
100. "Court Rules against Rosebud Tribe," *Winner Advocate*, 6 April 1977.

minated areas (except, of course, for the scattered patches of "outlying" trust land).

In the 1970s, however, this geographic arrangement of jurisdiction and rights was called into question. Activist lawyers and tribal leaders, who were energized by a new vision of tribal sovereignty rooted in a new reading of federal Indian law (a vision that they had been instrumental in creating), sought to revisit the question of whether Congress had "wiped out" three-quarters of the reservation. These advocates were convinced by their reading of the law that not only were tribes and Indian country *permanent* legal entities—a status enacted into law by the Indian Reorganization Act—but that tribes are also *sovereign governments* with *treaty rights* (such as guarantees in the 1889 act that tribes would be free from state jurisdiction) that could not be wished away and that withstood, as a legal matter, the ravages of the political winds. The tribal advocates posed a fundamentally new definition of the rights of people living in a large chunk of south-central South Dakota and it frightened—and was a source of resentment for—many non-Indians.

Clearly, both the old geographic allocation of rights, and the claimed revision based on treaties, could find justification in law. Both sides presented remarkably persuasive arguments—equally persuasive because federal Indian law is so fundamentally contradictory. The courts were forced to seek a resolution of the historical contradiction of fundamentally opposed laws that were equally operative by narrowing the judicial question to a highly abstract matter, far removed from the substantive rights involved. No compelling body of law concerning rights-claims would easily provide a principled answer in this case. The choice between the two possible answers hinged on a single narrow question: what was the intent of Congress regarding the reservation boundaries at the time the reservation was opened? This was, in fact, a question based on a *legal fiction*. To begin with, the concept of "intent of Congress" is a highly problematic determination in any instance.[101] How is it epistemologically possible to divine a coherent "intent" from an instrument written by several authors and ratified by congressmen who could not possibly all have thought through the complexities of a statute or agreed on the precise intentions and technical legal effects of the act?[102]

101. Abraham 1988:121.
102. Abraham 1988; Brennan 1988; Brest 1988; Frickey 1990:1143, 1210.

The notion of fixing definitively the "intent of Congress" in the matter of the Rosebud surplus land acts, however, is particularly problematic because Congress had no reason to have any particular intention regarding reservation boundaries in those acts. As the United States pointed out in its amicus brief to the Supreme Court, "Congress was concerned with *land* not *jurisdiction*," a concern that did not necessitate definitive reservation boundary lines.[103] In fact, the Supreme Court itself recognized, in effect, the fiction of the quest for congressional intent in reservation boundary cases in its 1984 *Solem* v. *Bartlett* opinion: "Members of Congress voting on the surplus land Acts believed to a man that within a short time—within a generation at most—the Indian tribes would enter traditional American society and the reservation system would cease to exist. Given this expectation, Congress naturally failed to be meticulous in clarifying whether a particular piece of legislation formally sliced a certain parcel of land off one reservation."[104] Such a question was simply beyond the conceptual horizon of lawmakers at the time—given their collective historical imaginary. Reservations, from the point of view of congressmen in the first decade of the twentieth century, were anachronisms waiting for the sweep of the broom of history; for that reason there was no need to be particularly careful with terms such as "cede," "sell," "diminished," and so on: these were not technical legal terms at the time. With the emergence of new laws, new policies, and a new politics in a new public sphere in the 1970s, trying to divine the intent of Congress in 1904, 1907, or 1910 regarding the boundaries of Rosebud Reservation required performing a counterfactual history experiment: what would Congress have done with the reservation boundaries back then *if* the members had believed that the question was important? While this is an interesting question, it is important to recognize that it admits only of a highly speculative "answer." There can be no epistemological guarantees that one answer is more correct—not to mention, likely be adopted by the Court—than another. Legal indeterminacy reaches its height in Indian law with this kind of abstract question based on a fictitious concept.

What serves as an answer to the question—that is, a *legal* answer in the Indian-law game—depends on what evidence judges choose to

103. Brief for the United States, filed September 1976, *Rosebud Sioux Tribe* v. *Kneip* (No. 75-562) file, Tobin Law Office.
104. 465 U.S. 463.

allow. These "rules of construction"[105] define what is admissible in interpreting the statute in question. If the evidence is limited to the operative language of the statutes themselves, read against the operative language of other surplus-land acts for comparative purposes—the "textualist" approach the tribe urged—a strong case exists for the assumption that the acts did not diminish Rosebud Reservation. The tribe advanced this approach, as against consideration of "extrinsic" materials, in its brief to the Supreme Court: "The court [of appeals] seems to have rested its conclusion, not on what Congress *did* in the law itself, but on what the court thought Congress understood from what was said during the debates. . . . But in the imperfect process of seeking out Congressional intent, there is no better evidence than the text of the statute itself. The language of the statute and the legal effect of the language control. A reservation may be terminated by what Congress *does*, not by what the court believes some members may have understood. The erroneous delivery or understanding of facts or law, by members of Congress, or even a committee of Congress, does not alter the meaning of the statute itself."[106] The state and counties looked for congressional intent "practically everywhere but the Rosebud statutes themselves."[107]

If, on the other hand, the evidence considered goes beyond the language of the acts and entails reconstruction of the "tenor" of the period on the basis of historical documents—as the state and four counties argued was justified under precedent—a strong case can be made for the intent of diminishment, since the assumption of the members of Congress was that the reservations were on the road to disappearance; they could not have imagined that the process of disappearance would become frozen in midstream in 1934. The tribe and the United States never referred to the compelling documentary evidence, the counties and state argued, and instead merely gave "their own opinions and not what Congress itself intended."[108]

The judicial holding in *Kneip* was not based on substantive matters in federal Indian law—matters concerning rights—but rather was based

105. See Clinton, Newton, and Price 1991:131–37; Getches, Wilkinson, and Williams 1993:345–48.

106. Petitioner's Brief, filed August 1976, *Rosebud Sioux Tribe* v. *Kneip* (No. 75-562) file, Tobin Law Office.

107. Petitioner's Reply Brief filed 7 January 1977, *Rosebud Sioux Tribe* v. *Kneip* (No. 75-562) file, Tobin Law Office. On this argument, see also Wilkinson and Volkman 1975; Tilleman 1976.

108. Respondents' Brief, filed October 1976, *Rosebud Sioux Tribe* v. *Kneip* (No. 75-562), 001337, 19761030, National Indian Law Library.

on a highly narrow *technicality* that could easily have gone—or could easily go—in the opposite direction. As two legal scholars put it in 1975, "the present state of the law [on treaty abrogation] is confused and could be expected to produce inconsistent results. There are several tests, with major practical distinctions among them. Moreover, the commonly used tests are sufficiently vague that courts have broad leeway in applying them. . . . [T]he fears of inconsistent adjudication have been realized."[109]

Indeed, in *Solem* v. *Bartlett* the United States Supreme Court took up the old question of the boundaries of Cheyenne River Reservation.[110] The question had been considered in ten different courts, beginning in 1911 (see p. 54, table 3). The South Dakota Supreme Court had held on five separate occasions that the reservation had been diminished, the United States District Court once that it had not been diminished, and twice that it had, and the Court of Appeals for the Eighth Circuit twice that the reservation was not diminished. Here was a question for Supreme Court clarification if ever there was one. What is interesting for present purposes is that the 1908 Cheyenne River surplus land act[111] is, in terms of text, almost identical to the Rosebud acts. The operative language authorized the Secretary of the Interior to "sell and dispose" of surplus reservation lands, just as in the Tripp and Mellette county acts. Critically, the statute declared that the United States was not bound to purchase the lands or find buyers, and that the Indians were not to be deprived "of any benefits to which they are entitled under existing treaties or agreements." It must have been more than a little disconcerting to Indian people on Rosebud Reservation, then, when the Supreme Court in *Solem* cited language identical to the acts considered in Rosebud to explain why Cheyenne River Reservation had *not* been diminished. The same kinds of historical documents that the court had seen as clear evidence of diminishment in *Kneip* were seen here as ambiguous and not dispositive. Thus, instead of being convinced by congressional references to reservation "diminishment" as it was in *Kneip,* the Court here seemed to stick more closely to the text and to be willing to entertain diminishment only by a showing of "an explicit expression of congressional intent," not by implication.[112] The

109. Wilkinson and Volkman 1975:634. For an argument that, constitutionally, the courts should not seek the *implied* "intent" of Congress in the face of its silence on treaty abrogation, see Wilkins, forthcoming.

110. 465 U. S. 463 (1984).

111. 35 Stat. 460.

112. 465 U. S. at 475.

Court held that Cheyenne River Reservation had not been diminished.[113]

The closeness of boundary cases is a direct result of the continuing legal validity of fundamentally opposed bodies of federal Indian law. That closeness and the narrowness and technicality of the legal calls have two important political consequences. First, legal rights for large numbers of people in and around Indian country are fundamentally unstable. Will thousands of non-Indians be put under tribal jurisdiction? Will city and state police officers be able to enforce the law on Indians? Will banks and businesses be able to enforce contracts against Indians? And when will all these questions be answered, and by which court? Very concrete matters—both for Indians and for non-Indians—are at stake in the outcome; both "sides" have a great deal to lose, win, or simply maintain.

Even when legal rights are relatively stable as a matter of decisioned law and actual exercise, rights remain politically contested. Because of the existence of opposed bodies of law, both sides can make convincing arguments because both sides have the law on their sides—even the losers, who see in the law their chance to fight another battle on another day.[114] Members of the tribe clearly felt that the *Kneip* decisions were arbitrary—and in a real sense they *were,* as the comparison of *Rosebud* with *Solem* certainly seems to indicate—unjust, anachronistic, and a

113. Standing Rock Reservation, opened under the same 1908 act that opened Cheyenne River Reservation, has also been held by the court of appeals not to have been diminished (*United States* v. *Long Elk,* 565 F.2d 1032 [8th Cir., 1977]).

114. A concrete example of this emerged during the completion of this book (see table 3). In October 1996 the Court of Appeals for the Eighth Circuit, in *Yankton Sioux Tribe* v. *Southern Missouri Waste Management District* (99 F.3d 1439) upheld a district court finding (*Yankton Sioux Tribe* v. *Southern Missouri Waste Management District,* 890 F. Supp. 878 [D. S.D. 1995]) that Yankton Reservation had not been diminished by an 1894 statute that opened surplus lands to homesteading. Nevertheless, *Indian Country Today* quoted the governor in March 1997: "Charles Mix County isn't an Indian reservation." The state will seek an appeal with the Supreme Court ("[Governor]: There's No Yankton Reservation," *Indian Country Today,* 24–31 March 1997, A1). Indeed, the Supreme Court ruled in January 1998 that Yankton Reservation had been diminished by the 1894 statute (*South Dakota* v. *Yankton Sioux Tribe,* 522 U.S. 329). But *South Dakota* v. *Yankton* had decided only the question of the lands ceded by the 1894 statute. The tribe wanted an answer to this question: What was the legal status of allotted lands that had been fee-patented? In August 1998 the federal district court held that these lands are still Indian country, even if they are owned by non-Indians (*Yankton Sioux Tribe* v. *Gaffey,* 14 F. Supp.2d 1135 [D. S.D.]). After South Dakota appealed this decision, the Court of Appeals for the Eighth Circuit reversed the district court holding in August 1999, finding that fee-patented former allotments are no longer Indian country (*Yankton Sioux Tribe* v. *Gaffey,* 188 F.3d 1010). As this book goes to press, the Yankton Sioux Tribe has petitioned the Supreme Court to take the case ("Yankton Jurisdiction May Go to High Court," *Indian Country Today,* 5 April 2000).

denial of justice to Indian people, a positive loss of Indian rights, that they intended to fight either in court or in Congress. After the Supreme Court decision, the tribal president was quoted: "This decision is a blow to justice all over. It's more a political decision than one based on law or treaty agreements. The U. S. has violated all its treaties at this point, we haven't given up the fight and we will continue."[115] The tribal council unanimously adopted a resolution which explained that "if the decision is allowed to stand it will mean that the Rosebud Sioux Tribe will be deprived of a significant amount of sovereign power over substantial areas of land." The council instructed the tribe's lawyers to petition the Supreme Court for a rehearing and called upon the National Congress of American Indians, the National Tribal Chairmen's Association, and other organizations to develop a publicity campaign supporting a rehearing or otherwise "to rectify the tremendous injustice perpetrated upon the Rosebud Sioux Tribe by the decision."[116]

The tribal public relations officer wrote in the *Todd County Tribune*: "The Great Sioux Nation is shocked." At issue was clearly a violation of law: "the message that seems to be coming out from our Nation's Capital is that our Treaties, Acts, and Agreements are not respected even in this day and age." "Neither the word 'Cession' or 'Public Domain'," the column reasoned, "was used in the Surplus Land Acts," and what passed for "congressional intent" was really the intent of the two legislators from South Dakota whose words were quoted heavily in the opinion. "[T]he decision was based on money and number [of non-Indians in the opened counties] instead of justice; it's a hollow victory and the history of rip-offs goes on even in our modern day age." Referring to the Lakota trickster figure who is known to kill and devour unsuspecting animals as they dance blindly to his songs: "It . . . leaves all Indians with a feeling, and rightfully so, that the Great 'Iktomi' the U. S. Government has been singing a tune to the Surplus Lands Acts of 1904, 1907 and 1910 and we have been dancing with our eyes closed ever since."[117] What better metaphor could there be for unpredictable Indian losses in the federal Indian-law game than the antics of a trickster?

115. "Court Rules against Rosebud Tribe," *Winner Advocate*, 6 April 1977.

116. Minutes, 12 April 1977, Rosebud Sioux Tribal Office; Minutes, 11 April 1977, Rosebud Sioux Tribal Office.

117. "Tribe Responds to Supreme Court Ruling," *Todd County Tribune*, 14 April 1977. The passage refers to a common story among Lakota people. One day Iktomi was traveling when he came upon some ducks. They asked him what he had in his bag, to which he replied "Dancing songs." Following Iktomi's invitation, the ducks got in a line,

The perfectly good federal law on the tribe's side undermined whatever "legitimacy" the Supreme Court decision might have had in the eyes of Indian people. There was strong resentment about violation of treaty rights—a violation clearly spelled out by Justice Marshall's dissenting opinion (which Indian people who followed the case read and understood). The case was far from "settled" in local knowledge: rights remained highly contested, notwithstanding the holding of the Supreme Court. As one tribal member who lives in Todd County told me, "We never say 'Todd County'" in referring to the reservation. When he speaks of Rosebud Reservation he means the area marked by the original exterior boundaries as defined in the 1889 act.

Furthermore, because the decision was so close, a slight variation in the details of the jurisdictional question may create a new opening for litigation, so that rights really do remain not only contested, but insecure. In 1979, for example, the South Dakota Supreme Court decided *State* v. *Hero,* a case in which two Rosebud Sioux tribal members appealed their convictions for violating state hunting laws on deeded land in Mellette County. They argued that Indian hunting and fishing rights in the opened counties had not been extinguished by *Kneip,* just as Menominee hunting rights had not been extinguished by termination (*Menominee* v. *United States*).[118] The court, however, insisted that *Kneip* covered Indian hunting and fishing, and sustained the convictions.[119] One of my Lakota informants believes that this case could have been pursued fruitfully in the federal courts: "There's aboriginal hunting rights. And I believe that they still exist today.... Take myself, I hunt a lot of what other people term 'off-reservation,' Mellette County, Tripp County,...with just a tribal license.... No...federal court case has ever said that Rosebud Sioux enrolled members cannot hunt or fish within the original boundaries of the reservation. The state says in *Rosebud Sioux Tribe* v. *Kneip* we lost all that. Well, I don't believe that to be completely true of everything. I don't believe you can take one lawsuit for one specific thing and apply it to everything."

Support for the *Hero* case that might have allowed it to go further was not forthcoming from the BIA, and the tribal council remains

---

closed their eyes, and danced as he sang some songs. Iktomi then slyly took a stick out of his bag and began to kill the ducks with it, one by one. Finally one of the ducks opened its eyes, saw what was happening, and warned the others. They flew away, but Iktomi had himself a meal.

118. 391 U.S. 404 (1968).

119. *State* v. *Hero.* 282 N.W.2d 70.

"gun-shy" about boundary cases because of the *Kneip* loss. But the potential for litigation is always on the horizon.

It is only a matter of time before a federal suit is brought by one side or the other to clarify the implications of *Kneip* for a slightly different fact situation. Under these conditions, are matters "settled"? Certainly, this unsettledness is one of the primary sources of "racial" tension in South Dakota. Because so much can be at stake in the rights involved, the greatest threat to the concrete rights of Indian people comes from the assertion of rights by non-Indians, and vice versa. Thus, Indian people come to see local non-Indians as their immediate political opponents regarding basic rights, and vice versa. The conflicting regimes of rights-claims, enabled by conflicting law, underwrite this "racial" struggle. It might be going too far to say that there would be no racial tension in South Dakota without the contradictions of Indian law, but the discourse of Indian law has crystallized an opposition in Indian and non-Indian political interests and called forth a bitter, zero-sum rights-game played against one's neighbors.

CHAPTER 3

The Mission Liquor Store
and Racial Hard Feelings

The city of Mission, it will be recalled from chapter 1, was incorporated under the laws of South Dakota, but within the boundaries of Rosebud Reservation, in 1932. Its population was composed predominantly of non-Indians residing on deeded land (see table 4). While the expectation had been that the reservation would disappear along with both trust land and the legal status of "Indian," the Indian Reorganization Act forever halted the withering away of the reservation, the tribe, and Indian status. One of the questions that resulted from this historical overlay of conflicting laws was whether Mission was subject to federal Indian liquor law, which for more than a century had prohibited the introduction of liquor into Indian country. In 1949 Mission, through a paid lobbyist, managed to get a federal statute enacted exempting "fee-patent lands in non-Indian communities" from the application of federal Indian liquor law. But just as the concept of "domestic dependent nation" in the *Worcester* v. *Georgia* decision was a legal oxymoron wishfully intended to reconcile irreconcilable principles, the concept of a "non-Indian community" within a reservation was (and remains) self-contradictory. The contradiction was merely papered over by the 1949 statute. Nevertheless, in 1956 the city of Mission opened a municipal liquor store. The liquor store was good for city revenue (see table 5), and because of the brisk business in alcohol,[1]

1. In 1983 the Mission Liquor Store had the third-highest sales of any municipal liquor store in the state, surpassed only by stores in Brookings, the home of South Dakota

TABLE 4.   POPULATION OF THE
CITY OF MISSION, BY RACE

	1940	1950	1960	1970	1980	1990
White	307	n. a.	337	438	372	267
Indian	145	n. a.	274	301	376	415
Total	452	388	611	739	748	682

SOURCE: 548 F. Supp. 1180; U. Department of Commerce, *Census of Population*, various years.
n. a. Not available.

TABLE 5.   MISSION LIQUOR STORE REVENUES
(IN DOLLARS)

Year	Sales	Net Income
1967	163,748	35,821
1968	184,945	43,456
1969	206,330	53,807
1970	240,226	60,699
1971	291,845	79,201
1972	342,156	91,961
1973	360,139	94,601
1974	387,463	99,956
1975	428,610	103,932
1976	n. a.	n. a.
1977	548,587	136,168
1978	586,534	127,438
1979	676,379	79,251
1980	769,414	56,275
1981	804,060	(3,110)[1]
1982	716,965	(57,030)
1983	713,213	(26,316)
1984 (first six months)	357,878	7,009

SOURCE: Statements of Operations, Liquor Store, 1967–84, city of Mission.
n. a. Not available.
1. The losses in net income were a result of heavy legal expenses associated with the liquor store litigation.

Mission survived without municipal taxes. A number of the residents I interviewed described the liquor store as the city's "golden goose."

The sovereignty movement that emerged in the 1970s provided Indian people on Rosebud Reservation with a framework for seeing clearly what was wrong with this picture and what to do about it. In 1971 the Rosebud Area Clergy Association reminded the Rosebud

State University, and Pierre, the state capital ("City Applies for Tribal Liquor License," *Todd County Tribune*, 13 July 1983.)

Sioux Tribal Council of a 1953 act of Congress that authorized reservation liquor sales only in conformity with a tribal liquor code; this, of course, gave tribes jurisdiction over liquor on reservations. The tribal council did adopt a liquor ordinance in 1971, and the tribal president asked the Interior Department whether liquor sales in the city of Mission would be legal without a tribal license. The Interior Department field solicitor responded that he had "heard recently that the majority of the residents in the town of Mission are Indian, and if so, it would appear that such town should not be considered to be a non-Indian community." Thus, at least in the opinion of the field solicitor, liquor establishments in Mission would have to conform to the tribal liquor code.[2]

The city of Mission was finally brought into federal court by the United States, in its capacity as trustee, in 1980. The conflict between the tribe's attempt to control liquor sales in Mission and the city's insistence on its autonomy came down to a narrow legal question: Is Mission a "non-Indian community"? This technical question, answered, as we will see, with highly abstract semantic and statistical analysis, was a direct consequence of the incompatibility of preserving the reservation and the tribe as a *government* on the one hand, and filling the reservation with non-Indians, their homes, businesses, and municipalities, on non-trust land, on the other hand. The statutory stopgap of an exempt "non-Indian community" in the midst of an Indian reservation was an anomaly in the law that was waiting to be litigated.

United States v. *Mission* may have been argued in technical terms, but from the point of view of both Indian and non-Indian people on Rosebud Reservation, its substance was a very concrete matter—the right to self-government. The litigation pitted local Indian and non-Indian people against one another in a struggle over rights that was bitterly contested and received widespread media attention both in South

2. Field Solicitor to Area Director, 27 July 1971, Mission Golf Club File, Rosebud Sioux Tribal Office; 67 Stat. 586; "Are Alcohol Sales Legal?" *Rosebud Sioux Herald*, 1 February 1971; Resolution 71-85, 8 July 1971, Rosebud Sioux Tribal Office; "Tribal Council Moves to Open Liquor Sales," *Todd County Tribune*, 15 July 1971; "Liquor Sales Now Legal on Rosebud," *Todd County Tribune*, 28 October 1971. The liquor ordinance was adopted, among other reasons, to accommodate the city of St. Francis, an incorporated, largely Indian town, which intended to open a municipal liquor store and could only do so under the terms of a tribal liquor ordinance ("Liquor Decision in Council Hands," *Todd County Tribune*, 17 June 1971).

The first target of tribal political action turned out to be not the city's liquor store but the Mission Golf Club, a private club that lay outside the city limits and that was for that reason more ambiguously covered by the non-Indian community exemption claimed by the city of Mission. Furthermore, the club was, as one resident recalled, "pretty controversial" among Indian people because of its "closed membership," which largely excluded

Dakota and beyond.[3] When the district court found in favor of the tribe, the *Todd County Tribune* reported: "Indian and non-Indian alike point out that the ... lawsuit and resulting decision have created an apartheid atmosphere in a community that has heretofore commingled compatibly."[4] When the city appealed the decision, the *Tribune* quoted a tribal member: "It is supposed to be our reservation, and [white] people should do what they have to do without making an issue out of it. It's just caused a lot more hard feelings."[5] This chapter will examine how these hard (racial) feelings were generated out of the struggle over the tribal liquor code.

LIQUOR IN MISSION

The introduction of liquor into Indian country was prohibited by Congress in the Trade and Intercourse Act of 1834.[6] When Rosebud Reservation was established in 1889, it naturally was subject to federal Indian liquor law. In the wake of non-Indians moving into Rosebud Reservation as a result of fee patenting, however, the question that

---

Indians. The issue, according to the tribal president, was "who controls commerce.... I think we should decide once and for all who has jurisdiction and how far this jurisdiction reaches." He sent a letter to the club stating that it was dispensing liquor on the reservation in violation of the tribal liquor code and insisting that the club comply with the tribal ordinance by obtaining a tribal license or cease selling liquor. The stockholders and board of the directors of the club retained an attorney who responded to the tribe: "[T]he liquor control ordinance ... raises very serious questions affecting many businesses and persons other than the Golf Club. Of particular significance are questions of the applicability of your constitution to non-Indians and the jurisdiction of the tribal court over non-Indians." The attorney also insisted that the club constituted part of the greater Mission non-Indian community, and thus was covered by the non-Indian community exemption. Although a complaint was filed in federal district court against the club, the tribe, preoccupied with the Kneip boundary case (see chapter 2) did not pursue the lawsuit (Resolution 72-120, 28 August 1972, Rosebud Sioux Tribal Office; "Tribe Serves Papers on Golf Club," *Todd County Tribune*, 11 January 1973; Resolution 72–143, 11 December 1972, Rosebud Sioux Tribal Office; "Tribe, Club Hearing Postponed," *Todd County Tribune*, 18 January 1973; "Rosebud Tribal Liquor Ordinance Finally Legalized," *Todd County Tribune*, 8 March 1973; Field Solicitor to Area Director, 4 February 1976, Mission Golf Club file, Rosebud Sioux Tribal Office; Acting Superintendent to Area Director, 9 March 1976, Mission Golf Club File, Rosebud Sioux Tribal Office; U. S. Attorney to Department of Justice, 2 April 1976, Mission Golf Club file, Rosebud Sioux Tribal Office; Field Solicitor to Associate Solicitor, 29 November 1979, Mission Golf Club file, Rosebud Sioux Tribal Office).

3. For example, "Inside a Sioux Reservation: Villages of Despair," *Washington Post*, 9 September 1984, 1.

4. "City Given until January 15 to Apply for Tribal Liquor License," *Todd County Tribune*, 29 December 1982.

5. "Public Opinion Poll," *Todd County Tribune*, 5 January 1983.

6. 4 Stat. 729.

arose was whether the city of Mission was Indian country—part of the reservation—and thus subject to federal Indian liquor law. Notwithstanding the 1922 *Black Spotted Horse* and 1943 *Kills Plenty Decisions* which held that fee-patented land within the boundaries of the reservation remains Indian country (see pp. 33–34), there were those in Mission who believed the city was not part of Indian country. Indeed, there had been a 1940 South Dakota attorney general's opinion to that effect.[7] Under these conditions it was a good bet that Mission was not legally Indian country and thus not subject to federal Indian liquor law. In fact, by 1948 someone *had* bet on it by opening a beer parlor in town. It was understood when the state liquor license was issued by the city that a test case might result, and when the operator was charged in federal court with criminal possession of liquor in Indian country and the beer parlor's stocks were confiscated by federal officials, nobody was surprised. The operator's attorney successfully argued that liquor possession and sales are exempted from federal Indian liquor law when they take place on deeded land within a reservation. Apparently the court was unaware of the *Kills Plenty* holding, and the operator was acquitted and resumed business.[8]

In the same year, however, Congress revised its definition of "Indian country" (see p. 34). In an attempt to avoid the jurisdictional confusion arising from deeded land (most of it owned by non-Indians) interspersed ("checkerboarded") with trust land within reservations, Congress defined "Indian country" in conformity with the *Kills Plenty* decision: Indian country would now include all land within the boundaries of an Indian reservation, notwithstanding the issuance of a patent-in-fee. The implications of this revision of "Indian country"—and federal Indian liquor law—for localities like Mission were immediately apparent, and the beer parlor closed down.

7. Relying on *State* v. *Big Sheep* (243 P. 1067 [Mt., 1926]), the attorney general opined that "the State courts have jurisdiction of all crimes committed by Indian wards of the Government, where such acts or crimes are committed upon land to which the United States has relinquished title" (*Biennial Report of Attorney General,* 1939–40: 483).

8. "Mission Beer Parlor Closed by Federal Authorities," *Todd County Tribune,* 22 May 1947; Order and Judgment of Acquittal, Criminal Case 3131, 9 July 1948, appended as supplementary exhibit 37; Attorney to Defendant, 17 July 1948, appended as supplementary exhibit 1; Attorney to Mission Businessman, 29 July 1948, appended as supplementary exhibit 2; Attorney to Mission Businessman, 3 August 1948, appended as supplementary exhibit 3; Attorney to Mission Businessman, 7 August 1948, appended as supplementary exhibit 4, Affidavit in Support of the Defendants' Motion to Set Aside the Judgement, filed October 1983, *United States* v. *Mission* (D. S. D., Civil Cases 80-3073 and 80-3074) file, City of Mission Office.

One Mission businessman (who owned the property on which the beer parlor was located) suggested to his attorney the strategy to lobby Congress to get "the East Side of Todd County taken out of the Rosebud Indian Reservation."[9] Although the attorney, a former governor of South Dakota, did not think it a practical solution, he did write to one of the United States senators from South Dakota, urging that the 1948 amendment to the definition of Indian country be repealed because "it certainly is going to cause confusion with various Indian reservations over the United States" where liquor had been sold on deeded land for years and where liquor was regularly transported on railroad and highway rights-of-way through the reservations.[10] Swayed by these arguments, Congress amended the United States Code in 1949 to exempt from federal Indian liquor law "fee-patented lands in non-Indian communities or rights-of-way through Indian reservations."[11]

The amendment was not entirely satisfactory from the point of view of non-Indian entrepreneurs within reservation boundaries. What is a "non-Indian community" when the community lies within the boundaries of a reservation? Is it one acre of deeded land owned by a non-Indian? Is there a minimum non-Indian population size involved? Is incorporation of a municipality under state laws either a minimum requirement or a guarantee of the non-Indian-community exemption? What if the municipality is predominantly Indian but has a substantial and civically involved non-Indian population? The phrase "non-Indian-community," as the attorney for the owner of the Mission beer parlor told a senator from South Dakota, had not been "specifically defined" by Congress or the courts, and therefore amounted to "an ambigu-

9. Attorney to Mission Businessman, 26 August 1948, appended as supplementary exhibit 15 to Affidavit in Support of the Defendants' Motion to Set Aside the Judgement, October 1983, *United States* v. *Mission* (D. S. D., Civil Cases 80-3073 and 80-3074) file, City of Mission Office.

10. Attorney to Assistant, 30 August 1948, appended as supplementary exhibit 17; Attorney to Senator, 16 March 1949, appended as supplementary exhibit 26 to Affidavit in Support of the Defendants' Motion to Set Aside the Judgement, October 1983, *United States* v. *Mission* (D. S. D., Civil Cases 80-3073 and 80-3074) file, City of Mission Office.

11. 18. U. S. C. 1154, codifying 63 Stat. 94 (1949). The attorney billed the owner of the beer parlor for the lobbying services, but he suggested that his client seek compensation from "the various other liquor houses and breweries" on South Dakota reservations because the 1949 amendment "practically opens up not only this Town of Mission but all Towns similarly situated in the State, and will literally mean thousands and thousands of dollars in business" (Attorney to Mission Businessman, 3 March 1950, appended as supplementary exhibit 37 to Affidavit in Support of the Defendants' Motion to Set Aside the Judgement, October 1983, *United States* v. *Mission* (D. S. D., Civil Cases 80-3073 and 80-3074) file, City of Mission Office).

ity."[12] In fact, he cautioned his client that "you will have to take some chances on opening up again" because of the ambiguity over whether Mission was defensibly a "non-Indian community."[13]

An informal opinion by the United States district attorney, however, made it clear that from the point of view of those charged with enforcing federal law, "Mission classifies as a non-Indian community."[14] With matters clarified, the former operator of the beer parlor opened a liquor store, the first within the boundaries of an Indian reservation in the United States.[15] The classification of Mission as a non-Indian community was formalized when the Interior Department solicitor officially opined in 1951 that Mission was a non-Indian community and that even fee-patented lands *adjacent* to the city were exempt from federal Indian liquor law under the non-Indian community exemption.[16]

Things looked promising for liquor consumption and sales in Mission, so promising that in 1956 the citizens of Mission adopted a ballot measure by a vote of 126 to 50 to open a municipal liquor store.[17] By 1970, in addition to the Mission Liquor Store, the Mission Golf Club—a private club with a bar—had opened south of town on fee-patented land, and two bars were operating within city limits. These were the only legal places to buy a drink in Todd County.

Meanwhile, in 1953 Congress authorized tribal governments to legalize and regulate reservation liquor sales pursuant to tribal liquor codes to be published in the Federal Register. An initial Rosebud Sioux tribal code was adopted in 1971, and a revised code was enacted in 1977 that provided for the licensing and regulation of all liquor sales on

12. Attorney to Senator, 2 April 1949, appended as supplementary exhibit 29 to Affidavit in Support of the Defendants' Motion to Set Aside the Judgment, October 1983, *United States* v. *Mission* (D. S. D., Civil Cases 80-3073 and 80-3074) file, City of Mission Office.

13. Attorney to Mission Businessman, 11 May 1949, appended as supplementary exhibit 33 to Affidavit in Support of the Defendants' Motion to Set Aside the Judgment, October 1983, *United States* v. *Mission* (D. S. D., Civil Cases 80-3073 and 80-3074) file, City of Mission Office.

14. Attorney to Mission Businessman, 7 July 1949, appended as supplementary exhibit 34 to Affidavit in Support of the Defendants' Motion to Set Aside the Judgment, October 1983, *United States* v. *Mission* (D. S. D., Civil Cases 80-3073 and 80-3074) file, City of Mission Office.

15. "Liquor Store Opens in Mission: First on Indian Reservation in U. S.," *Todd County Tribune*, 28 July 1949.

16. Acting Solicitor to Attorney General, 28 September 1951, Mission Golf Club File, Rosebud Sioux Tribal Office.

17. "Mission Voters Favor Municipal Liquor Store by Overwhelming Vote," *Todd County Tribune*, 26 April 1956.

the reservation. By March 1979 the tribal liquor commission was accepting applications for liquor licenses under its new code,[18] and in April it "gave notice to all establishments within the Rosebud Reservation that they would have to comply with tribal law by purchasing a tribal license."[19] Mission's attorney informed the city council that in his opinion "the City is not legally required to submit this application and that it should not do so."[20]

In May the Rosebud Sioux Tribal Council discussed the situation of non-compliance by non-Indians in Mission. A tribal attorney argued, "The people that are operating in Mission, [a bar], Country Club, and Mission Liquor Store, refuse to have tribal license[s] and they just snub their noses at us." The council voted unanimously "that BIA be requested to take whatever action necessary to insure that the tribal liquor Ordinance as posted in the Federal register is enforce[d] by their people."[21] Shortly thereafter the chair of the liquor commission wrote to the superintendent: "The Rosebud Sioux Tribal Liquor Commission has been made aware of the fact that four establishments in the City of Mission have no intention of complying with this aspect of tribal law," and were therefore in violation of federal Indian liquor law. The letter pointed out that the council had voted to request BIA assistance and asked, "please take this letter as a formal request to invoke whatever federal intervention is necessary to bring these establishments into compliance."[22]

Three main intentions underlay the tribal government's determination to regulate liquor. Certainly some tribal members were opposed to liquor sales on the reservation and wanted the establishments closed down in order to facilitate sobriety. It was particularly disconcerting to some that whites were selling the liquor that was causing problems for Indian people and Indian families. An Indian resident of Mission told me that it was commonly said that "it's those white people in Mission that are selling booze to the Indians out in the communities and getting them drunk." Another characterized the Indian money that changed

18. 67 Stat. 586; 43 Federal Register 47,291 (13 October 1978); "Tribe Accepting Liquor Applications," *Todd County Tribune,* 29 March 1979; Ordinance Legalizing the Introduction, Sale, or Possession of Intoxicants, 29 June 1978, Rosebud Sioux Tribal Office.
19. Liquor Commission to Superintendent, 1 June 1979, Mission Golf Club file, Rosebud Sioux Tribal Office.
20. Attorney to Attorney General, 4 May 1979, Liquor Store file, City of Mission Office.
21. Minutes, 10 May 1979, Mission Golf Club file, Rosebud Sioux Tribal Office.
22. Liquor Commission to Superintendent, 1 June 1979, Mission Golf Club file, Rosebud Sioux Tribal Office.

hands in the Mission Liquor Store as "blood money." This must have been painfully obvious on many occasions. My extended visits to Mission began after the liquor store was closed in 1984, but accounts of the effects of alcohol sales painted a grim picture. One non-Indian Mission resident recalled that at the beginning of the month (around "check day" when paychecks, social security, and welfare checks are issued) "people would be standing ten, twelve, deep, fourteen, fifteen deep, many of them inebriated, and the liquor store simply selling whatever it could to whomever wanted it for the best price possible." The liquor store "sometimes opened early and stayed open [past closing-time] maybe by just a few minutes just to get that last dollar. It was so greedy it was sickening." Another non-Indian told me, "You'd go down the street and there'd be people talking to the telephone poles, . . . or just passed out there, fighting. . . ." When I moved into a house on Main Street in 1985 to begin fieldwork, I was told that it had not been uncommon to hear gunplay on Main Street when the liquor store had been open. An Indian resident of Mission told me that the town was "real western" back when the liquor store and the two bars in town were doing business.

Some tribal members saw the liquor store proceeds as a potential source of revenue, either for the general tribal government fund or for a special fund for alcohol treatment and prevention programs. One member of the tribal council at the time characterized the motive for the license requirement thus: "we want some of this money that's been generated by all our people's miseries."

Others saw the conflict neither in terms of alcohol policy nor revenue *per se,* but in terms of the need to establish a range of tribal regulatory policies under the general heading of sovereignty. A man who had been a member of the tribal council during the liquor store dispute explained it thus: "The liquor itself was pretty much secondary. The main thing was being able to regulate . . . , to award licenses . . . , have that hearing process . . . just like regular county and city ordinances would have. But in this case, the tribe would have a say." In the context of the sovereignty-based reading of Indian law that emerged in the 1970s, the conduct of liquor sales, without tribal regulation, on an Indian reservation was a glaring inconsistency. It profoundly violated the new identification of treaty rights with sovereignty that was emerging among Indian people.

The superintendent asked the BIA area office in Aberdeen, South Dakota, for legal grounds to enforce the tribal liquor ordinance; he was

advised of the 1975 Supreme Court decision in *United States* v.
Mazurie.[23] *Mazurie* involved a non-Indian couple who owned the Blue
Bull Bar on fee-patented land on the outskirts of Fort Washakie, an un-
incorporated town on Wind River Reservation in Wyoming. The
Mazuries dispensed liquor without a tribal license, in violation, it was
argued, of federal Indian liquor law; they were arrested, and a federal
court convicted the couple, finding that they had introduced alcohol
into Indian country. The Court of Appeals for the Tenth Circuit reversed the conviction on the grounds that the prosecution had not
proven beyond a reasonable doubt that the Blue Bull was not excluded
from Indian country under the "non-Indian community" exemption.
Echoing the concerns voiced earlier by the Mission beer parlor's attorney, the court of appeals held that the problem, was the ambiguity of
the language of the statute: "the terminology 'non-Indian community' is
not capable of sufficiently precise definition. . . . The statute is thus fatally defective by reason of this indefinite and vague terminology."[24]

The Supreme Court, however, reversed, holding that the court of appeals was incorrect in demanding more precise definitions of the terms
"Indian" and "community." The commonsense understanding of the
average citizen was sufficient here: "The prosecution was required to do
no more than prove that the Blue Bull was not located in a non-Indian
community where that term has meaning sufficiently precise for a man
of average intelligence to 'reasonably understand that his contemplated
conduct is proscribed.' "[25] Of the 212 families within 20 square miles of
the Blue Bull, 170 were Indian, 41 were non-Indian, and 1 was mixed.
Of the 243 students in the local public school, 223 were Indian. The bar
was located near a large Indian housing complex, and Fort Washakie
was the headquarters of the BIA and the tribal government. "Given the
nature of the Blue Bull's location and surrounding population, the
statute was sufficient to advise the Mazuries that their bar was not ex-
cepted from tribal regulation by virtue of being located in a non-Indian
community."[26] The Blue Bull, the Court ruled, was in an Indian community and therefore in Indian country.

23. *United States* v. *Mazurie*, 419 U.S. 544 (1975); Superintendent to Area Director,
6 June 1979, Mission Golf Club file, Rosebud Sioux Tribal Office; Acting Assistant Area
Director to Superintendent, 17 August 1979, Mission Golf Club file, Rosebud Sioux
Tribal Office.
24. 419 U.S. at 549–50.
25. Ibid., 553 (quoting *United States* v. *National Dairy Products Corp.*, 372 U.S. 29,
32–33 [1963]).
26. 419 U.S. at 553.

Finally, after a good deal of prodding by the tribal council, the tribal liquor commission, the Rosebud superintendent, and the BIA area office in Aberdeen, an investigation of the Mission Country Club's liquor sales was authorized by the Department of Justice in January 1980.[27] Under the guidance of the United States attorney in Sioux Falls (himself a Rosebud Sioux tribal member), the BIA and the tribal government began to collect detailed evidence on the composition of the area within a five-mile radius of the club, using the Supreme Court's *Mazurie* analysis as a guide. A count of voter registration lists showed that the population within five miles of the club comprised 709 Indians and 421 non-Indians. Perhaps because these statistics so strongly indicated the "Indian" character of the area surrounding Mission, the Mission Liquor Store was also targeted for suit and became the principal defendant.[28]

UNITED STATES V. MISSION GOLF COURSE AND CITY OF MISSION

THE DISTRICT COURT CASE

In December 1980, the United States attorney filed suit against the city of Mission and the Mission Golf Club in federal district court. The United States sought an injunction enjoining the defendants from selling liquor except in conformity with the tribal liquor ordinance.[29] Strong sentiment prevailed in Mission against complying with the injunction sought by the United States. The bases of this sentiment varied. Certainly there were those in populist rural South Dakota who balked at

27. The golf club was chosen as the target for the suit because it lay outside city limits and thus more clearly fell under the circumstances at issue in *Mazurie* than did the liquor store.

28. Superintendent to Area Office, 3 October 1979, Mission Golf Club file, Rosebud Sioux Tribal Office; Liquor Commission Chair to Superintendent, 22 October 1979, Mission Golf Club file, Rosebud Sioux Tribal Office; Superintendent to Area Director, 23 October 1979, Mission Golf Club file, Rosebud Sioux Tribal Office; Assistant Area Director to Field Solicitor, 19 November 1979, Mission Golf Club file, Rosebud Sioux Tribal Office; Field Solicitor to Associate Solicitor, 29 November 1979, Mission Golf Club file, Rosebud Sioux Tribal Office; Field Solicitor to Assistant Area Director, 22 January 1980, Mission Golf Club file, Rosebud Sioux Tribal Office; Special Report, 28 January 1980, Mission Golf Club file, Rosebud Sioux Tribal Office; Liquor Commission Chair to Superintendent, 1 April 1980, Mission Golf Club file, Rosebud Sioux Tribal Office; Superintendent to United States Attorney, 9 April 1980, Mission Golf Club file, Rosebud Sioux Tribal Office; Superintendent to Area Director, 15 April 1980, Mission Golf Club file, Rosebud Sioux Tribal Office; Minutes, 8 July 1980, Mission Golf Club file, Rosebud Sioux Tribal Office.

29. Complaint, filed 5 December 1980, *United States v. City of Mission* (D. S. D., Civil Case 80-3074), Liquor Store file, City of Mission Office; "United States, Tribe File Suit against City and Golf Club," *Todd County Tribune,* 18 December 1980.

the idea that any government (here, the tribe) that denied representation to a class of people (here, non-Indians) would presume to assert jurisdiction over that class of people. This seemed not only unconstitutional but un-American, a point raised in the city's defense as a claim of denial of equal protection for non-Indians. One Mission resident framed the argument in the following terms: "When the city of Mission put in a paved street, it wasn't for white people, it was for everybody—or water, or sewer, or curb and gutter. And if the money from the liquor store were to go to the tribe, no services would be returned to non-Indians, no voting in any election, no voice, can't sit on any jury, can't run for office.... It's taxation without representation ... it's jurisdiction without representation."

For some, the idea of *Indians* telling white people what to do was the crux of the matter, and the author has often heard—from both Indians and non-Indians—that certain local whites' "red-neck attitudes," "bigotry," or just plain "racism" were the source of the liquor store suit. One tribal member saw the attitude of some members of the city council as bigotry, plain and simple: "They weren't going to have that damn tribe dictating anything to them, period. That was the attitude.... [I]n my opinion it was ... racial...." Another Indian man explained what seemed to him deep-seated racism behind the liquor store case in this way: "I know some white native Todd Countyians ... who just have that ... racist idea of what Indians are and who they are, the fact that they don't measure up to, they're not like, them. And I don't necessarily mean just because their skin's brown.... 'I'm smiling at him and shaking hands with him, ... I'm even sitting here eatin' a hamburger with him, ... and I work with him. But he's a little bit ... inferior to me.'"

For some, resistance to tribal jurisdiction over liquor sales was a purely pragmatic matter of revenue. One non-Indian resident recalled the concerns of purchasing a tribal liquor license: "OK, it's $2,500 this year, then maybe in six months they'll want $2,500 more, and then maybe next time they'll want $3,500, and ... it would just go like that." Given all these concerns—which were, no doubt, stirred together in the thinking of individuals—the city council voted unanimously to contest the suit rather than submit to tribal jurisdiction.[30]

The central legal question in the suit was whether Mission was a "non-Indian community" under the 1949 statute that exempted "fee patented lands in non-Indian communities" from federal Indian liquor

---

30. "City to Contest Liquor Lawsuit," *Todd County Tribune,* 25 December 1980.

law. The answer, of course, depended upon the definition of "community" and "non-Indian." A trial on the question was held in federal district court in Pierre, South Dakota, in March 1982.[31] The United States
made the argument, based on the Supreme Court's reasoning in
Mazurie, that Mission and the *surrounding territory* constituted a single, larger community; when that community was examined, its *Indian*
character was clear. In its brief, the United States pointed out that the
Court of Appeals for the Eighth Circuit, in *United States* v. *Morgan,*[32]
had set out the criterion of "cohesiveness" in defining a community; a
community was not necessarily limited to an area circumscribed by
legal boundaries. Under this definition, and using evidence of interaction between people in Mission and in its environs introduced at the
hearing, it was clear that Mission and the surrounding area were "all
one community" and that the community was clearly *Indian* in character. Sixty-five percent of Todd County was composed of Indian trust
land, and the 1980 census showed that Indians comprised 5,688 of
county's total population of 7,328. Of the 1,768 students in the Todd
County School District, 1,465 were Indian. Regarding Mission, the
1980 census indicated that 376 (50.28 percent) of the 748 residents
were Indian. Two of the six members of the city council were Indian,
and one of the non-Indians was married to an Indian. Of the 38 businesses in Mission, 15 were owned by tribal members.[33]

The defense sought to show at the trial that the Indian and non-
Indian populations in and around Mission were distinct communities.
The defense attorney argued that non-Indian interaction with Indian
people ended at the corporate limits of the city; non-Indians were not
significantly involved with Indian people outside of Mission. The city's
brief noted at the outset that Mission was incorporated under state law,
had its own police department and provided municipal services without
BIA or tribal assistance, and had incurred long-term financial obligations in order to provide for public improvements. The city argued as
well that Mission's Indian and non-Indian communities were socially
and culturally distinct: "The Indian people in and around Mission,
South Dakota sponsor all-Indian activities, such as bowling tourna-
ments, and rodeos.... The Indian culture is separate and distinct from

31. Transcript of Trial, 3–4 March 1982, *United States* v. *Mission Golf Course and City of Mission* (D. S. D., Civil Cases 80-3073 and 80-3074) file, Finch, Viken, Viken and Pechota, Attorneys-at-Law, Rapid City, S. D.
32. 614 F.2d 166 (8th Cir., 1980).
33. Plaintiff's First Post-Trial Memorandum, filed 22 July 1982 (D. S.D., Civil Case 80-3074), Liquor Store file, City of Mission.

the non-Indian culture.... Native dancing and singing, and other cere-
monies differ from other cultures, and there is very little interaction between the Indians and non-Indians except for those interactions that
occur from activities at the Todd County school system and through
normal trade. [H]owever, there is little social interaction between the
two cultures. The Indians conduct their 'pow-wows' in Antelope [a
housing area east of Mission] and not in Mission.... The pow-wows
are predominantly attended by Indians who participate in native dancing and music."[34]

The district court was convinced by the government's argument and
in October 1982 issued a permanent injunction against the city and the
club, requiring them to operate in conformity with the tribal liquor
code or close. Based on the rationales in *Morgan* and other cases, the
decision itemized the "points to be considered in deciding what is a
non-Indian community": (1) the racial composition of the population in
the area, both historically and at the present time, and the extent of the
population's use of area services other than the liquor establishments at
issue; (2) a comparison of the role of state, federal, and tribal governments in the area; (3) a determination of who holds title to the land in
the area; and (4) the racial composition of the clientele of the establishments selling liquor.[35] The court presented a detailed factual analysis of
the proportion of Indian and non-Indian persons in Todd County and
Mission since 1940, of the proportion of businesses owned by Indians
and non-Indians in Mission, of the Indian clientele of Mission businesses in general and of the liquor store in particular, of the racial composition of the city council and the school board, and other facts
brought out in the trial, stipulations, and exhibits. The opinion concluded: "The Court has little difficulty in finding from the evidence...
that defendants City of Mission and the Mission Golf Course are not located within non-Indian communities."[36] Furthermore, the opinion rejected the 1951 Interior Department Solicitor's opinion defining Mission as a non-Indian community: "Whatever the validity of this finding
in 1951, it is of little significance thirty years later."[37] What was once a
non-Indian community, the court found, had evolved into an Indian
community.

34. Defendant's Brief, 11 August 1982 (D. S. D., Civil Case 80-3074), Liquor Store
file, City of Mission.
35. 548 F. Supp. 1177, 1179–80 (D. S. D., 1982).
36. Ibid., 1183.
37. Ibid., 1183, note 4.

The opinion rejected the defendants' argument that the community to be examined for Indian/non-Indian classification was the city of Mission itself: "Defendants seem to imply that this Court is limited solely to an examination of the City of Mission within its legal boundaries. Yet every case dealing with the concept of a 'non-Indian community' has looked to the surrounding territory. In *Mazurie* the Supreme Court considered the nature of the twenty square miles surrounding the bar, and found it to be primarily Indian; here the population within just a few square miles around the defendants is primarily Indian."[38] The opinion concluded:

> The sum total of the various ways the Indian presence in Mission is manifest demonstrates "an element of cohesiveness" which is inconsistent with a view of Mission and surrounding area as a "non-Indian community." It is true that there are substantial non-Indian elements to the area, but it cannot be said that these elements predominate. Put in the terms used in *Morgan*, the business, education and social "focal point" which the [Mission] locality provides year round for the surrounding [housing areas, and indeed, county] could give a man of average intelligence the understanding that as an inhabitant in this area, he lives in a "community." . . . Given the totality of evidence in this case, defendants have failed to prove that this "community," which includes the City of Mission and surrounding environs, is "non-Indian."[39]

THE APPEAL

The Mission City Council held a special meeting two days after the district court decision was handed down, attended by twenty-six citizens—an unusually high number for a city council meeting—at which the city attorney explained the decision. There was clearly great concern that the tribe would gain control of the liquor store revenue if the city submitted to tribal jurisdiction. Would the tribe provide police protection for the liquor store and the club in return for the revenue? Since liquor revenue was used by the city to maintain streets, would the tribe now provide this service? Would controlling the liquor store and its revenue become a political football, as so many tribal enterprises had become?[40] The city hired a new attorney—a key figure on the defense team for *Rosebud Sioux Tribe* v. *Kneip* (see chapter 2) to pursue its appeal. Based

38. Ibid., 1183.
39. Ibid.
40. Minutes, Mission City Council, 14 October 1982, Liquor Store file, City of Mission; "City of Mission to Seek Tribal Liquor License, Will File Appeal," *Todd County Tribune*, 20 October 1982.

in the town of Winner, the attorney had an office in Washington with access to archival materials not available locally. He advised the city council that new facts could be introduced in the appeal but cautioned that the appeal would cost about $20,000, and that the chance of success was no better than even. The city council nevertheless voted to pursue the appeal.[41]

The resentment of at least some residents in Mission toward the district court holding was apparent in the pages of the *Todd County Tribune*. One article reported: "Public opinion has been decidedly negative toward [the district court's] decision." There was an idea afoot to initiate "a countersuit alleging that all or portions of [the United States Code] may be racially discriminatory against people who are not Indian and may violate the U. S. Constitution."[42] Indeed, at a meeting of the city council in December 1982, attended by a handful of citizens, discussion "centered on constitutional rights, . . . the fact that though the City is ordered to submit to Tribal jurisdiction in the case of liquor, the City has no voice, no vote and no legal resource from tribal government as it has guaranteed under State and Federal government." A tribal member present said "he didn't think the 'sky would fall in' if the City applied and received a tribal liquor license." But a non-Indian resident pointed out that many Indian people had been victimized by the tribal government "and he didn't want to see the same thing happen to the City."[43]

The *Tribune* published a sampling of local opinion on the issue. One non-Indian voiced a sentiment apparently shared by many: "As far as I'm concerned, if the [federal] government thinks this is an Indian community, let the government pay our expenses. . . . Everybody in Mission—Indian and white alike—are [sic] benefiting from the liquor store by keeping our streets, sewer, water, snow removal, and maintenance going. I think the Tribe is pushing too much and not taking care of their own business." Another faulted the judge's holding: "I always felt [the district court judge] was wrong. I can't go along with him. Mission has always been a non-Indian community and I don't see why it should be

41. Minutes, City Council, 21 October 1982 and 26 October 1982, Liquor Store file, City of Mission; "[Attorney] May Handle Appeal," *Todd County Tribune,* 27 October 1982; [Attorney] Will Represent City, Golf Club in Liquor Appeal, *Todd County Tribune,* 3 November 1982.

42. "City Given until January 15 to Apply for Tribal Liquor License," *Todd County Tribune,* 29 December 1982.

43. "City Applies for Tribal Liquor License Under Protest," *Todd County Tribune,* 5 January 1983.

any different now. I think the City is right in fighting it and I think that's the route to go."[44] Clearly the court was quite literally incorrect in its assumption that "a man of average intelligence" would understand Mission to be an Indian community.

Several tribal members polled by the *Tribune* had a different take:

Number one, how can you bite the hand that feeds you? That's what all these people are doing here[,] the non-Indians who live on the reservation. How can the City expect to get a license from the Tribe when they're fighting them in court? . . . The City expects to get a license? Nuts. That's all I've got to say. Antelope Community is also officially on record to oppose any and all attempts by the City to get a tribal license. . . . Like I always said to everybody here—doctors, BIA police, Indians and non-Indians—there's four roads leading off this reservation for anybody who doesn't want to live here. If they don't like it here, they can get out.

I'm kind of disappointed when they started going to court over [the appeal]. The non-Indians said that they got along good with us and were friends. When the judge came down and said the City had to apply to the Tribe, then the City didn't want to go under tribal jurisdiction. It makes it sound like we're friends as long as it goes their way but when it doesn't, the people go another way.[45]

The central question in the appeal was the definition of "community": Could it refer to a municipality standing on its own, as defined by its corporate boundaries? Or was a community necessarily based on social interaction, the bounds of which must be empirically established on a case-by-case basis? The city argued for the first approach, the United States for the second.[46] One month after the oral arguments in the case, a panel of three judges announced its *per curiam* decision: "We have carefully examined the briefs and record in this matter, and conclude that the district court's findings are not clearly erroneous and that no error of law appears." The district court decision was affirmed.[47]

Three days later, the city's attorney explained to the city council and a large group of citizens the steps necessary for an appeal to the Supreme Court, pointing out that a case accepted by the Court would

44. "Public Opinion Poll," *Todd County Tribune*, 5 January 1983.
45. Ibid.
46. Opening Brief for Appellants, filed 27 January 1983, *United States* v. *Mission Golf Course and City of Mission*, Civil Case 82-2516 (8th Cir.); Brief of the United States, filed 10 February 1983, *United States* v. *Mission Golf Course and City of Mission*, Civil Case 82-2516 (8th Cir.).
47. Per Curiam Decision, 16 May 1983, Civil Case 82-2516 (8th Cir.), Liquor Store file, City of Mission Office.

cost the city approximately $10,000 plus expenses. There was only a one-in-ten chance that the court would take the case, and only a one in two chance that the city would win. The council nonetheless voted to proceed with an appeal to the Supreme Court.[48]

The city's petition for a writ of *certiorari* argued that the court of appeal's holding that a community's boundaries must be established factually and were not coterminous with the legal boundaries of a functioning municipal government was a dangerous precedent, which if left standing would invite further litigation. The holding left open the opportunity "for any interested party—the United States, the affected tribe, an individual seeking to avoid or establish federal jurisdiction—to litigate the community issue in a way which suits its position and without regard to municipal boundaries." The holdings of the district court and the court of appeals were inconsistent on this point in a number of cases, "apparently interpreting the term in a manner which best favors federal jurisdiction." A clear definition of "Indian country" by the Supreme Court was needed to avoid "uncertainty for all concerned." Moreover, the case had potential impact beyond reservation boundaries. If a community was not coterminous with its legal boundaries but had to be identified on a case-by-case basis by an examination of the local social and historical facts, what about dependent Indian communities *off* reservations? Could ceded areas that contained some trust land and more Indians than non-Indians be *put back* into Indian country status? The South Dakota attorney general, in an amicus brief filed with the states of Idaho and Montana, also expressed concern about opening up litigation over off-reservation, dependent Indian communities if the definition of community was left as a purely factual case-by-case matter. Clearly the specter of undermining *Kneip* loomed.[49] Nevertheless, the Supreme Court denied *certiorari* in January 1984.[50]

48. "City Council to Appeal Liquor Decision, People Are More Important than Things," *Todd County Tribune,* 25 May 1983; Minutes, City Council, 19 May 1983, Liquor Store file, City of Mission Office.

49. Petition for a Writ of Certiorari, filed 7 October 1983, no. 83-606 (U. S.), Liquor Store file, City of Mission; Brief of the States of South Dakota, Montana, and Idaho as Amici Curiae, filed November 1983, *Mission v. United States,* no. 83–606 (U. S).

50. The city was not done yet, however, and in 1983 filed a motion with the district court to set aside the motion on the basis of new documents uncovered by its attorney showing that the non-Indian community exemption had been enacted by Congress precisely because of situations such as that of Mission. When the motion failed in the district court, the city appealed to the court of appeals, where it also lost (Memorandum of Points and Authorities in Support of the Motion to Set Aside the Judgment, filed October 1983, Civ. 84-2129 (8th Cir.), Liquor Store file, City of Mission Office; Per Curiam Decision, 14 March 1985, Civ. 84-2129 (8th Cir.), Liquor Store file, City of Mission Office;

DEALING WITH THE TRIBE

Early in 1984 the tribe sent to the city's attorney a proposal that sought to allow both the tribe and the city to carry on liquor businesses in Mission. The Supreme Court had held in *Rice* v. *Rehner* that both states and tribes have jurisdiction over liquor sales on reservations;[51] to satisfy this ruling, the tribe proposed that the city issue four state licenses to the tribe; the tribe, in turn, would issue four tribal licenses to the city. The city council made a counteroffer in which the tribe would issue the city liquor store a tribal license, and the city would cede the tribe a cut of the profits—say, ten percent.[52]

In response to the city's counteroffer, the tribal president, the tribal attorney, and two other tribal representatives attended a city council meeting in August 1984. Clearly the tribe had something more than ten percent of the liquor store profits in mind. The tribal president explained that the tribe was obligated to address the social problems generated by alcohol abuse and therefore was entitled to a substantial cut of the liquor store revenues for treatment and prevention programs. One of the other tribal members attending argued that "by selling alcohol the City provides the vehicle to alcoholism and it is time they accept the responsibility of that vehicle by spreading the profit around for such programs as alcohol treatment.... [T]oo much money has been made on the misery of people and... the tribe inherits the problems of alcoholism." The tribal president suggested a fifty-percent cut for the tribe from the liquor store's net profits; the proposal was rejected by the city council, which proceed to submit an application for a tribal liquor license. After considering the city's rejection of the fifty-fifty offer, however, the tribal council unanimously adopted a resolution stating that the "Rosebud Sioux Tribe is of the opinion that no sale of alcoholic beverages should be permitted on the Rosebud Indian Reservation."[53]

Petition for Rehearing, 25 March 1985, Civ. 84-2129 (8th Cir.), Liquor Store file, City of Mission; Docket Sheet, *United States* v. *Mission,* Civil 84-2129 (8th Cir.).

51. 463 U.S. 713 (1981).

52. Memorandum, 26 March, 1984, Liquor Store file, City of Mission Office; Minutes, 11 July 1984, Rosebud Sioux Tribal Office; Attorney to Mayor, 26 July 1984, Liquor Store file, City of Mission Office; Finance Officer to Tribal President, 27 July 1984, Liquor Store file, City of Mission Office; Minutes, City Council, 2 August 1984, Liquor Store file, City of Mission Office; Attorney to Tribal President et al., 3 August 1984, copy in author's possession; "City Council Discusses Liquor Issue, Lawsuits," *Todd County Tribune,* 8 August 1984; "City Offers Choices on Liquor to Tribe," *Todd County Tribune,* 15 August 1984.

53. Minutes, City Council, 29 August 1984, Liquor Store file, City of Mission Office; Resolution 84-169, 31 August 1984, Rosebud Sioux Tribal Office; "City Council in Dilemma over Budget," *Todd County Tribune,* 15 September 1984.

The Rosebud Sioux Tribal Liquor Commission held a hearing on liquor license applications in September. It lasted three hours, and 140 people attended. Several tribal members testified against the sale of liquor on the reservation in principle. Others urged against allowing the city of Mission to operate a liquor concession.[54] The city was denied a liquor license in November in a notice that added, "you should immediately cease the sale of all liquor." The liquor commissioners cited public hearings on the license, as well as the tribal council's resolution opposing the sale of alcohol on the reservation. The central consideration in its decision was the "rampant" alcoholism among Indian people.[55] The city council voted to appeal the decision in the Rosebud Sioux Tribal Court, but its attorney advised the council, "I am not spending a great deal of time in preparing legal citations and the like since I believe each one of us knows the outcome of this matter." The tribal judge found in favor of the tribe in April 1985.[56]

The liquor store remained open after its federal court remedies were exhausted and after being denied a tribal license. In fact, the mayor had even gone so far as to comment on television "that he would not submit to the tribal authority but would [only] comply with a U. S. Marshall closing the liquor store."[57] In November 1984 the Rosebud Sioux Tribal Council unanimously moved that federal officials be urged to "effect the closing of the Mission Liquor Store and the Golf Club immediately."[58] Finally, after the United States attorney contacted the mayor, the liquor store was closed. Signs were put up in the windows indicating that it had been closed by the United States attorney (that is, by federal, not tribal, officials). An Indian resident of Mission told me that he believed that the signs were meant to tell the public that the city

54. Record of Proceedings, Rosebud Sioux Tribal Liquor Commission, 19 September 1984, *In the Matter of the Appeal, City of Mission and Mission Golf Course from Denial of Licenses*, Civil Case 84-45, Rosebud Sioux Tribal Court, Rosebud, S. D.

55. Notice of Denial, 6 November 1984, Liquor Store file, City of Mission Office.

56. Attorney to Finance Officer, 31 December 1984, Liquor Store file, City of Mission Office; Attorney to Mayor, 8 November 1984, Liquor Store file, City of Mission Office; Attorney to Attorney, 9 November 1984, Court Cases—Rulings, 1984, Frank Lapoint Papers, Lakota Archives and Historical Research Center; "City Appeals Liquor License Denial," *Todd County Tribune*, 14 November 1984; Memorandum Decision, 16 April 1985, *Appeal, City of Mission*, Civil Case 84-45, Rosebud Sioux Tribal Court, Rosebud, S.D.

57. "Tribal Council Seeks Closing of Liquor Outlets," *Todd County Tribune*, 14 November 1984; Application, Affidavit, and Order to Show Cause, 14 November 1984, *Appeal, City of Mission*, Civil Case 84-45, Rosebud Sioux Tribal Court, Rosebud, S. D.

58. Minutes, 13 November 1984, Rosebud Sioux Tribal Office.

would not be pushed around by the tribe—or "by Indians." Certainly, many must have read the signs that way.[59]

THE AMBIGUITY OF "NON-INDIAN COMMUNITIES" IN INDIAN COUNTRY

The political and legal conflict over the Mission Liquor Store was set into motion by the same kind of conflicting laws that were at the root of the *Kneip* boundary case. An earlier period of fostering the withering away of the reservations and Indian country through fee patents issued by the Secretary of the Interior had been followed by a repudiation of fee patenting and a federal commitment to protecting Indian trust land and preserving the special jurisdictional status of Indian country. By the "modern period" of tribal sovereignty, the tribe sought to regulate the sale of liquor on the reservation. However, by the time the tribal government became permanent and energized by the pursuit of self-determination, thousands of non-Indians were farming and ranching within the reservation, hundreds were living and operating businesses in Mission, and the city had been incorporated under the laws of the state of South Dakota. These non-Indians, or many of them, came to believe that they were not subject to whatever powers the tribe might seek to assert.

If reservations were understood as anomalous and anachronistic under laws enacted during the "civilization" period, the Indian New Deal and its progeny during the self-determination period made Mission a kind of anomaly, even an anachronism—a product of an earlier time when reservations were supposed to disappear. In 1949, when Congress was more or less committed to the protection of Indian country from state incursions, business interests in Mission were able to influence certain legislators to make an exception in the law pertaining to Indian country for anomalous localities such as Mission; thus was born the "non-Indian community" exemption. But this was a stopgap rather than a solution to a recurring contradiction in Indian law. Since it was not clear when a reservation town is and when it is not a non-Indian community, the law was—and remains—fundamentally ambiguous, as the attorney for Mission's beer parlor pointed out at the time of the enactment of the federal statute. And while the matter was "settled" by the courts in narrow terms, by defining what federal authorities will

59. "City Closes Liquor Store," *Todd County Tribune*, 21 November 1984.

allow in Mission, it was hardly settled from the point of view of those
local non-Indians who do not believe they live in Indian country—
whatever the court says. If the court insisted that "a man of average intelligence"[60] in Mission would realize that he was living in an *Indian*
community, it is important for us to recognize to what degree some men
and women in Mission see their community very differently. And it has
to do with what local people see as basic, constitutional rights. To be a
non-Indian community, white residents of Mission might well argue, is
to enjoy the civil rights that all American citizens are guaranteed. To be
an Indian community, by contrast, is to be engulfed by the reservation
and tribal jurisdiction, authority that conflicts fundamentally with
white civil rights—indeed an authority *racially discriminatory*. In the
district court case, the city's attorney argued that Mission would be "denied equal protection [on the basis of race] and due process of law in
that the Rosebud Sioux Tribe and its liquor commission denies non-
Indians representation on said Tribal council and liquor commission
based solely on race."[61] This was not simply a legal ploy but a deeply
held conviction on the part of many non-Indians in Mission, even if it
was rejected by the district court.[62]

One white resident whom I interviewed faulted the judge's capacity
to render a decision that took fair account of complex ethnic relations
within the city: "As far as I'm concerned he's an outsider looking in,
judge or no judge. He says,... 'that's an Indian community because
they're predominantly Indian.'... You know, the people that set up the
townsite years ago,... I don't think it was their reasoning...." Like the
homesteaders who settled the opened counties (chapter 2), the city's
non-Indian population expected to be free from Indian country; certainly, they never anticipated tribal jurisdiction over the city or its non-
Indian citizens—especially a jurisdiction that denied them "equal
rights." Why, this man must have wondered, did "settled expectations"
on the part of non-Indians who had bought former Indian land in good
faith come into the equation in the *Kneip* case but not in the *Mission*
case?

60. 548 F. Supp. at 1183 (quoting *Morgan*, 614 F.2d at 170).
61. Answer, 17 December 1980, *United States* v. *City of Mission* (Civil Case 80-
3074), Liquor Store file, City of Mission. The district court questioned whether a municipality or a corporation could "have standing to urge a claim of racial discrimination."
Even if that were true, however, the court held that the tribal liquor ordinance does not
expressly prohibit a non-Indian from serving on the tribal liquor commission (548 F.
Supp. at 1184).
62. 548 F. Supp. at 1184.

The non-Indian community exemption was a legislative attempt—prompted by the city of Mission itself—to ameliorate the contradiction of a non-Indian municipality within the boundaries of a permanent Indian reservation with Indian-country status. The two federal laws that facilitated the establishment of Mission—the General Allotment Act (1887) and the Burke Act (1906)—and the law that made permanent the reservation and its tribal government—the Indian Reorganization Act (1934)—remain in effect. But they are in fundamental conflict, and the non-Indian community provision constitutes an attempt to juggle them. It is thus, necessarily, an ambiguity that gives rise to profound political and legal conflict. The classification is always a fact-driven, case-by-case determination—there are no legal "bright lines"—and a particular community's status can change with time, as Mission's did. Any judicial decision on the question, thus defining a specific allocation of rights, must necessarily seem arbitrary to the people who lose in court and who have to live with the decision. A white resident of the city described the arbitrariness of defining Mission as "not a non-Indian community" by arguing that even the category *Indian* is a legal fiction. He pointed out the many families that have both Indian and non-Indian members in Todd County. "What is an Indian? Quarter-breed, a half-breed, what is it? . . . When you can be three-quarters white, but one-quarter Indian, and [be legally Indian]. . . ." So how was it possible, he asked, to characterize Mission racially if so many "Indians" have so much non-Indian ancestry—and claim the characterization was objective or principled?

An Indian resident of Mission told me that he sees such abstract and ambiguous legal concepts as the opening for non-Indian attacks on tribal sovereignty through unjust loopholes: "To me [the city's non-Indian-community argument is] kind of like a half-truth or a mistruth, or a misjustice. . . . [T]hat's why South Dakota has been so aggressive against us, is that you can get into these theoretical situations . . . and they're willing to take a chance everytime that they'll be able to make another little dent."

Of course, the law being what it is, taking a chance on "theoretical" interpretations works both ways. Ambiguities in federal Indian law have been exploited by those opposed to tribal government authority, and they have been and will continue to be exploited by the tribes as well. The concerns voiced before the Supreme Court by the city and the state attorney general that a case-by-case, fact-driven determination of the boundaries of "community" might set off a litigation explosion may not have been unfounded, even if they have not as yet come to pass. Some tribal members believe, for example, that it might be possible to reclaim Mellette County as Indian country "by the numbers." If land can be purchased by the tribe in an opened county and put back into trust status, those counties, or substantial tracts, might be returned to Indian-country status by raising the trust-land component of the county land base above fifty percent, or the Indian component of the population above fifty percent. Whether such a strategy for reclaiming Indian country would be accepted by the federal courts or not, the courts' fact-driven understanding of an "Indian community" in the *Mission* case has some tribal members convinced that areas of lost Indian country may be reclaimed by an argument regarding Indian "communities." Rights—both Indian and non-Indian—are not simply contested, they are unstable: the possibility of litigation or legislative action successfully reversing the status quo is always on the horizon for everyone who lives in the Rosebud country.

Rights are unstable in another way. The "settlement" of one case in federal Indian law regarding jurisdiction only *displaces* legal uncertainty and political conflict into other equally problematic areas. One tribal member who was active for years on the Mission city council told me: "these problems, they go on forever. You never get away from them. It's the same issue, they just come up in a different context, it's the same basic issues." Indeed, no sooner was the liquor store dispute settled than the tribe and the city came into conflict over the 2 percent sales tax that the city imposed in 1985 in lieu of liquor store revenues.[63] Neither the state nor its subdivisions have authority to collect taxes from Indians within Indian country; this remains "black letter" law. The Rosebud Sioux Tribe has an agreement with the state that authorizes South Dakota to collect a 4 percent sales tax on all sales within Todd County and return a percentage (based on the Indian proportion of the county population) to the tribe. This allows the state to collect the sales tax on purchases over which it does have jurisdiction—those involving *non-Indian* customers. It simply collects the tax on all purchases and rebates to the tribe the revenue estimated—by population count—to have been raised from sales to Indian customers. This method avoids the awkward—and possibly illegal—need to ask the customer her or his race to determine the applicability of the state tax to a particular sale.

63. "Additional Sales Tax Effective March 1," *Todd County Tribune,* 13 February 1985.

The city of Mission, however, is not a party to this agreement and has no authority to tax tribal members. Tribal members have the lawful option to decline to pay the city sales tax, but how many will do this in front of other customers waiting in line behind them in the supermarket? Angered, the tribal council passed a resolution calling for "a boycott of all non-Indian businesses in Mission who are imposing an illegal tax on Indian people." "The purpose of the boycott," the tribal president explained, was "to show our contempt for the City Council's actions. Especially the redneck attitudes and action of the mayor."[64] The tribe placed a notice in the *Tribune* announcing that tribal members were not subject to the city sales tax and directing members to simply show their identification cards (available at the tribal enrollment office) to the clerk.[65] Merchants would not inquire about the customer's race because of potential civil rights violations; it was the customer's responsibility to advise the clerk that a sale was exempt from the city sales tax.

Antelope Community, just east of Mission, held a meeting on the matter, to which the chair of the Mission chamber of commerce was invited. A tribal official told the visitor: "[Y]ou have the gall to tax us Indians to pay your bills." The Antelope Community chairman added: "The City owed us the responsibility and courtesy to see if it was a fair and equitable tax and that it would go to the proper government which is the Rosebud Sioux Tribe and to hold public hearings and tell people. I want to know . . . how is the tax going to benefit me?"[66]

Others felt differently. According to the *Tribune*, "Some Mission residents are offended by the exemption, even though claimants have apparently been few in number, because the City tax is used to benefit all area citizens *with no discrimination*. When snow-covered streets are plowed, the City plows in front of an Indian's house as well as in front of a non-Indian's house. Indian and non-Indian children together have used the City's Swimming Pool. All people can drive Mission streets. . . . Fire protection is offered equally to all."[67]

This was a notion of rights very different from that enunciated by the Antelope Community's tribal official. The collision of two such views directly creates racial hard feelings.

---

64. "Boycott Has Little Impact," *Todd County Tribune*, 6 March 1985.

65. "Notice," *Todd County Tribune*, 13 March 1985.

66. "Antelope Community Members Want Facts on Taxes, Jurisdiction," *Todd County Tribune*, 1 May 1985.

67. "City Councilman Would Like Attorney General's Input in Tribal-State Sales Tax Agreement," *Todd County Tribune*, 1 May 1985 (emphasis added).

CHAPTER 4

State Jurisdiction in Indian Country

In the spring of 1989 the members of the Rosebud Sioux Tribal Council were facing the possibility of being jailed for contempt of court. The tribe and the state of South Dakota were embroiled in litigation in federal court on the right of the state to exercise jurisdiction over highways running through the reservation. The tribe had sued the state in United States district court, arguing that the state's claimed jurisdiction over highways was unlawful. After the judge decided that the state and the tribe had concurrent highway jurisdiction, the tribal president issued an executive order: "In recognition of the 1851 and the 1868 Treaties and the fact that the congress of the United States has never diminished the current boundaries of the Rosebud Sioux Reservation, I am hereby ordering that the State Highway Patrol not be allowed on any highways within the Rosebud Reservation Boundaries."[1] South Dakota responded with a motion for an order to show cause why the Rosebud Sioux Tribal Council and its president should not be "punished for contempt of court."[2]

Although the president later rescinded the order,[3] the tribal council overrode the recission at a special meeting at which it was decided that

1. Executive Order, 89–01, Rosebud Sioux Tribal Office, Rosebud, S.D.
2. Motion for Order to Show Cause, filed 21 April 1989, *Rosebud Sioux Tribe* v. *South Dakota*, Civil Case 86–3019, D.S.D.
3. The tribal president's rationale for rescinding the ban on the state police was that the original purpose of the executive order was to leverage support from the BIA, and since the BIA had responded that it could not legally enforce the order, the order was no longer necessary. Also, the president was concerned, on the advice of a tribal attorney,

the tribe needed to stand up to the state. The vice president of the Oglala Sioux Tribe, from neighboring Pine Ridge Reservation, spoke at the meeting and assured the council members that "your brothers to the west . . . will go to battle with you in the court of law." He also reminded the council of the need to be on perpetual guard against state incursions into the tribe's autonomy: "if the state has a precedent case . . . of assuming jurisdiction . . . on reservations, they're not going to stop there. Till they get everything we hold. And we all know the real picture: they're after our resources." Even though a tribal attorney assured the council that the district court decision affected only public highways and that state police would not be seen patrolling Indian communities, council members were concerned. "How far will they go?," one asked: Would they drive into the yards of Indian people? At one point, a tribal member took the floor to deliver an impassioned speech to the council:

> I always heard the word "sovereignty," but I've never seen an expression of it. I've worked for tribal government for a number of years, and . . . I always see the infringement of state regulation, federal regulation, and I don't see the tribe really taking a strong stand and saying "tribal regulation." There was a time when we controlled the whole state of South Dakota, and more. And now we're down to one county, thanks to [the] *Kneip* case. And I think that if the council doesn't stand strong, we're not even going to have Todd County. [W]hen is it going to stop, when are we going to [quit] giving it away . . . ? And if there is a threat of contempt of court, it shouldn't scare a person. I think that as elected leaders . . . you have taken a oath of office to defend the members of this tribe. And I know there are other council members of other tribes that sat in jail for fighting for their fishing rights. And I think if it means you have to be jailed to hang onto our jurisdiction, it has to be that way. [*aho*][4] Because you are the leaders. . . . I really want to encourage you as the elected governing body of this tribe to stand your ground against the state, irregardless of threats of contempt of court, or whatever else. . . . [applause]

The council voted unanimously to reaffirm the executive order banning the highway patrol from the reservation, and the president complied.[5]

---

that the order might jeopardize the appeal. The state withdrew its motion when the ban was rescinded (Executive Order 89-02, Exhibit C, Second Motion for Order to Show Cause, 9 May 1989, *Rosebud Sioux Tribe* v. *South Dakota* File [D. S. D., 86-3019], Dakota Plains Legal Services, Mission, S. D.; Tape of Rosebud Sioux Tribal Council Meeting, 5 May 1989, Rosebud Sioux Tribal Office).

4. Word of approval in the Lakota language.

5. Tape of Council Meeting, 5 May 1989, Rosebud Sioux Tribal Office; Minutes, 5 May 1989, Rosebud Sioux Tribal Office. The council reconsidered the action at their next meeting, but a motion to withdraw the ban was defeated by a vote of 14 to 6 (Minutes, 11 May 1989, Rosebud Sioux Tribal Office).

The South Dakota attorney general's office renewed its motion for an order to show cause against the tribal council and its president,[6] noting its concern that "tribal reluctance to use peaceful, constitutional means to resolving disputes" might lead to "actual violence."[7] Although the judge declined to issue the show-cause order,[8] the possibility that members and officers of the tribal council might be held in contempt and jailed was by no means farfetched.

As with the reservation boundary and Mission Liquor Store cases, the conflict was rooted in the historical overlay of fundamentally conflicting laws: on the one hand, the termination legislation of the 1950s, drawing its charter from the "uniformity" paradigm of Indian law, and, on the other, the more recent protection of Indian self-determination, appealing to a "uniqueness" reading of the status of Indians. Of direct relevance here are Public Law 280, enacted in 1953, which authorized states to assume jurisdiction over Indian country, and the Indian Civil Rights Act of 1968, which gave tribes protections against state jurisdictional incursions. Each of these acts grounded a different and profoundly inconsistent regime of rights for Indian people. The choice between them in the federal Indian law game hung by a remarkably abstract and technical thread.

As did the boundary and Mission Liquor Store struggles, this conflict directly contributed to "racial" tension in South Dakota. To tribal members who were involved in the highway jurisdiction case, "whites" and "white racism" were the issue. Racism explained why "they" wanted jurisdiction, and prejudice was the only explanation for egregious misreading of the law—from the point of view of tribal advocates—when the United States district court found in favor of the state. When I asked a Lakota resident why the state was so insistent about asserting jurisdiction over the reservation, he recalled the mural that hung until 1997 in the governor's office in the capitol in Pierre. To him, the painting was indicative of the "white attitude" behind the jurisdictional conflict and all other forms of racial conflict in the state: "[T]ake out the evil, which is Indian, make way for the good, which is European.... [I]t's Manifest Destiny." Given these Indian standpoints on what underlay the state's assertions of jurisdiction, it is not difficult to understand

6. Second Motion for Order to Show Cause, filed 9 May 1989, *Rosebud Sioux Tribe v. South Dakota* File (D. S.D., 86-3019), Dakota Plains Legal Services.

7. Reply to Response to Request for Expedited Discovery, filed 13 June 1989, *Rosebud Sioux Tribe v. South Dakota* File (D. S.D., 86-3019), Dakota Plains Legal Services.

8. Order, 20 June 1989, *Rosebud Sioux Tribe v. South Dakota* File (D. S.D., 86-3019), Dakota Plains Legal Services.

why Lakota people were willing to go to jail to keep the state highway patrol off the reservation.

TERMINATION AND STATE JURISDICTION

With a radical reversal of the Indian New Deal in mind, Congress adopted House Concurrent Resolution 108 in 1953, declaring its intent, "as rapidly as possible, to make the Indians . . . subject to the same laws and entitled to the same privileges and responsibilities as . . . other citizens . . . , to end their status as wards . . . , and to grant them all of the rights and prerogatives pertaining to American citizenship."[9] A more direct statement of the *anomalous* nature of a separate and unique status of Indian people—at least according to the uniformity reading—would be difficult to articulate, and this policy must have come as good news to officials in South Dakota. Although local law enforcement and judicial officers on Rosebud Reservation were early on exercising jurisdiction over Indians in Mission and on arterial highways in Todd County without legal authority (see chapter 1), state officials in Pierre—the capital—recognized the need for a lawful basis for state jurisdiction over Indians on South Dakota reservations.[10] Some local officials—such as states attorneys and judges—also may have doubted the legality of exercising state jurisdiction over Indians in Todd County and recognized the possibility that convictions could be reversed on appeal.

Some local people perceived a law enforcement gap, despite the extralegal assertion of jurisdiction over Indians. One of the attorneys I interviewed recalled the problems of law enforcement in rural reservation areas and predominantly Indian towns on Rosebud Reservation in the 1950s. Thefts by Indians of cattle owned by non-Indian ranchers, for example, would not be prosecuted by the United States attorney—who legally had exclusive jurisdiction under the Indian Country Crimes Act—because they were considered "too minor." He described an incident in a largely Indian town on Rosebud, indicating his recollection of desperate need for lawful state jurisdiction over Indians: "In the little town of St. Francis . . . in front of the general store a car was parked. Another car comes in broad daylight, . . . parks beside it. A number of men get out of the second car, have jacks and tire tools, and they jack up the

9. 67 Stat. B132.

10. For a concise history of attempts by South Dakota to assume jurisdiction over reservations from 1950 through 1964 and Indian resistance to those attempts, see Clow 1981.

... first car, take all the wheels and tires off ... and drive off. This is in full view of ... ten, twelve, people, who identify all of the participants by name.... The U. S. Attorney refused to prosecute. 'Minor matter.' What were the tires worth? Probably very little. But it was a crime that occurred in public view. Not only were white people offended ... but the Indian people were offended because nothing was done." He also recalled incidents in which Indian voters in Todd County registered and voted in more than one precinct in general elections; state authorities charged with administering voting laws could not enforce them against Indian violators.

As early as 1950 the South Dakota Indian Affairs Commission[11] discussed the problem of inadequate federal law enforcement on Indian reservations. State patrolmen would drive through the reservations "so that people may feel that there are police officers around," but they could not act as police because they had no jurisdiction over Indians. At an Indian Affairs Commission meeting, Dillon Myer—the commissioner who would begin to shepherd termination policies in the BIA[12] —suggested that "the ultimate answer is the assumption of full jurisdiction by the state." While everyone—except, of course, Indian people—might have preferred this, the problem was the expense involved. One state official responded to Myer that since Indian reservations are "a national affair," states with Indian reservations should be able to count on "federal subsidization."[13] The governor wrote to Commissioner Myer in 1952: "[there is] no question in [my] mind but that some day, Indian reservations will be done away with and the laws of the States will be the only laws that will apply," but "if the federal government is going to leave the job of law enforcement up to the counties and the state and not provide the necessary funds, I would be opposed to the transfer."[14]

Two weeks after adopting House Concurrent Resolution 108 in 1953, Congress enacted Public Law 280, which transferred to state governments jurisdiction over crimes committed by or against Indians and

11. The Indian Affairs Commission was established by the legislature in 1949 "to consider and study living conditions among the Indians residing within the state, with the purpose of establishing a method of absorbing the Indian people into the economy of the state" (South Dakota Session Laws, 1949, chap. 244).

12. See Drinnon 1986.

13. Minutes, 16 August 1950, Indian Affairs Commission Minutes, South Dakota State Historical Society, Pierre.

14. Anderson to Myer, 14 March 1952, Indian Commission File, Box 5, Departmental Files, Sigurd Anderson Papers, Richardson Archives, University of South Dakota, Vermillion.

civil actions involving Indians in Indian country in California, Minnesota,[15] Nebraska, Oregon,[16] and Wisconsin.[17] The act also authorized any other state with a jurisdictional disclaimer in its constitution—such as South Dakota—to amend state law in order to assume jurisdiction over Indians in Indian country.[18]

Under the authority of Public Law 280, in 1957 South Dakota enacted a law assuming "jurisdiction of all criminal and civil causes of action arising in Indian Country." To answer the attendant fiscal concerns, the act conditioned the assumption of jurisdiction upon reimbursement by the United States for the added costs. In addition, jurisdiction over any reservation would not be transferred to the state until a majority of the tribal voters had approved the transfer.[19] The Rosebud Sioux Tribal Council held a tribal referendum in January 1958, and the assumption of jurisdiction by the state of South Dakota was defeated by a vote of 811 to 227. In conveying the results of the referendum to county commissioners in Todd, Tripp, Gregory, Mellette, and Lyman counties, the council declared that it "does hereby abide by the wishes of the Rosebud Sioux people and shall continue to remain under Federal jurisdiction and shall continue to operate under the approved Tribal Law and Order Code."[20]

By October 1960, the Taxpayers League—a local organization in Todd County that represented non-Indians—was lobbying for state jurisdiction over Indians. (The effort again suggests that at least some local non-Indians realized that the state and its subdivisions did not have lawful jurisdiction over Indians, even though Mission and Todd County officials were exercising jurisdiction.) In January 1961 a bill was introduced in the South Dakota House of Representatives, drafted by a lobbyist acting for the taxpayers leagues of Todd County and Shannon County (Pine Ridge Reservation), that would have assumed jurisdiction over all criminal and civil matters in Indian country under the provisions of Public Law 280. The lobbyist recalled in an interview

15. Except Red Lake Reservation.
16. Except Warm Springs Reservation.
17. Except Menominee Reservation.
18. 67 Stat. 588. For the history of the termination policy, see Fixico 1986; Philp 1999.
19. South Dakota Session Laws, 1957, chap. 319.
20. Resolution 58-50, 18 July 1958, Rosebud Sioux Tribal Office, Rosebud, S. D. Since the federal government did not arrange for reimbursement of state subdivisions in conformity with the provisions of this state jurisdiction law, the law did not become effective anywhere in the state.

with the author in 1993 that the primary concern of the Taxpayers
League was "lawlessness," especially drunken driving on the highways.[21]

Enforcing such a law, however, raised the usual cost concerns. Taxpayers in Tripp County, which was responsible for enforcing state law
in Todd County (Todd County was unorganized and was attached to
Tripp for administrative and judicial purposes), worried that any ex-
panded jurisdiction over Indians would entail large costs.[22] Because of
these concerns, the bill was amended to assume jurisdiction only over
"criminal offenses and civil causes of action arising on any highways"
in Indian country; it provided for assumption of general jurisdiction,
however, if federal reimbursement was forthcoming. The bill became
law on 9 March 1961.[23]

The law would not become effective until 1 July 1961, and the governor wrote almost immediately to the BIA seeking to arrange grants-
in-aid for reimbursement of the added expenses anticipated in assuming general jurisdiction. He was informed by the commissioner of
Indian affairs and by the state's congressional delegation, however, that
the BIA was not authorized to enter into such contracts with states or
counties and that proposed legislation that would make this possible
was opposed by the Secretary of the Interior.[24] State officials must have
realized that federal subsidization of state jurisdiction would "never

21. Lobbyist to Gubbrud, 14 January 1961, Indian Affairs File, Box 2, Boards and
Commissions, 1961–63, Archie Gubbrud Papers, Richardson Archives, University of
South Dakota, Vermillion; House Journal, 19 January 1961, 175. The lack of sufficient
law enforcement delivery by the federal government on Rosebud Reservation was a concern not limited solely to the non-Indian Taxpayers League. Indian people as well were
concerned. In 1957 when the Rosebud Sioux Tribal Council was discussing the state's
new jurisdiction bill, the council representative from the Corn Creek community reported
that "the members of my community have so far expressed in favor of the state assuming
jurisdiction" because of inadequate police protection (Minutes, 8 April 1957, Rosebud
Sioux Tribal Office).

22. Correspondent to Republican Chair, 14 February 1961, Indian Affairs File, Box
2, Boards and Commissions, 1961-3, Gubbrud Papers.

23. House Journal, 20 February 1961, 777–78; Senate Journal, 28 February 1961,
922; South Dakota Session Laws, 1961, chap. 464; "Legislative News," Todd County
Tribune, 9 March 1961; Schell 1975:315. South Dakota also enacted a statute in 1959
accepting "concurrent police jurisdiction" over reservation highways (South Dakota Session Laws, 1959, chap. 144). Congress, however, never authorized South Dakota to take
"concurrent police jurisdiction" over reservation highways, and the law was ineffective
as a basis for assertion of jurisdiction.

24. Gubbrud to Commissioner, 27 March 1961; Congressman to Gubbrud, 29
March 1961; Senator to Gubbrud, 7 April 1961; Commissioner to Gubbrud, 13 April
1961; Senator to Gubbrud, 29 April 1961; Indian Affairs File, Box 2, Boards and Commissions, 1961–63, Gubbrud Papers.

happen."[25] Indeed, one intent behind the Republican-supported termination move in Congress was to reduce the federal budget. Thus, general state jurisdiction under the 1961 law never went into effect, but highway jurisdiction became effective on 1 July because it had not been conditioned upon federal reimbursement.[26]

The state legislature was not through yet, however, and in 1962 the Interim Investigating Committee, composed of members from both chambers, issued a report on Indian jurisdictional problems and the operations of the state department of the public welfare. The most serious problems were found in the administration of the Aid to Dependent Children (ADC) caseload, of which forty-five percent was Indian. The report noted that the state was prohibited from enforcing state law among this population, and it recommended that "to promote economy and efficiency in the operations of the Department of Public Welfare, the Legislature should accept criminal and civil jurisdiction over Indian Country insofar as such jurisdiction relates to the public welfare program and the related areas of juvenile affairs, commitments, and domestic relations."[27] "The Department of Public Welfare advises that its hands are tied and that it is hamstrung at the present time under existing laws because the state does not have jurisdiction over these selected causes of action." The $2.1 million spent annually on welfare for Indians made the matter of jurisdiction "extremely important to the taxpayers of this state."[28]

At an Indian Affairs Commission conference, the director of the state welfare department offered examples of the welfare inefficiencies owing to the lack of state jurisdiction:

25. South Dakota Director of Legislative Research to North Dakota Director of Legislative Research, 27 December 1961, Indian Affairs File, Box 2, Boards and Commissions, 1961–63, Gubbrud Papers.

26. In fact, Indian country jurisdiction being ever complicated in South Dakota, it was not clear in 1961 whether the highway jurisdiction provision was in effect. A University of South Dakota law professor conversant with jurisdictional issues, for example, could not determine from the wording of the statute whether highway jurisdiction was conditioned upon federal subsidization. He wrote to the governor that it appeared to him "that the state did not make that qualification," but he wanted clarification. The governor's office responded that "the Governor sees no authority for declaring the whole law ineffective"—that is, the assumption of highway jurisdiction would become effective 1 July; the professor, however, was warned that this was "by no means to be construed as a 'legal' interpretation . . . [but as merely] the interpretation of this office" (Professor to Gubbrud, 25 October 1961; Executive Assistant to Professor, 25 October 1961, Indian Affairs File, Box 2, Boards and Commissions, 1961–63, Gubbrud Papers).

27. Interim Investigating Committee 1962, 8. The report claimed that the problem cases did not "care very much whether they are in jail or out," and the extent to which the assumption of state jurisdiction in itself would have solved the problems is uncertain.

28. Ibid., 17–18.

[I]n one county the ADC mother and children are living off the reservation while the deserting father is living on the reservation. The mother has filed a complaint with the states [sic] attorney who cannot take action because he does not have authority on Indian land. This father is employed and earning enough to support his family. . . .

Another Indian family living off the reservation obtained a divorce through the state court. The divorce decree was granted and support payments of $100.00 per month were ordered. After the divorce the father returned to the reservation and it became impossible to enforce the court's actions by contempt proceedings.[29]

Taxpayers might take comfort in one aspect of the transfer of jurisdiction over Indian country from the federal government: if the state was wasting large sums on deadbeat Indian welfare recipients every year because it could not enforce state law against individuals residing on reservations, the powers granted by the legislation—even with the added expense of hiring enforcement personnel—might result in a net savings to the state budget.

The legislature passed a general jurisdiction bill in 1963. An amendment had been proposed on the floor to require tribal consent before the assumption of jurisdiction, but this motion was defeated.[30] The governor received a good deal of correspondence on the bill as it lay on his desk for signature. Numerous Indian writers from Rosebud urged the governor to veto the bill.[31] One of the concerns of Rosebud Sioux tribal members was the lack of impartial law enforcement, due process, and a fair hearing in state courts for Indian people. One letter to the governor advised him of the conditions in the Mission city jail, where there had been three suicides.[32] Another warned that Indians could not trust local authorities: "In Mission they sell liquor to the Indians and when he is so drunk, [he] leaves town. The cops wait for him and then picks him up for drunken driving and the likes and hauls him off to Winner to get per diem."[33] The

29. Conference on Civil Jurisdiction, 15 November 1962, Minutes File, Indian Affairs Commission Records, South Dakota State Historical Society.

30. House Journal, 27 February 1963, 804; "State Passes Law to Assume Jurisdiction on Reservations," Todd County Tribune, 7 March 1963.

31. Some letters were apparently written at the instigation of the Jesuit community at St. Francis Mission on Rosebud (Parish Bulletin, n. d., Indian Jurisdiction File, Box 1, Miscellaneous Subjects, 1963, Gubbrud Papers). Some were written by students in more-or-less organized letterwriting campaigns in the schools; some had substantially identical text and were written on identical stationery.

32. Correspondent to Gubbrud, 11 March 1963, Indian Jurisdiction File, Box 1, Miscellaneous Subjects, 1963, Gubbrud Papers.

33. Correspondent to Gubbrud, 8 February 1963, Indian Jurisdiction File, Box 1, Miscellaneous Subjects, 1963, Gubbrud Papers.

vice president of the Native American Church of South Dakota, from St. Francis, advised the governor that church members from Rosebud Reservation were "strictly against the Bill of State Jurisdiction over us Rosebud Indians. We prayed to the Great Spirit to guide your conscience upon a proper decision."[34] Certainly the church's sacramental use of peyote must have raised concerns among its members about the enforcement of state drug laws.[35]

One correspondent wrote, "If this bill passes, I know the Determination [termination] will also be passed."[36] Indeed, the connection between the bill and termination was not farfetched. The governor himself had been quoted in the *Sioux Falls Argus Leader* to the effect that Indians should pay property taxes just like everybody else. A resident of Mission was "pleased" to read the governor's comment: "I know several Indians that have from 200 to over 500 cow herds that refuse to pay taxes. ... I don't mind paying taxes because it is the duty of every good citizen, but it doesn't look fair for those that can afford it to ride along on a free ticket."[37] Many Rosebud residents believed that the effect of the bill would be to tax Indian lands and eventually convey them into the hands of non-Indians when the Indian owners fell into arrears on their taxes and the lands were sold for back-taxes. One writer insisted, "If this bill is passed many people will not be able to pay taxes on their land. This is just what the cattle people want."[38] Another wrote that the Indian people would be "like babies"—that is to say, vulnerable—under state law

34. Vice President to Gubbrud, 13 March 1963, Indian Jurisdiction File, Box 1, Miscellaneous Subjects, 1963, Gubbrud Papers.

35. In 1925, for example, a member of the Native American Church was found guilty in state circuit court of furnishing peyote to another Indian on Rosebud Reservation and was fined fifty dollars (Criminal Case 6409, 1925, Lyman County Courthouse, Kennebec, S. D.).

36. Correspondent to Gubbrud, 9 March 1963, Indian Jurisdiction File, Box 1, Miscellaneous Subjects, 1963, Gubbrud Papers.

37. Correspondent to Gubbrud, 7 March 1963, Indian Jurisdiction File, Box 1, Miscellaneous Subjects, 1963, Gubbrud Papers.

38. Correspondent to Gubbrud, 9 March 1963, Indian Jurisdiction File, Box 1, Miscellaneous Subjects, 1963, Gubbrud Papers. Another tribal member was even more direct about the interests of the non-Indian ranchers behind this bill: "The Stockgrowers Association of South Dakota are [sic] forcing the State tax payers to take on a huge burden, which a great many would object to if given the true facts. It is a known fact that this powerful organization is the silent force behind passage of this bill. They set the wheels in motion to have this bill enacted soon after several members of their association lost their case in a court-of-law to the Tribal government concerning the tribal tax on rental of their lands.... [T]hey have their greedy eyes on the fine grazing lands owned by the poor Indian. With their present economy most of the Indians would be unable to pay taxes on their trust lands" (Correspondent to Gubbrud, 11 March 1963, Indian Jurisdiction File, Box 1, Miscellaneous Subjects, 1963, Gubbrud Papers).

and that "all their lands" would be taken from them through "taxes and what not."[39]

The governor, of course, also received correspondence in favor of the bill. Bank managers in White River, Winner, and Mission urged him in a telegram to sign the bill, as did the publisher of the *Winner Advocate*.[40] A resident of Mission wrote, "We who live on the Reservation know how badly we need State Jurisdiction.... The only Indians here that don't want Jurisdiction are the Trible [sic] Council Officers."[41] A resident of Norris, in Mellette County, urged signature of the bill and complained: "When I came to my present home forty-five years ago the nearest neighbors in all directions were Indians. And some wonderful people they were. Well behaved, law-abiding and crime was seldom a problem. Now two generations later crime is so common and the Indians' immunity from prosecution for crimes committed on Indian land so fixed that they get away with murder as well as any lesser crimes and nothing is done about it."[42]

A resident of Mission wrote to the governor, asking that his letter be kept in strictest confidence since "my life as well as that of my family might be jeopardized." He complained of "lawlessness...that you would never believe could have even taken place in the darkest sections of uncivilized Africa. One of our established ranchers had approximately seventy stacks of fine hay completely burned away [by arson] last fall." He noted the recent killing of a man at Okreek and reported that the murderers had been "turned loose as a result of this confusion over division of authority under law and order." The BIA police force was "a farce and a sham."[43]

In addition to this "lawlessness" argument,[44] non-Indians invoked equal rights and responsibilities as justification for state jurisdiction. A Mission resident pointed out that state jurisdiction would "be an important step toward the integration of the Indian and non-Indians on

39. Correspondent to Gubbrud, 13 March 1963, Indian Jurisdiction File, Box 1, Miscellaneous Subjects, 1963, Gubbrud Papers.

40. Correspondent to Gubbrud, 7 March 1963, Correspondent to Gubbrud, 14 March 1963, Indian Jurisdiction File, Box 1, Miscellaneous Subjects, 1963, Gubbrud Papers.

41. Correspondent to Gubbrud, 7 March 1963, Indian Jurisdiction File, Box 1, Miscellaneous Subjects, 1963, Gubbrud Papers.

42. Correspondent to Gubbrud, 8 March 1963, Indian Jurisdiction File, Box 1, Miscellaneous Subjects, 1963, Gubbrud Papers.

43. Correspondent to Gubbrud, 7 March 1963, Indian Jurisdiction File, Box 1, Miscellaneous Subjects, 1963, Gubbrud Papers.

44. For an Iowa version of the "lawlessness" discourse, see Foley 1995:21–23.

the reservation."[45] A Norris correspondent wrote, "I feel that all citizens of South Dakota should have equal responsibility to abide by the laws of our state." The BIA and tribal leaders were "trying to set up the Indian as a citizen apart without responsibility to state laws." "Picture a classroom—with a flag of our country, a room full of our young citizens studying civics, and the teacher explaining our form of government, building citizenship, loyalty, and the spirit of America to confused young people whose tribe is not a part of that same citizenry. They are not covered or protected by the same code without state law."[46]

The governor himself spoke of equal rights when he signed the bill into law in March 1963. He was quoted in the *Todd County Tribune*: "We'll be giving the Indian equal protection under the law. We hear a lot about civil rights. But until all South Dakotans are treated the same, we'll never achieve the full potential of our state." The law assumed and accepted jurisdiction, pursuant to the provisions of Public Law 280, over "all criminal offenses and civil causes of action arising in the Indian Country."[47]

Indian people in South Dakota were not ready to accept defeat. The South Dakota tribes formed a statewide organization—the United Sioux Tribes—to refer the bill to the voters and defeat it in a referendum.[48] The United Sioux Tribes contracted with a Sioux Falls advertising firm and a Rapid City law firm to handle the drive for a referendum, and the petition in support, with more than 20,000 signatures, was eventually filed.[49]

One of the major concerns of Indian people raised during the initiative opposing the 1963 jurisdiction law was the alleged mistreatment of Indian people in county and city jails. In August 1963, a tribal member who was also the executive director of the National Congress of American Indians asked the Tripp County state's attorney to hold a hearing to consider evidence of abuse of Indians by law enforcement and of illegally

45. Correspondent to Gubbrud, 7 March 1963, Indian Jurisdiction File, Box 1, Miscellaneous Subjects, 1963, Gubbrud Papers.
46. Correspondent to Gubbrud, 13 March 1963, Indian Jurisdiction File, Box 1, Miscellaneous Subjects, 1963, Gubbrud Papers.
47. South Dakota Session Laws, 1963, chap. 467; "State Jurisdiction Bill to Become Effective on July First," *Todd County Tribune*, 21 March 1963.
48. See Clow 1981.
49. "Sioux Tribes Seek to Refer Jurisdiction Law to Voters," *Todd County Tribune*, 28 March 1963; Minutes, 30 March 1963, United Sioux Minutes File, Box 4, Cato Valandra Papers, Richardson Archives, University of South Dakota, Vermillion; Clow 1981: 179.

asserted state jurisdiction over Indians.[50] A closed hearing, at which a large number of witnesses testified, was held before a justice of the peace in Winner. The extent to which treatment of prisoners in county jails was a concern among Indians in the early 1960s reflects the circumstances of the civil rights climate at the time. It was legal in South Dakota, for example, for prisoners to be fed only bread and water as long as they were given a full meal every fourth day. A state official who had been involved in the 1963 hearing told me in 1993 that there had clearly been abuse of Indian prisoners, but apparently no action was taken.[51]

County jails were not the only source of contention; many Indian people felt that state courts meted out unequal justice. Proceedings in a criminal case in state circuit court in 1959, involving a Rosebud Sioux tribal member who had been arrested and charged with third-degree burglary for breaking into a store in Mission, suggest that these concerns were not unfounded. The complaint charged that the defendant, "was caught in the store by the owner but escaped out the back door taking with him some check blanks which he threw away in the alley behind the store. The Defendant was intoxicated at the time of the commission of this offense." Papers filed with the court by the state's attorney faulted the defendant's "bad habits," "irresponsible reputation," and alleged that his associates were "men and women of questionable character."[52] At the trial the judge questioned the defendant:

Q: The court informs you that you are entitled to be represented here by counsel. In other words, you are entitled to have a lawyer here to represent you at this time, and the court would give you time to obtain the services of a lawyer if you want one. Do you want a lawyer?

A: No sir.

    ...

Q: The court further informs you that if you do not have money or property with which to hire a lawyer, the court would appoint a lawyer at public expense to represent you. The court again inquires, do you want a lawyer?

A: No sir.

Q: Have you ever been arrested before?

A: Yes sir.

Q: How many times?

A: Quite a few times.

50. "John Doe Hearing Asked," *Rosebud Sioux Herald,* 19 August 1963.
51. "Rosebud Indians Renew Charges," *Rosebud Sioux Herald,* 2 September 1963.
52. Official Statement, 11 September 1958, Criminal Case 844, South Dakota Circuit Court, 11th Cir., Tripp County Courthouse.

Q: Have you ever been arrested for a felony?

A: Yes sir.

...

Q: For what?

A: Same thing.

Q: How much sentence did you receive at that time?

A: Four years.

...

Q: What is your plea, "Guilty" or "Not Guilty"?

A: Guilty.

Q: What were the circumstances surrounding this burglary?

A: I was just intoxicated is all I have to say.

Q: You were drunk?

A: Yes.

V: What did you take?

A: I didn't take very much. I don't know what I took.

...

Q: How many years did you serve in the penitentiary for the first burglary?

A: Thirty-four months.

Q: You didn't learn much by that, did you?

A: It doesn't seem like it.

Q: Breaking into buildings is something that society will not stand for, do you understand that?

A: Yes sir.

Q: Do you have any reason to show why the court should not pronounce sentence on you at this time?

A: No sir.

Q: Anything you want to say to the court on your own behalf?

A: No sir.

The defendant was sentenced to eighteen months in the penitentiary.[53] It is not clear whether the state's attorney or the judge knew that their jurisdiction in the case was of questionable legal validity. At the time of the trial, convictions such as these had not been challenged in state circuit courts, even when defendants were represented by attorneys.

A 1964 letter to the editor of the *Rosebud Sioux Herald* during the campaign against the jurisdiction bill summarized widespread concerns about the rights of Indian people in the courts: "The scales of justice in

53. Sentence, 11 September 1958, Criminal Case 844, South Dakota Circuit Court, 11th Cir., Tripp County Courthouse.

state courts have been heavily weighed against the Dakota people. Many of them immediately enter a plea of guilty, because of not being properly advised of their rights." The writer noted that even when court-appointed attorneys were present and aware of the "multitudes of federal laws that apply directly to our Dakota people for their protection," the attorneys "realize the futility of trying a case without proper funds." The writer complained that "city police court judges, county judges, justice of the peace courts and the circuit court judges deliberately violate their own oath of office to execute acts of injustice against our Dakota people residing within the geographic limits of their respective reservations." The writer described the situation as nothing less than "a police state," in which Indian people were "victimized daily by courts having no [lawful] jurisdiction." The letter ended: "Vote 'no' on [the] jurisdiction referendum."[54]

Indian people expressed concern about the civil implications of state jurisdiction as well. In March 1964 the *Rosebud Sioux Herald* ran a letter

54. Letter to the Editor, *Rosebud Sioux Herald*, 28 September 1964. The first defense challenge to state jurisdiction over Indians on Rosebud Reservation that I have found in my examination of county courthouse records took place in 1961. A Rosebud Sioux tribal member was charged with escape from the Mission jail—a felony—and was being held in the Winner jail pending trial. His attorney filed a petition for a writ of *habeas corpus* on the grounds that the court was "without jurisdiction... for the reason that the crime... is alleged to have been committed in the town of Mission... and said town is within the closed portions of the Rosebud Indian Reservation," where the state had no jurisdiction over Indians (Petition, filed 14 September 1961, Criminal Case 959, South Dakota Circuit Court, 11th Cir., Tripp County Courthouse). The writ was granted by the circuit court, which then considered whether the state had assumed jurisdiction under the 1961 statute. It was pointed out that the governor had not issued a proclamation of federal reimbursement as required under the 1961 statute for general jurisdiction, but the court did not release the prisoner. The defense attorney then demurred on the same grounds of lack of jurisdiction, but the defendant stood trial. He was, however, found not guilty (Criminal Case 959, South Dakota Circuit Court, 11th Cir., 1961, Tripp County Courthouse). The defense attorney, more than thirty years later, told me that the sheriff released the tribal member, who walked all the way from Winner to the Todd County line. Just before he crossed onto the reservation, the authorities arrested him on another charge. "They were mad" at the acquittal, the attorney recalled.

The earliest case that I am aware of to have been thrown out of court on the basis of the jurisdiction argument was a prisoner desertion case in 1963. The judge dismissed the case against the tribal member on the grounds that the state only had jurisdiction on highways through the reservation, and the alleged crime had not taken place on a highway (Order, 5 February 1963, Criminal Case 1013, South Dakota Circuit Court, 11th Cir., Tripp County Courthouse). But in other cases in which the defense did not raise the jurisdiction question, the court continued to try cases and impose judgment.

As a former Legal Services attorney explained to me, before Legal Services was instituted in 1964, a court-appointed lawyer would receive only fifty to one hundred dollars even for a case as serious as murder; the only logical course of action with such limited resources was to plead guilty. This may have been the reason the Indian defendant in the Mission burglary case quoted in the text waived his right to an attorney and simply pled guilty.

that traced the potential ramifications of the law: "How about the civil . . . aspects? Such as lawsuits, particularly in liabilities, contracts, suing for damages, marriage-settlements, especially where the wife is white. Aid to Dependent Children might be eliminated by a state civil court order, and the father forced to give up his lease money[55] each year to the county welfare. Draining the money in this and other ways will eventually lead to the confiscation of individual personal property, such as household merchandise, or even the house and any non-trust Indian property. It may even go so far as confiscation of wages. Eventually this will mean a land sale for the poverty-stricken Indian, in line with the white's long range plan to get the Indian land." Of course, such civil jurisdiction was precisely what the South Dakota Department of Welfare had in mind.[56]

The 1963 general jurisdiction law passed by the legislature and signed by the governor was resoundingly defeated in a 1964 referendum by a statewide vote of 201,389 to 58,289. A victory dance was held at Rosebud to celebrate. Certainly one of the factors in the referendum's success was fiscal—the costs to taxpayers of transferring jurisdiction from the federal government to the state. In the Rosebud country, however, the concerns of non-Indians about cost were to some extent overridden by their concerns for law and order. Tripp and Mellette counties returned majorities in favor of the law (see table 6). The precinct breakdown in Todd County indicates more precisely how Indian and non-Indian voters on the reservation felt about the question: Rosebud and St. Francis, with predominantly Indian populations, defeated the transfer of jurisdiction by votes of 318 to 61 and 210 to 95, respectively. The Mission precinct, with a heavy concentration of non-Indian merchants, favored the assumption of state jurisdiction by a vote of 331 to 173, and Lakeview, a predominantly non-Indian ranching community, voted 130 to 20 in favor of the 1963 law.[57]

THE *HANKINS* DECISION AND THE END
OF STATE JURISDICTION

In 1962 an Oglala Sioux tribal member was arrested by the state highway patrol for drunken driving on U. S. Highway 18, running through

55. The reference is to rental fees for lease of individual allotments to ranchers.
56. "Is Jurisdiction Simple?" *Rosebud Sioux Herald,* 30 March 1964.
57. Sioux Dump [. . .], State Jurisdiction," *Rosebud Sioux Herald,* 9 November 1964; Editor's Note, *Rosebud Sioux Herald,* 23 November 1964; "Jurisdiction Victory Dance Held at Rosebud," *Rosebud Sioux Herald,* 7 December 1964.

TABLE 6.   TALLIES OF THE 1964 STATE
JURISDICTION REFERENDUM, BY COUNTY

County	Yes	No
Gregory	1,304	1,976
Mellette	761	390
Tripp	2,273	1,600
Todd	875	1,130

SOURCE: Referred Laws, Jurisdiction File, Lakota Archives and Historical Research Center, Sinte
Gleska University, Rosebud, S. D.

Pine Ridge Reservation. Incarcerated in the Fall River County jail (unorganized Shannon County on Pine Ridge was attached to Fall River
County), the defendant petitioned the state circuit court for a writ of
habeas corpus. The circuit court held that the state's claim to jurisdiction under the 1961 State Highway Jurisdiction Act was invalid and released the defendant from custody. South Dakota appealed to the state
supreme court, which upheld the lower court's decision, in *In re Hankins' Petition,* determining that "partial" state jurisdiction—in this case,
solely over highways—was inconsistent with Congress's intent in Public
Law 280. Section 6 of the act authorized "disclaimer" states such as
South Dakota "to remove any legal impediment to the assumption of
criminal and civil jurisdiction" in accordance with the act's provisions.[58] The court reasoned that this language did "not expressly authorize the assumption of jurisdiction in the manner attempted by" the
state's 1961 law. The five "mandatory" states (California, Minnesota,
Nebraska, Oregon, Wisconsin) listed in Public Law 280 had been given
complete criminal and civil jurisdiction over Indians on reservations by
Congress; assuming that this scheme reflected the intent of Congress,
anything less than complete state jurisdiction, the court held, would be
inconsistent with congressional intent. Section 6 did not provide for the
assumption of anything less than unqualified jurisdiction over Indian
country, and the court concluded that the phrase could not be interpreted to allow jurisdiction only over reservation highways.[59]

    The 1964 *Hankins* decision immediately changed what state law en-
forcement officers could legally "do" in Todd County and Mission. The
Tripp County state's attorney (who handled prosecutions for Todd
County) ordered the municipal officers of Todd County and Mission not

58. 67 Stat. 590.
59. 125 N. W.2d 839, 842 (S. D. S. Ct., 1964).

to arrest any Indians and reportedly issued warnings to motorists that traveling through the reservation would be at their own risk because the state could not enforce law against Indians.[60] Although the *Hankins* decision concerned only reservation highway jurisdiction lawfully claimed by the state since 1961, the case apparently made the state's attorney question the long-*exercised* jurisdiction over Indians on the reservation: he asked the state's attorney general to issue an "official opinion as to whether the State of South Dakota has jurisdiction to prosecute Indians for the commission of crimes in the City of Mission." The attorney general confirmed that, indeed, state authorities did not have jurisdiction over Indians anywhere on Rosebud Reservation,[61] a holding that raised concerns among merchants in Mission, Winner, and Valentine (an off-reservation border town in neighboring Nebraska). [62] In a editorial, the *Todd County Tribune* asked "just where that leaves law enforcement in the City of Mission. Local police can arrest no Indians and so far as we have been able to determine the Rosebud Tribal [actually, BIA] Police are not on the job here." The paper invited state legislators to visit Mission "on any day following Indian pay days or when lease money is paid to the Indians" (a reference to drunkenness[63]) in order to be convinced of the need for state jurisdiction. The *Hankins* decision had immediate repercussions, according to the *Tribune*: "Last Friday night following the supreme court announcement numerous fistfights broke out on the streets of Mission. Local law enforcement officers were around but were powerless to intervene. Tribal police were conspicuous by their absence."[64]

Although in legal terms the *Hankins* decision did not change the situation that existed before 1961, it forced Todd County and Mission officials to recognize (if they hadn't already) that they had no jurisdiction over Indians anywhere on Rosebud Reservation, including the city of Mission. For the purposes of this chapter, the significance of the *Hankins*

60. Jurisdiction—Who Has It?" *Todd County Tribune*, 6 February 1964; "Halt Local Rosebud Sioux Violators," *Rosebud Sioux Herald*, 17 February 1964.

61. *Biennial Report of Attorney General*, 1963–1964:382. The attorney general pointed out that *Kills Plenty* (133 F.2d 292 [8th Cir., 1943]) had specifically held that the federal courts had jurisdiction over a crime committed by an Indian within Mission. *Hankins* provided additional authority for preventing state jurisdiction over Indians in Mission. As we saw in chapter 1, it was apparent that state's attorneys and local law enforcement officials were either unaware of, or had chosen to ignore, the *Kills Plenty* decision.

62. "Local Businessmen Fret," *Rosebud Sioux Herald*, 2 March 1964.

63. The *Tribune* neglected, of course, to note that the alcohol had been purchased at the city of Mission liquor store.

64. "Jurisdiction—Who Has It?" *Todd County Tribune*, 6 February 1964.

decision, in conjunction with the referendum, is that it ended—both in law and in fact—the assertion and exercise of state jurisdiction over Indians on Rosebud Reservation in 1964.[65]

STATE JURISDICTION AND TRIBAL
SELF-DETERMINATION IN THE 1970S

The pressure to extend state jurisdiction to Indian reservations was reinvigorated in the 1970s as a result of the unrest associated with the American Indian Movement (AIM), and the purported failure of tribal and BIA law enforcement to handle the situation. Early in 1974 the governor of South Dakota wrote to the Secretary of the Interior, warning of "a near breakdown of proper law enforcement in many reservation areas" that could "easily lead to citizens taking the law into their own hands in order to protect their property and personal safety."[66] When he received

---

65. Several subsequent court cases reiterated and clarified the state's lack of jurisdiction on the reservation. State civil jurisdiction on the reservations was prohibited in 1967 by the South Dakota Supreme Court in *Smith* v. *Temple* in which it was held that state courts had no jurisdiction over a suit involving an automobile accident on Pine Ridge Reservation where the defendant was an Indian (152 N. W.2d 547). In the 1968 case of *Kain* v. *Wilson*, the South Dakota Supreme Court held that the state court had no jurisdiction over a cattle trespass case against a tribal member on Pine Ridge Reservation, notwithstanding that the alleged trespass had taken place on non-Indian fee-patented land (161 N. W.2d 704). Federal jurisdiction was reiterated specifically with respect to Mission by the Court of Appeals for the Eighth Circuit in its 1967 *Beardslee* v. *United States* holding. The court upheld the federal murder conviction of a Rosebud Sioux tribal member who had committed the crime on non-Indian-owned, fee-patented land in Mission. The court pointed out that fee-patented land within a reservation was still Indian country, even if it was owned by a non-Indian (387 F.2d 280). This point was restated by the same court in a second *Beardslee* v. *United States* case (541 F.2d 705 [1976]).

In 1971 the state of South Dakota conceded that it had no authority to collect sales taxes from tribal members on the reservation—after a Rosebud Sioux tribal member brought suit, with assistance from South Dakota Legal Aid, against the state commissioner of revenue. The state made it clear that the city of Mission had never been excluded from the reservation and was part of the reservation ("No Sales Tax," *Rosebud Sioux Herald*, 11 January 1971; "No Tax on Sales for Sioux," *Todd County Tribune*, 15 January 1971; "Sales Tax Evokes Discussion," *Todd County Tribune*, 21 January 1971; "Tax Talk," *Rosebud Sioux Herald*, 22 February 1971; "Chamber Discusses Sales Tax Opinion," *Todd County Tribune*, 25 February 1971; "Lawsuit Behind No Sales Tax," *Rosebud Sioux Herald*, 22 March 1971). In 1972 the United States District Court for South Dakota held in *Soldier* v. *Carlson* (350 F. Supp. 65, 66) that the state had no authority to tax mobile homes owned by Rosebud Sioux tribal members in Todd County, even if they resided on fee-patented land. Such an action, the court determined, "interferes with the internal sovereignty of the Rosebud Sioux Tribe," since it violated the rule enunciated in *Williams* v. *Lee* (358 U. S. 217 [1959]) that reservation Indians have the right "to make their own law and be ruled by them" (350 F. Supp. at 66).

66. Kneip to Secretary of the Interior, 11 April 1974, Law Enforcement on Reservations File, Box 179, Richard Kneip Papers, Richardson Archives, University of South Dakota, Vermillion.

no reply he reminded the secretary of the federal government's "clear responsibility ... to ensure the protection of communities and individuals" within reservations.[67] By August, the executive branch of state government was receiving "numerous telephone calls from Indians and non-Indians who are afraid that we are on the verge of open warfare on the reservation."[68] The secretary of the South Dakota Department of Public Safety warned the governor of "bloodshed" if the federal government did not take action.[69] As will be recalled from chapter 2 (this was also in the midst of the *Rosebud Sioux Tribe* v. *Kneip* reservation boundary case), the governor also sent a message to the president, warning of the danger. Strong sentiment prevailed among non-Indian local and state government officials that Indian activism on the reservations was more a "criminal problem" than political struggle.[70] The problem was not only with those who identified themselves as Indian activists, however, and local non-Indians were also concerned about reservation crime in general: a letter to the governor from a Winner attorney, for example, alleged that Indian criminals were exhibiting increasing "boldness" and "acting in broad daylight."[71]

Arguments associating purported lawlessness on reservations with the state's lack of jurisdiction and the insufficiency of federal and tribal enforcement underlay the creation of the grassroots organization Civil Liberties for South Dakota Citizens (CLSDC) (see pp. 58–59). But as had been the case in the 1950s, the demands of local non-Indians for state

67. Kneip to Secretary of the Interior, 22 May 1974, Law Enforcement on Reservations File, Box 179, Kneip Papers. The governor was particularly concerned about AIM's planned 1974 International Indian Treaty Conference on Standing Rock Reservation: "The recent history of violence accompanying convocations of the American Indian Movement in South Dakota has resulted in deep concern among citizens" (ibid.). The secretary of the Interior eventually responded with federal plans "providing protection to citizens and property in the cities of Mobridge and McLaughlin and Corson and Wolworth counties during the pending AIM meeting" on Standing Rock Reservation. The plans involved deputizing state officers with BIA commissions, detailing additional BIA officers, and placing on standby "our Special Operations Services (SOS) Unit which has specific training in handling civil disturbances" (Secretary of the Interior to Kneip, 13 June 1974, Kneip Papers).

68. Correspondent to Kneip, 26 August 1974, Law Enforcement on Reservations File, Box 179, Kneip Papers.

69. Secretary of Public Safety to Kneip, 20 August 1974, Kneip Papers.

70. Memo to Governor, 7 July 1975, Law Enforcement of Reservations File, Box 179, Kneip Papers. One non-Indian rancher from Rosebud complained to the governor's office "of one instance where he was fishing when a group of young Indians came up to him, threatened him, even pointed a rifle at his head, slashed the tires on his pickup and forced him to leave the area where he had been fishing" (ibid.).

71. Winner Attorney to Governor, 17 October 1975, Law Enforcement on Reservations File, Box 179, Kneip Papers.

jurisdiction were not solely based on a perceived law enforcement gap. A rancher who had been involved in CLSDC recalled that "basically ... what started it was a feeling of nonprotection or nonenforcement of the law. But then, they got to looking at it, and then it becomes an issue of certain groups of people having certain special liberties, with no re-sponsibility. . . . [T]here should not be people to which the law applies differently."[72] "Unequal treatment based on ... race" and "special priv-ileges" for Indians, as a resident of Mission described the situation,[73] appeared to many non-Indians as profoundly inconsistent with Ameri-can democracy—an essentially wrong-headed policy simply on the basis of first principles.

Even the state's governor, a Democrat who depended upon Indian votes, voiced this concern in his 1974 letter to the president: "What I am describing here is a complex legal situation where persons living side by side and interacting in a society and economy of interdependence are subject to different laws and differing applications of justice. . . . It seems clear to me that such a system where we have two legal classes of citizens with differing obligations and rights of citizenship living to-gether encourages tension." It seemed inevitable that non-Indians would find it difficult to stomach the fact "that Indian persons are not subject to taxation by the state, yet they enjoy other rights of citizenship such as voting for state officials." Although the governor did not call for state jurisdiction over the reservations, and recognized that a solution might "require years of careful and tedious negotiation to resolve the matter" both legally and politically, his letter clearly gave voice to a

---

72. In a 1993 interview the rancher laid out for me what might be called the militia theory of state jurisdiction in Indian country:

> [RANCHER:] Under the Constitution the sheriff of a county is the only legal law en-forcement. . . . I don't know if that goes back to the old *posse comita-tus* where the sheriff can conscript any member fifteen years of age or over. . . . So that comes . . . into the . . . legality of firearms, and what the militia consists of and so on. . . . The National Rifle Association has something about that, that the sheriff . . . has the only constitu-tional law within the county because you vote for him. . . .

> QUESTION: So . . . you don't go for any of this [Indian] "sovereign nation" stuff.

> ANSWER: Not a bit, not a bit. If a tribe would decide that they were going to be a sovereign nation, I'd say "Fine, put up a chain-link fence around it." Then see how they like, you know, not letting anybody in or out. . . . And I think constitutional law says that there will be no nation within the nation. . . . [A]n Indian reservation's not a sovereign nation.

73. Correspondent to Kneip, 24 September 1974, Task Force on Indian-State Gov-ernment Relations File, Box 51, Kneip Papers.

common sentiment among non-Indian South Dakotans—especially those living within the boundaries of Indian reservations.[74]

If the Democratic governor of South Dakota was not about to support doing away with a special legal status for Indian people, there were politicians who were prepared to argue for that. In 1977 the American Indian Policy Review Commission issued a report strongly supporting tribal sovereignty. But the senator who served as the commission's vice chair issued a dissenting opinion in which he underscored the equal responsibilities of Indians as citizens, now that they had equal rights as citizens: "[O]nce reservation Indians became citizens of the United States, they became citizens of the States where they resided [as a result of the Fourteenth Amendment] and were then eligible to vote in State and local elections, run for State and local public office, and enjoy State services, such as public education. Hence they help create and administer law which is not applicable to them. They enjoy State services without sharing in the burden of financial support. This creates enormous hostility among non-Indians who feel (1) with the rights of citizenship go its burdens, and (2) if Congress is to insulate Indians from State taxation, it is the burden of Congress to provide the Indians' fair share of support to State services."[75]

While statements of this kind may have emboldened local non-Indians who wanted "equal rights for everybody," in fact, the pressure for state jurisdiction during the 1970s did not result in federal legislation. The political gestures that ensued from the debate were little more than symbolic victories. CLSDC, for example, managed to get a resolution introduced and passed by the South Dakota legislature memorializing Congress and the federal executive to "fulfill their respective responsibilities" in solving the jurisdictional controversy in South Dakota, since "these undesirable conditions are largely a result of acts of the United States government and the state of South Dakota is virtually powerless to achieve their fundamental solution."[76] Although the resolution clearly articulated the concerns of CLSDC members who resided on Rosebud Reservation,[77] it had no legal effect; the jurisdictional status quo remained unchanged until 1979.

74. Kneip to Ford, 10 September 1974, Indian Affairs File, Box 11, Kneip Papers.
75. American Indian Policy Review Commission 1977 581–82.
76. Senate Concurrent Resolution No. 7, *Congressional Record*, vol. 121 (8 April 1975), 9287.
77. One clause, however, which asserted that "the state of South Dakota recognizes the right of tribal self-government" (ibid.), provoked objection from the CLSDC. In hearings on the resolution before the State Affairs Committee, tribal members agreed not to oppose the measure if the clause was added. An attorney representing CLSDC opposed

ROSEBUD SIOUX TRIBE V. SOUTH DAKOTA

THE *WASHINGTON* OPINION AND THE ORIGINS OF THE HIGHWAY SUIT

The opportunity to assert state jurisdiction on the reservation would eventually come not from a legislative act but from the South Dakota attorney general's reading of the U. S. Supreme Court's 1979 opinion in *Washington* v. *Yakima Indian Nation.*[78] The case involved the question of how states with constitutional disclaimers of jurisdiction over Indian

---

such an amendment, pointing out that it violated both the intent of the resolution and Supreme Court decisions (Minutes, Senate Committee on State Affairs, 27 February 1975, South Dakota Legislative Research Council, Pierre, S. D.). Nevertheless, the resolution reflected the interests of CLSDC more than the interests of the tribes. Indeed, the state coordinator of Indian affairs complained to the governor that "the underlying meaning is pointed at State Jurisdiction" and that the resolution was "a statement of [CLSDC's] prejudicial and discriminatory attitude towards Indian people" (Coordinator to Governor, 13 February 1976, Indian Affairs File, Box 87, Kneip Papers).

Legislators made other symbolic gestures toward the "equal rights and responsibilities" paradigm. One of South Dakota's senators even entered into the *Congressional Record* a 1977 position paper on Indian-white relations in South Dakota authored by the board of commissioners of Corson County, on Standing Rock Reservation. The paper laid out the "riddles and frustrations" of Indian country jurisdiction in the criminal and civil domains, and concluded, "Citizens in 'reservation' counties must manage to survive without the benefit of 'justice for all' which is a presumed right of all American citizens. In Corson County, justice is not blind—it is forced to see racial differences and go by a different set of rules according to skin color and geographic location." To solve this problem, the authors proposed that Congress "enact legislation to bring all of the State of South Dakota, including Indian Country, under State law." This position paper was endorsed by nine other counties in or adjacent to Indian country, including Tripp County. The board of commissioners of Tripp (which acted for unorganized Todd County) adopted a resolution endorsing the recommendations of the Corson County position paper ("Tripp-Todd Commissioners Support Corson County Idea Re State Law on Reservations," *Todd County Tribune,* 10 February 1977; Kneip to Chair of Human Resources Cabinet Subgroup of Health, 24 February 1977, Indian Affairs—Misc. 1977 File, Box 395, Kneip Papers). In response, the Rosebud Sioux Tribal Council adopted a resolution that declared the commissioners' resolution a "direct attack on the sovereignty of the Rosebud Sioux Tribe" ("Rosebud Sioux Tribe Answers Commissioners' Resolution," *Todd County Tribune,* 3 March 1977).

The South Dakota legislature's State Affairs Committee investigated the possibility of removing the constitutional disclaimer of jurisdiction over reservations in 1977, and a bill to that effect was introduced during the 1977 session (Minutes, 9 August 1977, State Affairs Committee, Indian Affairs—Misc. File, Box 395, Kneip Papers; Testimony, 18 January 1978, State Affairs Committee, Indian Affairs File, Box 396, Kneip Papers). On the federal level, a bill was introduced in the House of Representatives in 1977 to "abrogate all treaties" and to assert that "no individual or group possesses subordinate or special rights" in the United States (H. R. 9054, 95th Cong., 1st Sess. [introduced 12 September 1977]). This was one of the notorious "white backlash" bills against Indian gains (see Testimony Given to the State Affairs Committee by Rosebud Sioux Tribe, 18 January 1978, Indian Affairs File, Box 396, Kneip Papers). Neither bill made it out of committee.

78. 439 U. S. 463 (1979).

country could lawfully assume such jurisdiction under the provisions of Public Law 280. In a highly detailed and technical semantic analysis, the Court found that "disclaimer" states such as Washington (and, by extension, South Dakota) could assume jurisdiction "at such time and in such manner" as they so chose by legislation—as long as their actions were consistent with the broader intent of Public Law 280: assimilating Indians into the general population, responding to a hiatus in reservation law enforcement, and shifting financial responsibility for reservations from the federal to the state government. Thus, the Court found, the assumption of full jurisdiction over reservations was not necessary; partial state jurisdiction was legally possible under Public Law 280.

This was good news for the South Dakota attorney general's office, which was engaged in "battle of will and a battle of power" with the tribes, as one of my informants familiar with the office's history put it. A lawyer who was conversant with the office's thinking at the time, recalled its broad outlines:

> [I]f you think like a military general, if you control all the means of transportation, you're the sovereign there, you control everything.... The definition of highways in both state and federal law at that time [was] all roads, section-line roads, alleys, town roads—the whole works. [The state] control[s] the road in front of the tribal building. So if... you step on the highway, now you're in state jurisdiction. From a sovereignty viewpoint, that basically gave the state total control because almost nothing could occur in Indian country without the state's permission. They couldn't deliver gas, they couldn't deliver food, they couldn't do anything. So now the state would have the upper hand....

The attorney general was thus inclined to interpret the United States Supreme Court's *Washington* decision as overruling the South Dakota supreme court's ruling in *Hankins*—thereby reactivating the 1961 highway jurisdiction law. "It was only a matter of waiting until a proper case could be obtained," as one lawyer described it to me, for the attorney general to test his theory in court. A "proper case" would involve facts that not only fit the new interpretation but that would also compel the court of public opinion to side with the attorney general.

Five months after the *Washington* decision was handed down, a police officer in Winner was allegedly beaten by four Rosebud Sioux tribal members.[79] One of suspects returned to Rosebud Reservation. On orders from the attorney general, the suspect was arrested by officers of

---

79. *South Dakota v. [Tribal Member]*, 310 N. W.2d 669 (S. D., 1981)

the state department of criminal investigation while he was pumping gas into his car at a gas station in Mission. According to his affidavit:

> [F]our men in an unmarked vehicle in plain clothes . . . parked near the island where I was filling my vehicle with gas, two men jumped out from the front seat and grabbed me and said, "you are under arrest." They showed me no identification and did not give me their names or [tell me] who they represented. Another man got out of the back seat of the vehicle and handcuffed me and I was placed in the back seat between two men, handcuffed with my hands behind my back. I asked the four who they were and they didn't answer.
>
> We no more than got on U. S. Highway 18 . . . when a message came over the CB radio asking "did you get him?" . . . Another transmission came through, "did anyone see you?" Answer by driver, "there were only a couple of kids. . . ."
>
> I asked the driver and the man in the fatigue shirt . . . if they were federal agents or marshals, and the driver spoke up and said, "no, we are from Pierre and the Attorney General sent us to arrest you." I said, "well, I thought it was an illegal arrest and transport of an Indian off of the reservation," and the driver said, "we'll see."

The suspect was transported to Winner; according to his testimony, he was mistreated by the officers during the trip and forced to crouch in the car's back seat to avoid being seen.[80]

The defendant's court-appointed attorney complained to the state's attorney that "there was a lot of secrecy involved in his arrest." As far as anyone was able to ascertain, it might as well have been "some men from Mars" that made the arrest. But "[s]ince Todd County is a closed portion of the Reservation it would appear . . . that his arrest was illegal."[81] The South Dakota attorney general responded that it indeed was not men from Mars who arrested the tribal member: "I gave the orders to arrest your client within the jurisdiction of the State of South Dakota. It is my opinion that all highways within the confines of Todd County are within the jurisdiction of the State of South Dakota."[82]

80. Defendant's Affidavit, Criminal Case 79-174, South Dakota Circuit Court, 6th Cir., Tripp County Courthouse. An individual familiar with the position of the attorney general's office on this case told me: "[W]hen you're the sovereign you're in charge of law enforcement, you don't want anybody standing in your state across a section line going 'na na na na na.' And . . . if this works, what we're going to have is guys racing down, doing a stop-and-rob, and screaming back to Mission Town, and nobody wants that."

81. Attorney to State's Attorney, 5 July 1979, Criminal Case 79-174, South Dakota Circuit Court, 6th Cir., Tripp County Courthouse.

82. Attorney General to Attorney, 6 July 1979, Criminal Case 79-174, South Dakota Circuit Court, 6th Cir., Tripp County Courthouse.

The Rosebud Sioux Tribal Council was quick to respond to the arrest. "The question is," the tribal president told the assembled council members, "does the State have jurisdiction on the land within the boundaries of the reservation." The council unanimously adopted a resolution condemning the arrest as an act of "abduction, kidnapping, and civil rights violations among other infringements" that put the "sovereignty, integrity and governmental organization of the Rosebud Sioux tribe...in jeopardy."[83]

The defense attorney moved for an order to quash the arrest warrant as "a void and illegal seizure" of the defendant, amounting to kidnapping. [84] In a letter to the judge, the attorney argued that the state's secretive tactics in the arrest suggested "that these officials had no business being in Todd County."[85] The jurisdictional question, however, was never reached by the court. In fact the judge, obviously unaware of the attorney general's new theory about the reactivation of the 1961 highway jurisdiction statute—it had not been alluded to in the state's attorney's brief[86]—did not deny that the arrest had been illegal but held that the court had jurisdiction in the case even if the arrest had been illegal.[87] A judicial test of the attorney general's theory would have to wait.

The jurisdictional issue remained relatively quiet on Rosebud until 1985,[88] when a tribal member was arrested by a South Dakota highway patrol officer for operating an overweight truck on U. S. Highway 18 in Mission and charged with a misdemeanor in state circuit court. The defendant's attorney filed a motion to dismiss the case, arguing that the state had neither subject matter nor personal jurisdiction in the case.[89] Another criminal case in Todd County also raised the question of juris-

83. Minutes, 17 July 1979, Rosebud Sioux Tribal Office.

84. Motion and Brief, filed 8 November 1979, Criminal Case 79-174, South Dakota Circuit Court, 6th Cir., Tripp County Courthouse.

85. Attorney to Judge, 8 November 1979, Criminal Case 79-174, South Dakota Circuit Court, 6th Cir., Tripp County Courthouse.

86. Brief in Opposition to Defendant's Motion to Quash, filed 18 December 1979, Criminal Case 79-174, South Dakota Circuit Court, 6th Cir., Tripp County Courthouse.

87. Memorandum Decision, 7 January 1980, Criminal Case 79-174, South Dakota Circuit Court, 6th Cir., Tripp County Courthouse.

88. Other cases regarding the exercise of state jurisdiction on the reservation arose in the aftermath of the Supreme Court's *Washington,* but they were less widely publicized than the case described above and did not involve a legal defense invoking Indian country. In 1981, for example, the Todd County sheriff, who was himself a tribal member, arrested two Indians for car theft on the reservation and turned them over to the court in Winner, where they were convicted ("Antelope Community Talks Law and Order," *Todd County Tribune,* 18 November 1981).

89. Brief in Support of Defendant's Motion to Dismiss, filed 7 August 1985, Criminal Case 85-26, South Dakota Circuit Court, 6th Cir., Tripp County Courthouse. Before filing

diction. In May of 1985 a non-Indian truck driver was arrested by the highway patrol at the scene of an accident that resulted in the death of a tribal member at the intersection of U. S. Highways 18 and 83 in Mission. The non-Indian was charged in circuit court with vehicular homicide, second-degree manslaughter, driving while intoxicated, and operating a vehicle without a license. This defendant's attorney moved to dismiss on the grounds that reservation highways are in Indian country and that therefore the state had no jurisdiction over a crime committed by a non-Indian against an Indian.[90]

The state's attorney for Tripp County answered the motions for dismissal in both cases with the same argument. Echoing the attorney general's new theory, the briefs argued that South Dakota had accepted criminal and civil jurisdiction over highways running through Indian country in 1961 by an act of the state legislature in conformity with Congress's offer of jurisdiction to states in Public Law 280. Although the state supreme court had struck down partial state jurisdiction in its 1964 *Hankins* decision, the United States Supreme Court's *Washington* decision, which authorized partial assumption of jurisdiction by states in Indian country, had the effect of reversing *Hankins* and reactivating

---

the motion, the defendant's attorney wrote to the tribal president: "It is my understanding that the Attorney General of the State of South Dakota has historically and remains anxious to assert State jurisdiction over State highways and roadways extending within the bounds of Indian reservations." Noting that the legality of the state attorney general's claim was uncertain, the defendant's attorney suggested that it was a question of interest to the tribe: "Allowing the State to assert this type of jurisdiction now allows the State an opportunity to establish a history of State assumption of such powers. Should the Tribe ever attempt to protect their tribal sovereignty and power over their reservation in the future, an established pattern of State authority exercised consistently over such incidents will bar any effective argument that the Tribe has historically maintained these powers." The attorney invited the tribe to submit an amicus brief in the case (Attorney to Tribal Chairman, 30 July 1985, State of South Dakota, 1978-85 File, Frank LaPointe Papers, Lakota Archives and Historical Research Center, Sinte Gleska University, Rosebud, S. D.).

90. Memorandum in Support of Defendant's Motion to Dismiss for Lack of Jurisdiction, filed 27 August 1985, Criminal Case 85-19, South Dakota Circuit Court, 6th Cir., Tripp County Courthouse. I asked an attorney familiar with this case why the U. S. attorney had not prosecuted the driver in federal court under the Indian Country Crimes Act. He said that both the South Dakota attorney general and the U. S. attorney (a Republican) were looking for a "vehicle . . . to assert state jurisdiction on the highways." This case was deemed a good vehicle "because the tribes would not want to be seen to be inconsistent by appealing a case in which the state had taken after a white guy that killed one of their brethren." Indeed, the U. S. attorney made it clear in a letter to the state's attorney in this case that the state had concurrent jurisdiction (United States Attorney to state's Attorney, 14 August 1985, appended to State of South Dakota's Brief, filed 21 August 1985, Criminal Case 85-19, South Dakota Circuit Court, 6th Cir., Tripp County Courthouse).

the 1961 highway jurisdiction statute.[91] Convinced by the state's argument, the circuit court judge upheld the exercise of state jurisdiction.[92]

THE HIGHWAY CASES IN FEDERAL DISTRICT COURT

At a January 1986 meeting, the Rosebud Sioux Tribal Council was briefed by one of its attorneys on the criminal cases pending in the Tripp County courthouse in Winner. The best approach, the attorney advised, would be a suit in federal district court, which offered, he argued, a better venue for an impartial hearing than the South Dakota supreme court. While there was some sentiment to take a strong political stand on jurisdiction ("I think this body needs a resolution kicking state patrol off the rez"), the council chose to proceed cautiously, instructing its attorney to explore a legislative solution and to draft a federal complaint for the council's consideration.[93] The Rosebud Sioux Tribe's complaint was filed in United States district court in Pierre in May 1986. It sought declaratory judgment and a permanent injunction to "restrain and prohibit South Dakota from exercising jurisdiction over

91. State of South Dakota's Brief, filed 21 August 1985, Criminal Case 85-19, and State of South Dakota's Brief, filed 21 August 1985, Criminal Case 85-26, South Dakota Circuit Court, 6th Cir., Tripp County Courthouse.

92. Memorandum Decision, 21 January 1986, Criminal Case 85-26, South Dakota Circuit Court, 6th Cir., Tripp County Courthouse. In December 1985, the question of state jurisdiction over reservations also came up in a dispute between the South Dakota attorney general's office and the Oglala Sioux Tribe. The state refused to recognize tribal licensure of vehicles owned by tribal members, and the attorney general pointed out in a letter to the president of the Oglala Sioux Tribe that under the 1961 law "it is clear that the State of South Dakota has jurisdiction over highways throughout the reservation and, therefore, a tribal license plate would not only be ineffective outside the borders of any Indian reservation, it would also be ineffective within the boundaries of any reservation" (Attorney General to Tribal President, 10 December 1985, Resolutions, 1984-6 File, LaPointe Papers). The Oglala president alerted the Rosebud president to "the emergency situation." "[T]he state is apparently," the letter advised, "planning to arrest all licensees of the Oglala Sioux Tribe . . . to get the South Dakota Supreme Court to reverse itself and rule that the state has criminal/civil jurisdiction over Indian People on reservation highways." He requested that Rosebud join the Oglalas in a federal lawsuit (Oglala Tribal President to Rosebud Tribal President, 2 January 1986, Resolutions, 1984-6 File, Frank LaPointe Papers). A tribal attorney advised Rosebud tribal officials that the issue was "very touchy and delicate" and "bears constant watching" because it would be easy for the state to get the matter heard in state court, where it would have an advantage, by simply "arresting an Indian on a State highway" (Attorney to Tribal President, 15 January 1986, Resolutions, 1984-6 File, Frank LaPointe Papers). The state had of course already managed to have two cases heard in state circuit court, which accepted the state's position on jurisdiction and created precedents for subsequent litigation.

93. Minutes and tape of meeting, 31 January 1986, Rosebud Sioux Tribal Office; Minutes, 14 February 1986, Rosebud Sioux Tribal Office.

Indians within the Rosebud Indian Reservation."[94] The Rosebud Sioux Tribe was later joined in the case by the Cheyenne River Sioux Tribe and the Oglala Sioux Tribe.

The case raised two fundamental questions of law: (1) was the 1961 state highway jurisdiction statute consistent with the intent behind Public Law 280 and therefore valid under the terms of *Washington;* and (2) what was the legal force of three historically overlain, but conflicting, legal benchmarks—the 1961 state highway jurisdiction statute, the 1964 state *Hankins* decision, and the 1968 federal Indian Civil Rights Act (ICRA)?[95] The tribes argued on the first matter that the provisions in the 1961 South Dakota law differed substantially from those of the state of Washington's statute, upheld by the Supreme Court in *Washington* v. *Yakima Indian Nation.* South Dakota had deliberately sought to "avoid state financial responsibility for law enforcement"; it had assumed responsibility only for highway jurisdiction, which generated income from traffic fines, and the state had conditioned general jurisdiction over reservations upon reimbursement by the federal government of the associated expenses—"a goal directly contrary to the purposes of [Public Law] 280."[96]

Regarding the second matter, the tribes argued that the 1968 ICRA, among other things, amended Public Law 280 to prohibit states from assuming jurisdiction in Indian country without tribal approval. In 1965 South Dakota's assistant attorney general testified before a United States Senate committee considering an early draft of the ICRA that the state had "never assumed jurisdiction in Indian country." Since South Dakota did not, as a matter of law, have jurisdiction over Indian country in 1968 (when the ICRA was enacted), the state would need to obtain tribal consent for such jurisdiction, as required by the ICRA, in the future. The 1961 law had been omitted from the 1974 revision of the

94. Complaint, filed 12 May 1986, *Rosebud Sioux Tribe* v. *South Dakota* (Civ. 86-3019, D. S. D.) File, Dakota Plains Legal Services.

95. 82 Stat. 77.

96. Memorandum Opposing the Motion for Summary Judgment and Supporting the Tribe's Cross-Motion for Summary Judgment, filed 2 March 1988, *Rosebud Sioux Tribe* v. *South Dakota* (Civ. 86-3019, D. S. D.), File MSC 0001—Cross-Deputization, 1988, Lakota Archives and Historical Research Center. The state of Washington's jurisdictional plan did not depend upon federal reimbursement but rather upon tribal requests for state jurisdiction. South Dakota's "strange scheme" did not address the gap in law enforcement—another congressional concern behind Public Law 280—raising concerns that it would in fact have increased "checkerboarding." Where exactly does a highway end and Indian country begin—at the pavement's edge, at the edge of the shoulder, at the fence line?

South Dakota Codified Laws (because it had been overturned by *Hankins* and was not believed to be in force), and the state had simply not exercised jurisdiction in Indian country for many years. Law enforcement on reservation highways had been left to the tribes and the federal government, which appropriated the funds and established the requisite police and judicial structures.

In response, the state argued on the first matter that the 1961 law had been perfectly consistent with the congressional intent behind Public Law 280. One of the goals of the legislation had been cost savings, an intent satisfied by substituting state and local law enforcement personnel for the Federal Bureau of Investigation, the U. S. attorney's office, and BIA and tribal police in cases originating on reservation highways. Highway fatality rates in Todd County, the state argued, were more than triple those for the state as a whole, a finding adduced as evidence for the insufficiency of law enforcement activities in the county. The state's brief argued that the failure of the tribal court to apply consistent and appropriate sentences in drunken driving cases indicated that tribal law enforcement "is simply unable or unwilling to face the challenges which face it." Exercise by the state of its highway authority under the 1961 law would thus address a "hiatus" in law enforcement on Indian reservations, another intent of Public Law 280. Noting that the 1961 legislation placed Indians under the same civil and criminal jurisdiction as other residents of the state—"clearly a first step to [bringing] about the process of assimilation of Indians into the general population," as anticipated by Public Law 280—the state concluded that "the decision of the South Dakota Supreme Court in *Hankins* is plainly wrong as a matter of federal law."[97]

On the second matter, the state's brief rejected the tribes' contention that the ICRA had any bearing on the case. South Dakota's assumption of jurisdiction had taken place in 1961 and had not been forfeited because of the erroneous *Hankins* decision; state officials had simply chosen (in conformance with the ruling in *Hankins*) not to *exercise* Indian country jurisdiction. Put differently, de jure jurisdiction had continued uninterrupted since 1961, even though de facto jurisdiction had been suspended between 1964 and 1985. The ICRA was not retroactive to 1961, when South Dakota validly *assumed* jurisdiction.[98]

97. State's Brief in Support of Motion for Summary Judgment, filed 11 January 1988, *Rosebud Sioux Tribe* v. *South Dakota* (Civ. 86-3019, D. S. D.) File, Dakota Plains Legal Services.
98. Ibid.

There was a great deal at stake in the litigation. During the summer of 1988, while the case was pending, the *Todd County Tribune* published an editorial in support of state jurisdiction over the reservation. Citing the "drug pushers, bootleggers, rapists, murderers, burglars, thieves, robbers, vandals, alcoholic drivers" and other criminals who "run loco on this reservation," the paper made the suggestion that "[i]f tribal government can't handle law and order on this reservation, maybe it's time we ask the state if it can. I constantly hear Indian and non-Indian saying it's also time to write our Congressmen. Congress established Indian reservations, they tell me, and Congress can disestablish Indian reservations. I hear more and more people saying it's time to invite state jurisdiction onto this reservation. Could they be right?"[99] The following week, the paper noted that "[r]eaders, most of them Indian ... called or stopped me during the past week to say 1) they liked and agreed with last week's discussion of disestablishing Indian reservation boundaries and bringing in state jurisdiction, 2) they have long wanted state jurisdiction but don't speak out publicly for fear of being harassed, assaulted and shot at and 3) they are very tired of the posturing and phoniness within tribal government and think, as several Indian readers put it, it's 'high time' state jurisdiction was brought to the reservation."[100] These editorials were not simply playing an imaginary "lawlessness" card; to the contrary, they gave expression to real concerns about the insufficiency of federal and tribal law enforcement on the reservation—concerns enunciated by Indian as well as non-Indian people. Indian people, however, did not necessarily draw the conclusion that the solution was state jurisdiction.[101]

Indeed, Indian people were, and continue to be, very suspicious of the motives behind the drive for state jurisdiction. At a tribal meeting with BIA and state department of transportation officials regarding highway jurisdiction in 1989, a tribal council representative articulated the dangers of state jurisdiction to the visitors: "We're fighting for our lives. If the state takes over this reservation, it's going to be like a concentration camp. Believe you me, there's nothing impossible that can happen.... I'm sorry you don't live here on this reservation to feel this prejudice, to feel this thing that we're going through daily. You don't

99. "Smoke Signals," *Todd County Tribune,* 20 July 1988.

100. "Smoke Signals," *Todd County Tribune,* 27 July 1988.

101. Some Indian people, however, believed and continue to believe that state jurisdiction is the solution to lawlessness, although it is difficult to gauge the numbers. Others, while not seeking state jurisdiction, believe that the solution is to cross-deputize state and tribal officers.

know those little things that are happening. You don't see the little Indian that been pushed aside so that this brand new . . . non-Indian person come [*sic*] in and take over his job at the higher pay. . . . [W]e're oppressed nations. The oppressors are the people that are doing this to us right here in the State of South Dakota."[102]

Given the stakes of both Indian and non-Indian people in the outcome, the highway case was more than an academic dispute over congressional intent; rather, it was a political question deeply tied to convictions about race-based basic rights on Rosebud Reservation.

The district court reached its decision in March 1989, holding that in the light of the Supreme Court's *Washington* opinion, *Hankins* was fatally flawed as law. The "flaws in *Hankins* severely erode the reasoning and holding in *Hankins*," the court wrote, "that the 1961 legislation was insufficient to empower South Dakota to enforce state law on Indians on highways within Indian country."[103] The court pointed out, however, that the 1961 law had a "checkered history," having gone "some two decades without being enforced."[104] Although it had never been repealed by the legislature, the act was literally not "on the books" from 1974, when it was removed from the codified laws because of the ruling in *Hankins,* until 1985 when it was reinstated in the code as a result of the *Washington* decision. This in itself made the district court question the statute's continuing validity, although it elected to defer to the South Dakota supreme court, which had already decided the issue. In its 1988 *State* v. *Onihan* decision,[105] the state supreme court struck down its own decision in *Hankins* and, as the federal district court put it, "resurrected the 1961 Act." The assumption of highway jurisdiction in 1961, the district court held, "remains an effective state statute notwithstanding its checkered history."[106] The result was that the state and the tribe had concurrent jurisdiction over reservation highways.

THE *ROSEBUD* V. *SOUTH DAKOTA* APPEAL

Neither the state nor the tribes were satisfied with the decision,[107] and cross-appealed the decision to the Court of Appeals for the Eighth Cir-

102. Tape of summit meeting, 25 May 1989, Rosebud Sioux Tribal Office.
103. 709 F. Supp. 1502, 1508 (D. S D., 1989).
104. Ibid., 1509.
105. 427 N. W.2d 365 (S. Ct. S. D., 1985).
106. 709 F. Supp. 1509.
107. The United Sioux Tribes, according to its press release, "reacted to the decision with disbelief and disagreement. South Dakota has not exercised jurisdiction for over 20

cuit. The *Todd County Tribune* quoted the tribal president: "When the Sioux Nation allowed the establishment of South Dakota[108]...the [state] may not have been aware of a disclaimer that says they don't mess with us tribes on our reservations. The State has *no* jurisdiction on any reservation. It was disappointing when [the federal judge] used the word 'concurrent.' He and his staff should know better."[109] The tribal president issued an order banning the highway patrol from the reservation. A compromise suggested by the governor in which the state would handle only drunken driving cases on the reservations provoked the president's hostile response: "While it may be the opinion of the State of South Dakota that a simple solution would be for Tribes to give up jurisdiction over certain violations of the law, it is the position of the Rosebud Sioux Tribe that we will not give up any jurisdiction to which we are legally entitled."[110]

This letter reflected the consensus of the Rosebud Sioux Tribal Council[111] and many Indian people that the district court's decision was not only a miscarriage of justice but a violation of the law, indeed, *black letter* law. Indian rights—commonly referred to as treaty rights—were clearly described as inalienable in acts of Congress and federal court precedents. The closeness of the legal question regarding two conflicting regimes of rights-claims based on equally effective bodies of law made the decision seem arbitrary and a violation of law to tribal advocates. As a tribal member commented in a letter to the *Todd County Tribune*, "The 1968 Indian Civil Rights Act overrode much of Public Law 280, and in one article of the act it says 'only'—the word only with Indian

---

years based on the South Dakota Supreme Court decision in *In Re Hankins*." The organization also argued that the decision was contrary to the 1964 state referendum, ignored the ICRA, and was "starkly inconsistent with the present federal policy of Indian self determination and government to government relationships" (Press Release, United Sioux Tribes, 6 April 1989, Jurisdiction File, Box 8, 1991 Accession, LaPointe Papers). The United Sioux Tribes passed a resolution to appeal the decision (Resolution, United Sioux Tribes, 6 April 1989, Jurisdiction File, Box 8, 1991 Accession, LaPointe Papers).

108. The reference is to the 1889 Great Sioux Agreement, which opened "surplus" reservation land to homesteading by non-Indians in western South Dakota (see chapter 1).

109. [President] Seeks Stay on Trooper Issue," *Todd County Tribune*, 7 June 1989.

110. President to Governor, 27 April 1989, Rosebud Sioux Tribal Office.

111. Tape of Council Meeting, 5 May 1989, Rosebud Sioux Tribal Office. There was, however, at least some disagreement over this stance. One tribal official challenged the tribe's response to the governor's offer: "Are you saying DWI's deserve a break?" He was criticized by others at the meeting for implicitly backing down on sovereignty and was told that a well-known and outspoken local non-Indian opponent of tribal sovereignty would be happy to hear his opinion on jurisdiction. Although he insisted that he was not "copping out" on sovereignty, it was clear his opinion was unpopular (Tape of Meeting, 2 May 1989, Rosebud Sioux Tribal Office).

consent. With Congress' passing the Indian Bill of Rights, the [state] must get tribal consent to pass through tribal land. It's simple: The state has no jurisdiction on Indian land without consent. The[re] cannot be 'but' or 'if' when the treaty [that is, the ICRA] spells out Indian rights. The U. S. District Court of South Dakota, which should protect Indian rights, shows it was prejudice[d] toward Indians of South Dakota. There is no balance of law for the reservation Indian. The blind lady of justice is no longer blind; she is dead."[112]

At a meeting with BIA and state department of transportation officials in May 1989,[113] a tribal official insisted that the court's decision "violates congressional law, it violates treaties, it violates statutes, everything that's in place. There is no possible way in this world that [the judge] could have ruled the way that he did." He also said: "I don't believe [the judge] has the authority to make a decision on a sovereign nation, such as us and any other tribe because we are . . . governed by treaty."[114]

The Eighth Circuit panel of three judges reached its decision in March 1990, reversing the holding of the district court: "We find that the district court erred. Absent tribal consent, we hold the State of South Dakota has no jurisdiction over highways running though Indian lands in the state."[115] The 1961 South Dakota law, in contrast to the law examined in *Washington*, "takes jurisdiction over . . . the only part of law enforcement which comes close to being self-financing."[116] Therefore, "[w]e believe South Dakota's limited excursion into the area of Indian jurisdiction is not responsive to the concerns underlying the passage of [Public Law] 280," and thus jurisdiction was not validly assumed in 1961.[117]

What is more, the intent behind the amendment of Public Law 280 through the ICRA was, the court reasoned, to prohibit unilateral actions by a state to assume jurisdiction over reservations without tribal consent. This prohibition necessarily extends to South Dakota's "retroactive application of a new statutory interpretation."[118] The

---

112. Letter to the Editor, *Todd County Tribune*, 31 May 1989.

113. The governor and the attorney general were invited to the summit but did not attend ("State Officials Invited to Summit Meeting," *Todd County Tribune*, 17 May 1989).

114. Tape of Summit Meeting, 25 May 1989, Rosebud Sioux Tribal Office.

115. 900 F.2d 1164 at 1166 (8th Cir., 1990).

116. Ibid., 1170, quoting 709 F. Supp. 1508.

117. 900 F.2d at 1170.

118. Ibid., 1171.

court insisted that "Congress intended to eliminate completely the ability of a state to assume jurisdiction without tribal consent, at any time and in any manner after 1968." The court acknowledged the legality of "requiring a change in statutory interpretation to be applied retroactively."[119] But the application of this rule must depend upon the particular facts of the case at hand. There was, in fact, judicial precedent for the countervailing rule that a "decision overruling a previous construction of a statute is not given retroactive application where to do so disturbs the vested rights of the parties.... We believe the tribes had a vested right in the protection offered by the 1968 tribal consent amendment." Thus even if arguably applicable to the 1961 South Dakota act, the court ruled that retroactive application of *Washington* "would disrupt the Tribes' 'justifiable expectations.'"[120]

Thus, early in South Dakota's "year of reconciliation"[121] the Rosebud Sioux Tribe won its dispute with the state over highway jurisdiction. The *Todd County Tribune* quoted the former tribal president, who was in office when the suit was filed: "The Sioux Nation won. In fact, all tribes won."[122] The *Tribune* also ran a letter from a former senator from South Dakota who voiced a hope that the court of appeals' decision would "put the matter to rest and that some overeager lawyer working for state government will not put the state and the tribes to further expense trying to overturn the decision in the Supreme Court." He insisted that the law was "crystal clear": South Dakota's attempt to assume jurisdiction was prohibited by the ICRA. "For the Attorney General and other government officials to keep beating the dead horse of state jurisdiction," he pointed out, "severely violates" the sentiment behind the year of reconciliation.[123]

"RESOLUTION" OF THE HIGHWAY CASE

Unhappy with the court of appeals' ruling, the state attorney general's office considered filing a petition for a writ of certiorari to the U.S.

119. Ibid., 1172.
120. Ibid., 1173.
121. The governor and South Dakota tribes signed a proclamation designating 1990, the centenary of the Wounded Knee Massacre, as a year for Indian–non-Indian reconciliation ("A Century After a Massacre, A New Peace Pipe in Dakota," *New York Times,* 3 February 1990; "Indians, Others Rise to Challenge," *Rapid City Journal,* 21 December 1990; "Year Is Start in Right Direction," *Rapid City Journal,* 21 December 1990; Iron Shield 1990–91).
122. "Indian Roads Ruled Off Limits to State Laws," *Todd County Tribune,* 21 March 1990.
123. "Letter: Quit Beating the Dead Horse of State Jurisdiction," *Todd County Tribune,* 11 April 1990.

Supreme Court. In October 1990, however, the Rosebud Sioux Tribal Council held a special meeting to consider a compromise offered by the state: If the tribe would agree to authorize the highway patrol, for a period of five years, to detain tribal members suspected of committing crimes for transfer to tribal authorities and prosecution under the tribal code, tribal officers would be authorized by the state to detain suspects who were not members of the tribe for transfer to state authorities and prosecution under state law. This five-year cross-deputization agreement also contained an assurance from the state attorney general that his office would not petition the Supreme Court for review of the court of appeals' decision—in effect guaranteeing that the decision would stand—if all the South Dakota tribes signed the agreement. Two attorneys from the Cheyenne River Sioux Tribe (which already had an agreement with the state to this effect) explained to the tribal council that the tribes might well lose the case in the Supreme Court, considering both the closeness of the call and the Court's recent disposition of Indian cases. They assured the council that the tribe would be giving up no sovereignty or jurisdiction, and that highway patrol officers would be enforcing *tribal law* and citing tribal members into *tribal court* only.[124]

The proposed agreement generated little support among the council members. One representative suggested that the visiting tribal attorneys "get back down to the real world" and look at the history of state law enforcement and how Indians had fared under it. There was obviously a fear that the state would zealously enforce tribal laws ("we'll be jamming that [tribal] jail up there") or otherwise abuse Indian people. Some expressed concern that any agreement that allowed the highway patrol to exercise police powers on the reservation was a dangerous precedent (although the attorneys pointed out that the tribe could not legally prevent the state officers from patrolling reservation highways, since they clearly had jurisdiction over non-Indians).[125] Another concern was that the state courts would not honor citations or arrests of

124. Minutes and Tape of Meeting, 11 October 1990, Rosebud Sioux Tribal Office; Explanation of Proposed Agreement between the Rosebud Sioux Tribe and South Dakota Pertaining to Highway Jurisdiction, 15 October 1990, Jurisdiction File, Box 8, 1991 Accession, LaPointe Papers.

125. The tribal council, however, questioned whether state officers needed to patrol the reservation in order to police non-Indians. One member reminded the council of the existence of the tribe's implied consent law: "[I]mplied consent should be on every Indian reservation. A white man comes over that line, that sign will say, 'By crossing this line you are implying you're subjecting yourself to the jurisdiction of the Rosebud Sioux Tribe.' Boom. If he doesn't want that, then don't cross it" (Tape of Meeting, 11 October 1990, Rosebud Sioux Tribal Office).

non-Indians by tribal officers under state law. The agreement was also faulted as "one-sided": in arrests made off the reservation, state courts had jurisdiction over all individuals arrested; why, therefore, should non-Indians arrested on the reservation be turned over to state officials in this case? The council voted to table the compromise and take it back to the communities.[126]

Not all the communities met on the matter, but those that did expressed opposition. The Ring Thunder Community passed a resolution stating that "the Rosebud Sioux Tribe and the Sioux Nation have battled too long and hard to consider any type of agreement with the State of South Dakota concerning jurisdiction," and that "the Sioux Nation should not let ourselves be blackmailed into any kind of agreements."[127] The Rosebud Sioux Tribal Council subsequently voted unanimously to adopt the Ring Thunder resolution.[128]

The South Dakota attorney general's office appealed the decision to the Supreme Court in a petition for a writ of certiorari. The case was in effect settled in May 1991 when the Supreme Court denied the state's petition.[129]

CONTRADICTION AND RIGHTS-CLAIMS

Just as the concurrent validity of fundamentally opposed bodies of law energized the boundary (chapter 2) and liquor store (chapter 3) cases, the contradiction between two bodies of law established during different historical periods is at work in the struggle over state jurisdiction in Indian country. The contradiction in this instance is between statutory and case law written during the "termination" period of the 1950s and early 1960s on the one hand, and more recent law that reasserts (or reinvents) Indian "self-determination" on the other. There is no question that Public Law 280 is still "on the books" and that South Dakota might legally assume jurisdiction under its terms. And just as certainly, the 1968 ICRA—which amended Public Law 280 to prohibit unilateral state assumptions of jurisdiction—is on the books, as is the other contemporary statute and case law that supports Indian self-determination

126. Minutes and Tape of Meeting, 11 October 1990, Rosebud Sioux Tribal Office.
127. Ring Thunder Community Resolution 90-13, 11 October 1990, Jurisdiction File, Box 88, 1991 Accession, LaPointe Papers.
128. Minutes and Tape of Meeting, 18 October 1990, Rosebud Sioux Tribe; Resolution 90-229, 18 October 1990, Rosebud Sioux Tribal Office.
129. 500 U.S. 915 (denial of petition, 13 May 1991).

and sovereignty. The contradiction between Public Law 280 and the ICRA came to a head in South Dakota because of the very concrete concerns of Indian and non-Indian people in Indian country. As we have seen, many non-Indians (and some Indians) sought state jurisdiction as a solution to a perceived reservation law enforcement "hiatus," and as a correction to "race-based, special privileges" or "dual citizenship" *fundamentally inconsistent with American democracy.* Indian treaty rights, for many in South Dakota, are "un-constitutional" and "un-American" in a very literal sense.

Indian people have opposed state jurisdiction for a variety of reasons: because they do not trust state police and courts, because they believe that they will fare poorly under state jurisdiction, because they worry about termination, and—on the level of principle—because they believe state jurisdiction is fundamentally inconsistent with Indian treaty rights and tribal sovereignty as repeatedly recognized by the federal courts and by Congress. Framing their arguments in the same terms as the opposing camp, they argue that it is state jurisdiction in Indian country without Indian consent that is fundamentally inconsistent with American democracy—"illegal," "un-constitutional," and "un-American."

Both sides in other words, literally have substantive law on their sides, and both sides have talented "politicians"[130]—newspaper editors, lawyers, elected and appointed government officials—familiar with the law and able to act on it. These politicians acted both politically, by mobilizing into "blocs" people with material interests at stake in the rights claims involved, and legally, through litigation and legislation. Each side has a vision of rights that, while intrinsically justifiable, is inconsistent with that of the other. Rights are, thus, both fundamentally contested and perennially unstable. Perhaps it was only a matter of time before one side would find an opening to assert its position.

This opening manifested itself in a sequence of historical accidents by which South Dakota had assumed jurisdiction (in 1961), then relinquished it (in 1964), then reclaimed it again (in 1985)—but only after Congress specified that such an assumption was ineffective without tribal consent. Which legislative or judicial act arguably had precedence under such circumstances: the 1961 jurisdiction law, the 1964 reversal of that law by a state court, the 1968 legislative prohibition on further

---

130. I mean no disparagement by the term. A better (and less judgmental) term might be Gramsci's "organic intellectuals"—intellectual workers who do the vanguard work of developing reasoned standpoints in ongoing struggles (Gramsci 1971).

unilateral assumptions of state jurisdiction, or the assertion in the 1980s that the 1964 decision in *Hankins* had never really rendered the 1961 law invalid? The various answers to that question could quite literally produce profound gestalt-shifts in the rights of Indian people throughout Indian country. The jurisdictional instability that this sequence of historical accidents called into existence provided the opening for a political bloc in favor of state jurisdiction to argue that the first historical event was controlling. The opening provided a opportunity for the state to make a dent—or attempt to do so—in tribal sovereignty.

The tribes, of course, also used openings in the law, to chip away at state sovereignty, for example, when the Oglala Sioux Tribe announced that tribal members need not register their automobiles with the state and that the tribe would issue its own license plates.[131] A staff member in the state's executive office told me that this particular challenge from the tribes was one of the motivating factors in the hard stance that the state had taken on highway jurisdiction; "tired of being on the receiving end of the lawsuits all the time," state officials felt pressed to draw a line against tribal incursions into state sovereignty. Law's contradictions, law's openings, "can cut both ways."[132]

Fundamentally contradictory bodies of concurrently effective law, combined with the sequence of historical accidents, meant that the judicial questions involved were, as in the boundary and liquor store cases, highly technical, and, therefore, extremely close.[133] Was the 1961

131. More recently the Rosebud Sioux and Cheyenne River Sioux tribes have obtained a holding from the Court of Appeals for the Eighth Circuit that the state of South Dakota has no authority to impose a vehicle excise tax on tribal members within the reservation (*United States on behalf of Cheyenne River Sioux Tribe v. South Dakota*, 105 F.3d 1552 [1997]).

132. This perspective was the philosophical basis for the state's stance of "linkage" on jurisdictional matters, a position that annoyed the tribes. The executive branch—at the time of my fieldwork, at least—insisted that the ground rule in state-tribal relations regarding jurisdiction should be to maintain the status quo. The state would relinquish jurisdiction only in exchange for concessions from the tribe involved. For example, in the gaming compact between the Rosebud Sioux Tribe and South Dakota, which authorized a tribal casino under the terms of the Indian Gaming Regulatory Act of 1988 (102 Stat. 2467), the tribe retained more civil and criminal jurisdiction (specifically, jurisdiction over nonmember Indians) than did other tribes in their compacts with the state in return for fewer gaming devices than other tribes. From the tribes' point of view, this kind of bargaining over sovereignty represents a basic disrespect on the part of the state toward the tribes as governments.

133. One of the attorneys I interviewed believed strongly that the political context in which a decision had to be made could have an influence on the outcome of close cases. When I observed that the same district court judge who had found in favor of the tribe in the Mission Liquor Store case (actually in favor of the United States), found against the tribe in the highway case, the attorney responded, "of course." In the highway case "he's

South Dakota law—in 1990 judicial hindsight—consistent with the intent of Congress in 1953? Did the 1964 state supreme court decision *really* invalidate the law, or did the law remain in effect even though it was not recognized? Did the 1968 passage of the ICRA mean that the 1964 court decision should not be revisited, even if it was wrong, because we no longer live in the "tenor of the times" (termination) that gave rise to the statute considered in that case? These were the questions entertained by the federal courts in *Rosebud Sioux Tribe* v. *South Dakota*. And since the questions were so abstract and close, the judicial answers were both unpredictable and unconvincing to the losing parties, since they still believed they had the law on *their* side and that the decision had been based upon a technicality rather than the substance of the law—which, of course, it was. One tribal member told me in 1993 that the district court's holding of concurrent highway jurisdiction was both "unjust" and "didn't make any sense" legally. Another, a practicing attorney, told me the district court decision had simply been "wrong"; "we felt that he had misinterpreted" the law. Naturally, interested non-Indian parties, particularly in state government, felt the same about the reversal in the court of appeals. In the next chapter, we will examine the extent to which federal decisions regarding tribal jurisdiction over non-Indians seem fundamentally wrong to white people living on Rosebud Reservation.

---

dealing with the state. The state's got a little more political pull than some little town sitting out in the middle of nowhere.... He can rule against the city of Mission and nobody's going to get pissed off other than the people in the city of Mission.... But if you rule against the state on something,... you catch a little more heat for it." This was pointedly not a commentary on the particular judge (indeed, the informant said he had no idea how this judge made decisions in his cases) but rather on the pressures that influence decisions in judicial close calls in Indian country.

CHAPTER 5

Tribal Jurisdiction over Non-Indians

In November 1972 a large group of American Indian Movement (AIM) and other Indian activists—including the man who would shortly become the chair of the Rosebud Sioux Tribe—marched on Washington in the "Trail of Broken Treaties," where they presented to the administration a position paper called "The Twenty Points." The Twenty Points represented "a new framework for . . . the status of Indian tribes,"[1] "a new paradigm for dealing with Indian nations":[2] treating them literally *as sovereign nations* with *treaty* rights.[3] During the occupation of Wounded Knee by AIM and its allies in 1973, this paradigm was taken to its logical and dramatic conclusion, with the declaration of the Independent Oglala Nation. For the Indian people of Rosebud Reservation, the meaning of sovereignty was brought home even more clearly in the criminal trial of the Wounded Knee defendants, at which the defense argued that "the Courts of the United States do not have the power and jurisdiction to judge the guilt or innocence of individuals who are citizens of *other Nations* for alleged crimes committed on the *soil of other Nations*."[4] The

1. Deloria 1985 [1974]:48. This book is particularly valuable for understanding the new framework and was, in fact, partly responsible for its emergence. For an analysis of the role of AIM activism in articulating the new paradigm, see Nagel 1997:224–27.

2. Smith and Warrior 1996:144.

3. See also Means 1995:228–30. Interestingly, the man who would become the Rosebud tribal chairman was initially suspicious of the Twenty Points (Burnette and Koster 1974:201) but came to champion tribal sovereignty.

4. *United States* v. *Consolidated Wounded Knee Cases,* 398 F. Supp. 235 (D. S. D., 1975) (emphasis added).

trial included a "treaty hearing" in Lincoln, Nebraska, at which Indian activists, lawyers, and native experts on treaties—including individuals from Rosebud—testified regarding the Lakota understanding of the treaty of 1868.[5]

The emerging conception among the indigenous public of an *other nation* status had a substantial legal and historical rationale: the notion of Indian sovereignty appears, more or less implicitly—and more or less persuasively—in the foundational cases of Indian law and the treaties and agreements themselves. Many non-Indians in Rosebud country, however, continue to ask how one can have a "nation within a nation." This position, as well, has its own rationale, to be found—according to its proponents—both in Indian law and in the foundational document of the United States, the Constitution.

This chapter examines the attempts by the Rosebud Sioux Tribe to exercise criminal and civil jurisdiction over the non-Indians residing within Todd County and Rosebud Reservation. These efforts have given rise to critical legal questions—with exceedingly close judicial calls. In the broadest terms, the judicial answers come down to choosing between the *inherent* sovereignty of Indian tribes or the *overriding* sovereignty of the United States. Choosing the former, tribal advocates argue, means fostering the right of tribes to govern their own territories; advocates of non-Indians, by contrast, argue that choosing the latter means defending the constitutional rights of United States citizens who happen to live in Indian country. The two alternatives are mutually contradictory and incompatible—"balance" does not seem possible—and neither policy experts nor lawyers have found a way to accommodate both positions simultaneously. The contradiction between these two regimes of rights-claims, moreover, is the source of serious "racial" tension in Indian country. A non-Indian resident of Mission articulated his understanding of the demand for tribal jurisdiction over non-Indians bluntly: "That's one goal of the Indian people: it's just to screw the whiteman."

THE SOVEREIGNTY DEBATE DURING THE 1970S

In 1955 the Rosebud Sioux Tribal Council unanimously declared that "non-Indians of course are not subject" to tribal jurisdiction, and replaced references in its law-and-order code to "any person," which the

5. Ortiz 1977.

council assumed had been an oversight, with the phrase "any Indian."[6] At the height of the termination period, and before the emergence of sovereignty as an interpretive framework for reading the law, no one in South Dakota—Indian or non-Indian—believed that tribes could, as *governments,* claim general jurisdiction over non-Indians on the reservation. In 1934 the Interior Department's New Deal lawyers argued in the solicitor's opinion they drafted, "Powers of Indian Tribes,"[7] that tribes have the inherent power to tax "nonmembers" who "accept privileges of trade, residence, etc.,"[8] "to impose license fees upon persons engaged in trade with its members within the boundaries of the reservation,"[9] and to "exclude private individuals from the territory within its jurisdiction, or prescribe the conditions upon which such entry will be permitted."[10] The opinion went so far as to argue that the tribe's right to "punish *aliens* within its jurisdiction according to its own laws and customs...continues to this day, save as it has been expressly limited by the acts of a superior government."[11] Eight years later, however, Felix Cohen's 1942 *Handbook of Federal Indian Law*—written for the Interior Department—advised: "attempts of tribes to exercise jurisdiction over non-Indians, although permitted in certain early treaties, have been generally condemned by the federal courts since the end of the treaty-making period, and the writ of habeas corpus has been used to discharge white defendants from tribal custody."[12]

Even if the right of general tribal jurisdiction over non-Indians could be read into the 1934 opinion—as, indeed, many Lakota in the 1970s came to interpret the "Powers of Indian Tribes"—that reading was not a common one during the 1950s and 1960s. The Rosebud Sioux had imposed a tax on non-Indian ranchers leasing trust land during the 1950s,[13] but had stopped short of any more generalized assertion of

6. Resolution 5511, 3 June 1955, Rosebud Sioux Tribal Office, Rosebud, S. D.

7. U. S. Department of the Interior 1974, 1:445. On the role of the solicitor's opinion in the construction of tribal government under the Indian Reorganization Act, see Deloria and Lytle 1984b. On the role of the opinion in the institution of tribal government on Rosebud Reservation, see Biolsi 1992: chap. 4.

8. U. S. Department of the Interior 1974, 1:465.

9. Ibid., 471.

10. Ibid., 467.

11. Ibid., 472 (emphasis added).

12. Cohen 1942:148 (footnotes omitted).

13. The tribe had been empowered under the terms of the Indian Reorganization Act and the tribal constitution to impose taxes on the reservation, regardless of Indian status. In the 1950s the tribal council instituted a tax on grazing leases, about which "many white ranchers [had] been hollering their heads off." Some paid the tax by check with the annotation "under protest." Tribal members responded, "If they don't want to follow

tribal authority over non-Indians on the basis of territorial jurisdiction. Tribal authority over non-Indians was understood as a subject-specific and limited matter. In 1970 the Interior Department solicitor opined explicitly that tribes generally do not have criminal jurisdiction over non-Indians.[14]

Matters changed significantly during the 1970s. In 1973 an Interior Department lawyer told a conference of the American Indian Lawyers Association that although the department had "fostered…for many years" the view "that the tribes have no jurisdiction over non-Indians…, [t]here is a very large question of whether that is really the law, or whether tribes do, in fact, have both criminal and civil jurisdiction over non-Indians and may take them into their courts involuntarily."[15] In 1974 the 1970 solicitor's opinion was formally withdrawn.[16]

In the context of this uncertainty about the jurisdiction of tribal courts over non-Indians, coupled with the emerging indigenous sovereignty movement, the Rosebud Sioux Tribe revisited its law-and-order code in 1972. The revision of the code was in this instance a modest one—limited to a section on broken seals—but the act of replacing the word "Indian" with the word "person" signaled an expanding notion of tribal jurisdiction.[17] Indeed, in 1974, under the leadership of a new, activist president, the tribal council enacted an ordinance giving the tribal court jurisdiction over "any person" within the boundaries of the 1889 reservation.[18] The position of the tribal president, at least, was made clear in testimony presented at a U. S. Senate hearing in 1975: "I think that the law [regarding tribal jurisdiction] should be as it is everyplace else. In other words, when you're in Rome, you do as the Romans do; when you're in New York, you're subject to the laws of New York;

---

regulations, let them get the h—— off the reservation. We're not forcing them to stay here" ("Local White Rancher Challenges Tribal Tax," *Rosebud Sioux Herald*, 5 August 1963, Lakota Archives and Historical Research Center, Sinte Gleska University, Rosebud, S. D.). The Court of Appeals for the Eighth Circuit upheld the validity of an Oglala Sioux tax on non-Indian ranchers in *Iron Crow* v. *Oglala Sioux Tribe* (231 F.2d 89 [1956]) and *Barta* v. *Oglala Sioux Tribe* (259 F.2d 553[1958]).

14. Criminal Jurisdiction of Indian Tribes over Non-Indians," 10 August 1970, U. S. Department of the Interior 1974, 2:2018. The opinion was based on *Ex Parte Kenyon* (14 Fed. Cas. 353 [Cir. Ct., W. D. Ark., 1878]) and on an 1855 opinion of the United States attorney general.

15. American Indian Lawyers Association, 1973, *The Indian Civil Rights Act, Five Years Later*, Law Library, Stanford University, Stanford, Calif., 16.

16. "Criminal Jurisdiction of Indian Tribes over Non-Indians," 10 August 1970, in U. S. Department of the Interior 1974, 2:2018.

17. "Tribal Jurisdiction Asked," *Todd County Tribune*, 24 August 1972.

18. Ordinance 74-07, 30 April 1974, Rosebud Sioux Tribal Office.

when you're in California, you're subject to the laws of California and when you are in the State of South Dakota—off Indian Reservations—you are subject to the laws of South Dakota, [and] when a person enters Indian Territory, they should be subject to the law which exists there at this time."[19] Looking back on the controversy, an attorney who had opposed the expansion of tribal jurisdiction explained in 1979 that "[the] shift from the defensive use of the doctrine of tribal sovereignty [staving off state jurisdiction] to its offensive use is a new phenomenon—born of the politics of the present."[20] He had in mind, of course, the emergence of tribal sovereignty as a political manifesto.

Politics were unquestionably part of the issue: non-Indians residing on Rosebud Reservation were concerned about the prospect that they might fall under the tribe's jurisdiction. The mayor of Mission wrote to his congressional delegation and the governor regarding the tribe's intention to try "South Dakota State Taxpayers" in tribal court.[21] Although the governor responded that the United State Department of Justice had assured him that "Indian tribes do not have jurisdiction over non-Indians in Indian country" and had pledged to "take every step possible to defend this position,"[22] these assurances did little to answer the concerns of non-Indian residents. The president of Civil Liberties for South Dakota Citizens (CLSDC), who resided in neighboring Bennett County, wrote to the governor in 1974, complaining of the governor's televised reference to tribes as "sovereign nations": "We recognize that tribal governments are vested with certain sovereign powers over members of their own tribes, but these sovereign powers do not extend

19. U. S. Congress, Senate 1975, 9. At the same hearing the tribal president explained that criminal activities on the part of some non-Indians on Rosebud had prompted the tribal council to enact the new guideline regarding personal jurisdiction. Referring to a series of haystack fires that had plagued local ranchers (see p. 59), he informed the subcommittee that the United States attorney had declined to investigate the incidents because they were not technically arson (and thus did not fall under the Major Crimes Act). Indians and non-Indians had perpetrated the crimes, which were associated locally with AIM activism: "This is what caused the Rosebud Sioux Tribe Office to enact a resolution which it passed into law to take jurisdiction over non-Indians on our reservation, because the FBI and the Federal people were not acting in accordance with the law. I advised the U. S. attorney of South Dakota if he didn't act, I was going to act. I meant that emphatically. We are not going to have lawbreakers running around Rosebud doing some of the things they have done in the past" (ibid., 5).

20. Martone 1979:830.

21. Mission Mayor to Abdnor et al., 29 August 1974, Law Enforcement on Reservations File, Box 179, Richard Kneip Papers, Richardson Archives, University of South Dakota, Vermillion.

22. Kneip to Mayor, 4 September 1974, Law Enforcement on Reservations File, Box 179, Kneip Papers.

beyond their own members." Claimed tribal jurisdiction over non-Indians was simply unconstitutional.[23] This letter likely represented the position of CLSDC members—and, no doubt, that of many other non-Indians—in Todd County. Indeed, a Mission resident wrote to the governor in 1975 on CLSDC stationery that "we in Todd Co. are being denied our Civil Rights."[24] The governor found the CLSDC's criticism of his description of Indian tribes as sovereign nations "well taken."[25] He was sufficiently convinced by the argument that he included the problem of claimed tribal jurisdiction over non-Indians in a 1974 telegram to the U.S. president about serious jurisdictional problems in South Dakota (see p. 58). In February 1975 CLSDC held its first annual meeting. Among other actions, the group adopted resolutions asking the South Dakota attorney general for an opinion on tribal jurisdiction over non-Indians and requesting that the U.S. Congress enact legislation clearly limiting tribal jurisdiction to Indians.[26]

As a result of this kind of political pressure from non-Indians, one of the South Dakota's United States senators, who was chair of the Indian Affairs Subcommittee of the Committee on Interior and Insular Affairs, floated legislation providing that (in the senator's explanation to the governor) "[w]ithin the boundaries of a reservation, on private land, tribal courts do *not* have jurisdiction over non-Indians. Should a non-Indian commit an offense, tribal law enforcement will then turn over the offender to state authorities. Of course, the tribe will not have the power to tax non-Indians on private land." The senator believed such an arrangement would both recognize the legitimate claims of tribal governments under the Indian Reorganization (IRA) and address the concerns of non-Indians. While the legislation was never formally introduced, that it was seriously contemplated at so high a level is evidence of the strong opposition to tribal jurisdiction over non-Indians.[27]

In the wake of the 1972 Trail of Broken Treaties and the occupation of Wounded Knee in 1973, Congress created the American Indian Policy

23. President of CLSDC to Kneip, 7 November 1974, Indian Affairs File, Box 11, Kneip Papers.

24. Correspondent to Kneip, 15 June 1975, Indian Affairs (Misc.) File, Box 71, Kneip Papers.

25. Kneip to President of CLSDC, 29 November 1974, Indian Affairs File, Box 11, Kneip Papers.

26. "Civil Liberties Group Adopts Resolutions at State Meeting," *Winner Advocate,* 12 February 1975.

27. Senator to Kneip, 10 February 1975, Indian Affairs (Misc.) File, Box 51, Kneip Papers.

Review Commission (AIPRC) in January 1975. The AIPRC, composed of three senators, three representatives, and five Indian people (chaired by a senator from South Dakota), was charged with studying the history and current state of federal Indian law and policy, and it in turn delegated the study of particular topics to eleven task forces.[28] The report of the task force that considered jurisdictional issues was published in 1976.

The report found that "there is no question that the case for Indian jurisdiction ... over non-Indians is rooted in fundamental, long established principles of international law and domestic constitutional law."[29] The analysis started with Felix Cohen's argument, known as the inherent-powers thesis, that a tribe possesses all powers of self-government logically associated with its aboriginal, preconstitutional state of sovereignty unless those powers are explicitly removed by Congress. The powers include "modern" powers, such as regulation, taxation, and criminal prosecution, that the tribe may not have had occasion to use as of yet, but that are implied by the status of sovereignty within the modern world.[30] The task-force report insisted that "sovereign tribes have full jurisdictional powers, except to the extent that specific components may have been limited by the United States" through explicit congressional action.[31] The report concluded that the solution for resident non-Indians who did not want to come under tribal jurisdiction was to return to a "situation where Indian reservations ... are owned and occupied almost exclusively by the individual Indian tribe." Put bluntly, the solution was to persuade non-Indians to "sell out and leave the reservation" through a federally financed reacquisition plan.[32] The 1977 Final Report of the AIPRC did not deal in detail with tribal jurisdiction over non-Indians, but noted—without objection—the "expanding role of tribes in civil and criminal matters involving non-Indians," and recommended that Congress not attempt to reverse this trend through legislative intervention.[33]

Of course, neither the argument that tribes had sovereign powers over non-Indians nor the proposal that non-Indians move off the reser-

28. See Prucha 1984a:1162–70.
29. American Indian Policy Review Commission 1976:89.
30. See "Powers of Indian Tribes," 25 October 1934, in U. S. Department of the Interior 1974, 1:445; Cohen 1942; Deloria and Lytle 1984b. The substance of this thesis was criticized by Justice Marshall in *McClanahan* v. *Arizona* as a "platonic" notion of sovereignty; 411 U. S. 164, 171 (1973).
31. American Indian Policy Review Commission 1976:89.
32. Ibid., 100–101.
33. American Indian Policy Review Commission 1977:19, 14.

vation, held much appeal for non-Indians living in Todd County—or on any other reservation in the United States. Speaking for this constituency, the vice chair of the AIPRC submitted a dissent with the *Final Report*. He criticized the report as a "product of one-sided advocacy in favor of American Indian tribes,"[34] and argued that the report erred fundamentally in its assertion that tribes are "sovereign," that is, are "governmental units in the territorial sense." A tribe, he argued, is a "body politic" that has been permitted by the United States merely to "govern itself and order its *internal* affairs, but not the affairs of others."[35] Contrary to Cohen's inherent-powers thesis, "not a single case of the United States Supreme Court . . . has ever held that tribes possess inherent tribal sovereignty such that in the absence of congressional delegation they could assume governmental power . . . over nonmembers of the tribe." Whatever powers they might have were a function of federal delegation, not inherent tribal sovereignty.[36] Allowing tribes to have jurisdiction over non-Indians would mean that citizens with "no say in the creation of Indian law and policy of the reservation . . . [would] be subject to tribal jurisdiction. In short, non-Indians would have all the burdens of citizenship but none of the benefits."[37] This would amount to a situation that "[o]ur forefathers" would not have countenanced: "taxation without representation."[38]

Indeed, the prospect was an even more basic violation of American democratic principles: "There are few values more central to our society than the belief that governments derive 'their just powers from the consent of the governed.' Government by Indian tribes over non-Indians, if allowed to take place, would be a clear exception to that principle. A heavy burden of justification should fall on those who would subject some of our citizens to the coercive powers of others without any opportunity or right to join in the deliberations and decisions which determine how that power is to be exercised."[39] The senator recommended, contrary to the AIPRC report, that "Congress enact comprehensive legislation which . . . makes it clear that the governmental powers granted tribes by the Congress are limited to the government of members and their internal affairs, and are not general governmental powers."[40]

34. Ibid., 571.
35. Ibid., 573.
36. Ibid., 578–79.
37. Ibid., 579.
38. Ibid., 582.
39. Ibid., 586.
40. Ibid., 583, 590.

The jurisdictional question became particularly pressing in the mid-1970s. Indeed, in the first Indian law textbook published after Felix Cohen's 1942 *Handbook*, Monroe E. Price predicted in 1973 that "[b]ecause of the influx of non-Indian persons into 'Indian Country' . . . an important question in the next few years will be the power of the tribe to regulate the conduct of the new [sic] arrivals."[41] Although some local non-Indians took strong exception to the notion that they might fall under tribal jurisdiction, some strands of emerging legal interpretation held differently. Price, for example, anticipating the AIPRC report, believed there was little legal basis for limiting tribal jurisdiction over non-Indians ("there has never been explicit federal legislation depriving tribal governments of jurisdiction over non-Indians") and argued that such limitation would be contrary to the congressional policy of strengthening tribal governments.[42]

In 1974 the U. S. District Court in Washington state held in *Oliphant v. Schlie* that a tribal government had the inherent authority to assert criminal jurisdiction over non-Indians. The case involved a non-Indian who was arrested on Port Madison Reservation by the Suquamish tribal police and charged in tribal court with assaulting an officer and resisting arrest. He petitioned the district court for a writ of *habeas corpus* on the grounds that the tribe had no jurisdiction over a non-Indian. The court denied the petition.[43]

Oliphant appealed the decision to the Court of Appeals for the Ninth Circuit. The reasoning in the court's 1976 decision started with Cohen's inherent-powers thesis: "Surely the power to preserve order on the reservation, when necessary by punishing those who violate tribal law, is a sine qua non of the sovereignty that the Suquamish originally possessed."[44] Given that, it remained only to determine whether Congress had expressly withdrawn the right to exercise this authority over non-Indians, and here it was *silence* that was significant. Although Oliphant argued that congressional action, including the Indian Civil Rights Act of 1968 (ICRA),[45] had divested the tribe of criminal jurisdiction over non-Indians, the court did not find evidence of any such action or intent in the legislative history and affirmed the holding of the district court.

41. Price 1973:171.
42. Ibid., 173.
43. The district court opinion was not published; the case is summarized here from the facts as described in the opinion of the court of appeals (544 F.2d 1007 [9th Cir., 1976]).
44. 544 F.2d at 1009.
45. 88 Stat. 77.

By 1976 the commissioner of Indian affairs was comfortable enough with the clarity of the existing case law to advise the Interior Department solicitor's office that "Indian tribes are sovereign governments possessed of the same attributes of any government," including criminal jurisdiction over non-Indians. *Oliphant* had merely affirmed the "logical implications" as to criminal jurisdiction of a line of Supreme Court cases—most notably *Williams* v. *Lee* (1959)[46] and *United States* v. *Mazurie* (1975)[47]— that recognized the right of tribes to exercise civil jurisdiction over non-Indians. The commissioner summarized the holding of the district court in *Oliphant:* "The court emphasized that pursuant to the Indian Reorganization Act of 1934, the Suquamish Tribe was authorized to organize and function as a local government body, possessing certain inherent sovereign powers. The court concluded that these powers of self-government must necessarily include jurisdiction over the person of a non-Indian who violates tribal laws." The commissioner conceded that there was a legitimate concern that "the procedural rights of non-Indian criminal defendants may be denied by either unjust or merely unsophisticated tribal administrators of justice," but the ICRA[48] and the federal review of tribal court proceedings safeguarded those rights; tribes, moreover, were upgrading the quality of law enforcement and judicial systems with BIA technical and financial assistance. "[I]t is our position," the commissioner concluded, "that the legal principles formulated in the *Oliphant* decision are correct. The right of tribal self-government means the power to govern over those matters which affect the interests of the tribes regardless of the race or political affiliation of the party involved."[49]

46. The case involved a non-Indian merchant on the Navajo Reservation who sought settlement of a claim against a Navajo couple in an Arizona state court. The Supreme Court held that the state court had no jurisdiction over a case involving Indians on a reservation, but it went on to consider the matter of tribal court jurisdiction over a non-Indian. The Court held that removing tribal court jurisdiction simply because the petitioner was a non-Indian had no merit and would "infringe on the right of the Indians to govern themselves": "It is immaterial that respondent is not an Indian. He was on the Reservation and the transaction with an Indian took place there.... The cases in this court have consistently guarded the authority of Indian governments over their reservations. Congress recognized this authority in the Navajos in the Treaty of 1868 and has done so ever since" (358 U.S. 217, 223 [1959]).

47. *Mazurie* rehearsed the holding in *Williams* regarding tribal jurisdiction over non-Indians, finding that "the authority of tribal courts could extend over non-Indians, insofar as concerned their transactions on a reservation with Indians" (419 U.S. 544, 558 [1975]).

48. The ICRA essentially applied the Bill of Rights, with some modification, to Indian tribal governments.

49. Commissioner to Deputy Solicitor, 3 September 1976, Jurisdiction File 00121-1, 2, 3, 4, Lakota Archives and Historical Research Center, Sinte Gleska University, Rosebud, S.D.

The commissioner's findings, however, proved premature. The plaintiff in *Oliphant* appealed the decision of the court of appeals to the Supreme Court. The jurisdictional question was a crucial one in South Dakota (as it was in other substantial areas of Indian country), and the South Dakota attorney general, joined by the states of Montana, Nebraska, Nevada, New Mexico, North Dakota, Oregon, and Wyoming, submitted an amicus brief in the case. The brief pointed out that the Rosebud, Cheyenne River, Crow Creek, and Sisseton-Wahpeton Sioux tribes had passed ordinances extending tribal jurisdiction over non-Indians since the district court decision in *Oliphant*, and that ninety-five instances of tribes asserting or attempting to assert jurisdiction over non-Indians had been reported to the attorney general of South Dakota. The court of appeals' decision had changed the "common understanding"—noted in Cohen's *Handbook*—that tribes did not have such jurisdiction. It disturbed "an almost one-hundred-year status quo" in states such as South Dakota: "Non-Indian citizens, who decades ago decided to reside or remain within the confines of an Indian reservation, may now suddenly find themselves subject to tribal jurisdiction. This event could not have been reasonably foreseen by those non-Indian citizens and would create undue hardships for them as they would be subject to the jurisdiction of a governmental entity in which they are virtually excluded from participation."[50]

The brief rejected the thesis of inherent tribal sovereignty as "a particularly elusive concept with no clear boundaries." The concept of "sovereignty" needed to be applied practically as the more modest right of a tribe to regulate "intratribal relations among its members." This understanding would be more consistent with case law, the apparent intent of Congress over the years, and longstanding practice: "the concept of tribal sovereignty has never been approved for use outside the context of intratribal relations and should not be so used at this time."

The state argued that the historical record made clear that Congress had, as a matter of course, assumed that tribes did not have jurisdiction over non-Indians, as indicated by Congress's occasional grants of such jurisdiction to tribes by explicit legislation. The 1791 treaty with the Cherokee,[51] for example, recognized the right of the Cherokee to "punish" non-Indians who settled illegally on their land. "It is difficult to ex-

---

50. Brief for the State of South Dakota, *et al.*, as Amici Curiae, filed 18 September 1977, *Oliphant v. Suquamish Indian Tribe*, 76-5729 (U.S.).
51. 7 Stat. 39.

plain the [presence] of this provision," the brief reasoned, "if the tribe already had such authority as an attribute of 'inherent sovereignty.'"[52] The 1859 Treaty of Port Elliott with the Suquamish,[53] by contrast, contained no such provision.[54] Clearly, congressional silence meant not that Congress had let stand Indian "inherent sovereignty" with implicit jurisdiction over non-Indians, but that Congress had not *given* such jurisdiction to the tribe—the only way the tribe could ever *have* such jurisdiction. The 1885 Major Crimes Act,[55] which granted the federal courts jurisdiction over certain crimes between Indians in Indian country, also constituted evidence that Congress intended that tribes not have jurisdiction over non-Indians. Could the Court really believe that Congress meant to allow tribes to keep criminal jurisdiction over non-Indians, while removing it for Indians? Thus, even if the tribes had originally had "inherent sovereignty" giving them jurisdiction over non-Indians, Congress had removed that jurisdiction by clear implication.[56]

The Supreme Court handed down its decision in *Oliphant* in 1978, essentially adopting South Dakota's argument.[57] The Court found that a careful reading of the case and statute law made it clear that although Congress had never expressly forbade the exercise of tribal jurisdiction over non-Indians, the "unspoken assumption" was that tribes did not have criminal jurisdiction over non-Indians.[58] When tribes became dependencies of the United States, they lost those powers *"inconsistent with their status"* as dependencies.[59] Tribes clearly continued to hold some inherent sovereign powers, but the tribes' incorporation into the United States also placed "inherent limitations on tribal powers"[60] and made them subject to the overriding sovereign's "great solicitude that its citizens be protected by the United States from unwarranted intrusions on their personal liberty." Indian tribes would, therefore, not be allowed to try non-Indian citizens of the United States "except in a manner

52. Brief for the State of South Dakota, *et al.*, as Amici Curiae, filed 18 September 1977, *Oliphant v. Suquamish Indian Tribe*, 76-5729 (U.S.)
53. 12 Stat. 927.
54. The treaty provided, moreover, that Indian offenders against U.S. law would be delivered up to federal authorities; it is for that reason unlikely that Congress expected the tribe to exert criminal jurisdiction over non-Indians while the federal courts were to exert criminal jurisdiction over Indians.
55. 23 Stat. 385.
56. Brief for the State of South Dakota, *et al.*, as Amici Curiae, filed 18 September 1977, *Oliphant v. Suquamish Indian Tribe*, 76-5729 (U.S.).
57. 435 U.S. 191 (1978).
58. Ibid., 203.
59. Ibid., 208 (emphasis in original), quoting 544 F.2d at 1009.
60. 435 U.S. at 209.

acceptable to Congress." That is, tribes could exercise such jurisdiction only by express delegation from Congress.[61]

Oliphant, however, pertained solely to criminal jurisdiction, and the question of tribal civil jurisdiction over non-Indians remained unanswered—or, more precisely, inconsistently answered. Frederick J. Martone, an attorney who had worked on the dissenting opinion to the AIPRC *Final Report*, insisted that as a function of their "dependent status," tribes had lost jurisdictional authority over anything but internal matters. His formula for establishing the validity of tribal jurisdiction was simple: "If the assertion of tribal power is over a member, then unless expressly prohibited by federal law and if otherwise consistent with its dependent status, the assertion is valid. If, on the other hand, the assertion of tribal power is directed to a nonmember, the assertion is invalid *per se* unless expressly permitted by federal law. The Supreme Court appears to have come upon these simple . . . rules in *Oliphant* and *Wheeler*."[62] In short, tribes have a right to "self-government" but not "sovereignty" in the sense of continuous governmental jurisdiction over a territory.[63] As a general rule, according to Martone, they do not have jurisdiction of *any kind* over non-Indians.

Richard B. Collins, a staff attorney with the Native American Rights Fund at the time, found a different threshold for tribal civil jurisdiction over non-Indians. Anticipating the Supreme Court's 1981 holding in *Montana* v. *United States*,[64] Collins argued that tribes have inherent civil jurisdiction over non-Indians "who enter into consensual relations with Indians or when their activities directly affect Indians or Indian lands."[65]

The Rosebud Sioux Tribe public relations officer had a third view in 1979. In his weekly column in the *Todd County Tribune*, he argued that the tribe had inherent powers of government retained from aboriginal sovereignty unless those powers were specifically removed by an express act of Congress: "Indian tribal organizations are, in fact, governments. [A]ll inherent powers remain intact until Congress expressly acts." Clearly this man did not believe that the Supreme Court's *Oliphant* holding was correct. Following Cohen—whom he had surely read—there was no necessity to find a justification for tribal jurisdiction

61. Ibid., 210.
62. Martone 1979:845.
63. Ibid., 829 note.
64. 450 U. S. 544, esp. 565–66 (1981).
65. Collins 1979:523.

over non-Indians in a treaty or an act of Congress; that power was *inherent*. Critically, one of the specific powers listed by the tribe's public relations officer was "the power to regulate non-Indian individuals in Indian Country." Non-Indians on Rosebud Reservation had clearly been put on notice.[66]

REGULATING NON-INDIANS ON ROSEBUD RESERVATION

THE TRIBAL COMMERCIAL CODE

The systematic exercise of tribal civil and regulatory jurisdiction over non-Indians residing on Rosebud Reservation began with the enactment of the tribe's uniform commercial code in 1989.[67] One impetus for the code was a notorious incident in 1989 in which an off-reservation automobile dealer attempted to repossess a vehicle from a tribal member. Knowing that the state court had no jurisdiction in the matter, and apparently assuming that a suit in tribal court would be fruitless, the dealer pursued the tribal member in a high-speed chase and repeatedly discharged a firearm. To provide an alternative in tribal court to any further attempts at this kind of "frontier" repossession (and for other purposes) the tribal council enacted a uniform commercial code modeled on the code used throughout the United States. The commercial code had been drafted by a Seattle law firm.[68] Among other provisions, the code required that "all persons engaged in business within the exterior boundaries of the Reservation" obtain a tribal business license.[69] The application procedure included submission of a "sworn statement that the applicant will comply with all Tribal law applicable to the applicants' business" as well as a "statement that the applicant consents to Tribal Court jurisdiction and service of process in matters arising from the conduct of business."[70]

Response from local non-Indian businesspeople was not long in coming. Although the *Todd County Tribune* praised the tribe's interest in "entering the mainstream of free enterprise" with its new commercial code, the newspaper's editor expressed concern about abuses of claimed

66. "Rosebud Sioux Tribe News," *Todd County Tribune*, 5 April 1979.
67. Rosebud Sioux Tribal Law and Order Code, Title 14 (Rosebud Sioux Commercial Code), Title 15 (Corporations and Tribal Entities), Title 16 (Businesses).
68. Resolution 88-72, Rosebud Sioux Tribal Council, 11 May 1988, Rosebud Sioux Tribal Office.
69. Rosebud Sioux Tribal Law and Order Code, 16-1-201.
70. Ibid., 16-1-202.

jurisdiction over non-Indian businesses: "Will it be used in power plays against non-tribal members? Will years of struggle by some business owners to make a decent living for their families be disregarded and negated by new legislation? The language of the tribe's commercial code seems to demand obedience of those within its jurisdiction.... Does it mean license holders will eventually be allowed the right to vote in tribal elections, the right to seek office and sit on tribal juries, rights of dual citizenship that tribal members now enjoy?"[71]

The South Dakota attorney general apparently agreed with the thrust of this editorial and told an audience in Winner: "People should be allowed to vote in any government that taxes or licenses them. To be allowed to tax people but to not let those who are taxed vote flies in the face of the foundational principle on which this country was formed. It's taxation without representation."[72]

The *Tribune* pursued the matter by claiming directly that "Whites should have tribal voting rights." After explaining that the newspaper would not apply for the tribal license until the editor had time to "think things through,"[73] the column recalled the 1975 *Little Thunder* v. *South Dakota* suit, in which local Indians successfully sued for the right to vote for the county officials who administer services to them.[74] "The same principle should hold true for whites who are now being asked to pay a fee and may eventually be asked to pay taxes to an Indian government." The solution was "naturalization laws...something that can be offered only by nations who consider themselves truly independent and sovereign."[75]

Matters continued to heat up when the tribal attorney general was reported by the *Tribune* to have insisted that the license requirement was a law with which resident businesses must comply, whether or not the proprietors understood the law to their satisfaction or felt comfortable with it. The tribe was, after all, a government and not a voluntary association. "I'd be willing to bet," the attorney general was quoted as saying, "[that] Winner merchants don't understand the South Dakota

71. "Smoke Signals: Tribe Should Delineate Impact of New Code," *Todd County Tribune,* 8 February 1989.
72. "[Attorney General, Tribal President] Trade Jabs on 'Abolishing'," *Todd County Tribune,* 15 February 1989.
73. "Smoke Signals: Whites Should Have Tribal Voting Rights," *Todd County Tribune,* 22 February 1989.
74. *Little Thunder* v. *South Dakota,* 518 F.2d 1253 (8th Cir., 1975).
75. "Smoke Signals: Whites Should Have Tribal Voting Rights," *Todd County Tribune,* 22 February 1989.

Uniform Commercial Code either." But, of course, they complied with that law. Answering the *Tribune*'s challenge, the attorney general added that tribal membership, and thus voting rights, could not be opened to non-Indians because enrollment required a minimum of Sioux Indian blood; voting rights, she argued, were in any event "a separate issue from whether the tribe has the power to tax." Some businesses were warned that thirty days had elapsed without submission of their license applications.[76] Indeed, three-fourths of the businesses in Mission had not applied, and second notices were posted.[77]

The *Tribune* responded to the attorney general's comments:

> [The] assertion that business owners would willingly pay a license fee to the state of South Dakota...may be true enough...because...the state of South Dakota...is obligated to return both money and services to its residents as well as voting and citizenship rights. As a business owner myself, I willingly pay a business license fee to the state of South Dakota because I am guaranteed certain constitutional rights in return—the right to hold office, vote in elections, sit on juries, receive money that builds roads, bridges and schools, etc.... While I agree with [the attorney general] that the tribe's new commercial code was written the same as the state of South Dakota's commercial code, the difference between them again lies in the fact that the state of South Dakota returns both voting and citizenship rights to fee-payers along with money and services. The Tribe does not.[78]

By the beginning of April 1989, twenty-nine of forty-five businesses in the Mission area had yet to submit license applications, and risked imposition of a $1,000 tribal fine. Some had contacted the state attorney general's office in Pierre about what they saw as a violation of their civil rights.[79] The extent of the objections to the tribal business-license requirement was made clear at a Mission chamber of commerce meeting attended by seventy people, including the tribal attorney general and other tribal representatives. The meeting "at times was slightly heated as businessmen and women questioned tribal officials about rights...and tribal jurisdiction over non-Indians." The attorney general explained that although the tribe had no criminal jurisdiction over

76. "Tribal Attorney General: Businesses Should Pay License Fee," *Todd County Tribune*, 22 March 1989.

77. "Commercial Code Meeting May Be Slated for April," *Todd County Tribune*, 29 March 1989.

78. "Smoke Signals: Fundamental Problem of Identifying What Works," *Todd County Tribune*, 29 March 1989.

79. "Tribal Officials Say No to Public Meeting on Code," *Todd County Tribune*, 5 April 1989; "New Tribal Business Code Worries Some Mission Businesses," *Todd County Tribune*, 19 April 1989.

non-Indians, it did have civil jurisdiction: "A U. S. Supreme Court decision granted the tribe that right."[80] The attorney general's legal theory was based on language in *Montana* v. *United States* (1981). There the Supreme Court held that "Indian tribes retain inherent sovereign powers to exercise some form of civil jurisdiction over non-Indians on their reservations" when the latter "enter consensual relationships with the tribe or its members through commercial dealings" or when non-Indian "conduct threatens or has some direct effect on the political integrity, the economic security, or the health or welfare of the tribe."[81]

It was clear from remarks at the chamber of commerce meeting, however, that many business owners were not convinced, and that they did not trust the tribal council or the tribal court.[82] A tribal official at the time recalled the tenor of the Mission chamber of commerce meeting: "[T]here were a lot of people who came in and were really angry. There were a lot of ranchers there who ... had an exemption from the business license.... But they were half hysterical ... and they were very angry.... [T]hat was the feeling I had, that they were really frightened that something terrible was going to happen as a result of [tribal jurisdiction], and they needed to protect themselves." Indeed, after the chamber meeting, nineteen businesses in the city of Mission and its environs signed a petition stating that "buying this license would be surrendering our constitutional rights" by requiring "that we subject ourselves to the Tribe's jurisdiction.... [W]e will not willingly buy this license and we will do all we can to help defend each other if a court encounter should become a reality."[83]

The position of the non-Indians who resisted tribal jurisdiction was not without legal basis. Indeed, the *Montana* decision itself appeared to come down *against* tribal jurisdiction, save for the exceptions mentioned—which are often seen by non-Indians who know the law as justifiably "narrow" exceptions. Undercutting an inherent-sovereignty argument in support of tribal jurisdiction, the Court noted that tribes

80. "Business Meeting Helps Clear Air on Tribal Business License," *Todd County Tribune,* 10 May 1989.

81. 450 U. S. 544, 565–56. The tribal government's reading of *Montana* as giving the tribe civil jurisdiction over non-Indians on the reservation was articulated in a *Todd County Tribune* editorial ("Willing Non-Indian Surrender Could Allow Leadership, Responsibility for Indians," *Todd County Tribune,* 14 June 1989).

82. "Business Meeting Helps Clear Air on Tribal Business License," *Todd County Tribune,* 10 May 1989.

83. [Petition,] Mission, South Dakota, 16 May 1989, Indian Affairs, General, General Files, George S. Mickelson Papers, Richardson Archives, University of South Dakota, Vermillion.

"lost many of the attributes of sovereignty" through their "original in-corporation into the United States,"[84] and that any authority to regu-late non-Indian activities was necessarily diminished by alienation of In-dian lands to non-Indians who had lawfully moved onto the reservations under the aegis of Congress. Articulating what must have been precisely the sentiment of the non-Indians at the Mission chamber of commerce meeting, the *Montana* Court insisted: "It defies common sense to suppose that Congress would intend that non-Indians purchas-ing allotted lands would become subject to tribal jurisdiction when an avowed purpose of the allotment policy was the ultimate destruction of tribal government."[85] Put simply, "exercise of tribal power beyond what is necessary to protect tribal self-government or to control inter-nal relations is inconsistent with the dependent status of the tribes, and so cannot survive without express congressional delegation."[86] The Court's language provided a charter for the non-Indians' resistance to tribal sovereignty.

Nor was their argument solely that that tribal jurisdiction over non-Indians violated the intent of Congress in the General Allotment Act; to the contrary, they argued that such jurisdiction violated the basic con-stitutional rights of non-Indians. The proprietor of a local business complained to a state legislator of the infringement of civil rights under the tribal commercial code. He had written to his congressman, but had been told that "businesses operating on the Rosebud Reservation are *re-quired by law* to have a license and *are [subject] to tribal jurisdiction.*" "By what law?," the correspondent asked; "[i]f there is such a law, how can Congress violate the constitution and give away our constitutional rights? . . . I do not care if the Rosebud Sioux Tribe governs its members, if they so desire, however, I do object to the Tribe taxing and governing me, a non-member. . . . It is simply *taxation and governing without rep-resentation.* It denies me my constitutional rights."[87] The writer ex-pressed white people's fear of being run out: "Rosebud Sioux Tribal officials, particularly [the president] has [sic] made it very clear during several public meetings that this is *'Indian Country.'* The Rosebud Sioux Tribe has jurisdiction and white people are not welcome here. 'This is our reservation and if you don't like it here, then get out.' That

84. 450 U. S. at 563.
85. Ibid., 560.
86. Ibid., 564.
87. Mission correspondents to Senator, 1989, South Dakota Legislative Research Council, Pierre (emphasis in original).

statement has been said over and over again by [the president] and others. . . . Recently an Indian fellow . . . [asked] me where my passport was. He then informed me that all white people are foreigners and are here illegally. I thought this was America—*one nation under God,* indivisible, *with freedom and justice for all.*"[88]

It is not difficult to understand the concern in this letter. While it requires some reading out-of-context, the tribal president was reported in the *Tribune* to have invoked the ruling of a federal judge that that Mission was an *Indian community.* Some non-Indians might resent that, the president was reported to have said, but "[t]hat's not my problem."[89] A tribal member's column in the *Tribune* pointed out: "Though non-Indians may complain of the dual system of government on the reservation, my feeling is *that's just the way it is.* It reminds me of the popular phrase seen on bumper stickers and recited by patriotic citizens: 'America: love it or leave it.'"[90] An expression commonly heard on Rosebud is that "there are four roads[91] off the reservation . . . " (the implication being that non-Indians who object to Indian governance are free to leave). In an interview with the author, a staff member in the state executive branch recalled an interchange between the governor and a tribal chair: "What do you really want?," the governor asked. "And this guy said to him, 'I want the white guys off the reservation.' And . . . he was honest, he wasn't joking, he was not ranting, raving, . . . he just knew what his goal was." As the staff member said of non-Indians in Indian country, "a lot of 'em are scared to death."

The state of South Dakota eventually became involved in the issue of tribal business-licenses through its department of transportation. At the time, the state was in the process of rebuilding U.S. Highway 18 through Todd County. Sections of the old road had been torn up with the aim of straightening, grading, and widening the right-of-way. The road was impassable during construction, and the department of trans-

---

88. Ibid.

89. "Emotions Pitched Following Attorney General's Remarks," *Todd County Tribune,* 22 February 1989. To be fair to the president, he was also reported to have said that he foresaw a day when non-Indian residents would have a vote in tribal government (ibid.).

90. "Around the Rosebud: [Attorney General] Not Current on Indian Law," *Todd County Tribune,* 22 February 1989 (emphasis in original). The columnist called, nonetheless, for non-Indian and Indian people to get beyond the jurisdictional squabbles—by accepting tribal sovereignty—and "unite and deal with the unemployment and poverty here together" (ibid.).

91. The reference is to U.S. highways 18 (running east-west) and 83 (running north-south), which lead in four directions "off" the reservation.

portation informed the tribe that work could not be completed until certain conditions were met. One of these was that the tribe waive its business-license requirements for the highway contractors. The problem, from the state's point of view, was not the requirement of a tribal license, but the provision in the tribal code for "consent to jurisdiction of Tribal Court and to service of process of Tribal Court."[92]

Tribal council members held a meeting and carefully considered the state's ultimatum. A letter to the tribe from the state's secretary of transportation noted that standing firm on tribal sovereignty might mean jeopardizing tens of thousands of dollars in tribal tax on the highway contracts and 150 seasonal jobs for tribal members.[93] This was a serious matter. "I just hate to see . . . unemployment lines," one tribal officer observed at the meeting, and would rather see tribal members working "than playing these games with the state."[94]

When the council met to take formal action on the proposal, the tribal president suggested the possibility of amending the tribal code to remove the objectionable *consent*-to-jurisdiction language. The tribal attorney general assured the council that this did not involve waiving tribal jurisdiction, since tribal jurisdiction was an inherent right of self-government and not conditioned on "consent." The tribal council, however, was not in the mood for compromise over a matter as serious as sovereignty. The tribal officer who had earlier wanted to avoid "playing games" with the state observed that after hearing the attitudes of business owners regarding tribal jurisdiction at the Mission chamber of commerce meeting described above, he realized that "we're gonna have to fight it all the way." One council member insisted that the council stand firm against the state's threat to delay completion of the road work: "We as Lakota people are used to living under these adverse conditions for eons of years, ever since the whiteman came to this continent. . . . [I]f anything, we should unite and strengthen this government, this Rosebud Sioux Tribe, and . . . tell the state to go you-know-where.

92. Secretary of Transportation to Tribal President, 1 May 1989, South Dakota Department of Transportation, Pierre; "State Gives Rosebud Ultimatum on Highway Project," *Todd County Tribune,* 3 May 1989; "No Agreement on 18 Construction," *Todd County Tribune,* 7 June 1989.

93. An ordinance enacted by the council (and applicable, by the state's consent, to highway construction) authorized the tribe to collect a one-percent tax on the contracts and ensured Indian preference hiring in seasonal road construction work ("Guest Editorial: Highway Issue Must Be Resolved," *Todd County Tribune,* 31 May 1989).

94. Tape of Meeting of Committees on Highway, 2 May 1989, Rosebud Sioux Tribal Office.

And we are really a sovereign nation then.... [W]e don't have to worry about a thing. We can delay this [construction]. It's alright. We can have alternate routes. Or we can buy a horse...." The council voted not to amend the commercial code at the same meeting during which it voted to keep the state highway patrol off the reservation (see pp. 100–101).[95]

In May the *Todd County Tribune* applied for its tribal business license. In an editorial, it called for one of two possible resolutions to the contradictions involved. "Though it may... be taxation without representation and though it's possible my constitutional rights are being violated, I can now ask the Tribe to come even further into the 20th century, and like Todd, Shannon and Washabaugh Counties were forced to do [for Indian citizens by the *Little Thunder* decision], offer a voice and a vote [for non-Indians] in tribal government in exchange for fees, taxes and other tribal civil requirements that may be imposed in the future." Alternatively, the editorial argued, "tribes should exercise their power only over their own people, not over people who have no legal, political or social remedy or voice. Let each people's government exercise their own power over their own land and their own citizens. Let each government leave the other's property and people alone."[96]

The non-Indian people I interviewed mentioned several concerns about the business license besides the required consent to tribal court jurisdiction. (The requirement was ultimately repealed.) One concern was that the price of the license, perceived as a tribal revenue scheme, would escalate. Another was the tribe's claimed right to audit the books of a licensee. Some were worried that the tribe would meddle in private business affairs by enacting regulatory ordinances, such as Indian-preference hiring requirements for all businesses on the reservation. Some also felt that non-Indian businesses could not obtain satisfactory justice in the tribal court. (One of my interviewees bluntly characterized the Rosebud Sioux Tribal Court as a "kangaroo court.")

The conflict with the state department of transportation was settled when the tribe agreed that contractors would not be required to sign a consent to tribal jurisdiction and would retain "the ability to assert that the Tribe lacks jurisdiction." The tribe would not "waive its jurisdiction, and the state, its employees and agents [would] not consent to the jurisdiction of the Tribal Court." The parties agreed simply that the

95. Tape and Minutes of Meeting, Rosebud Sioux Tribal Council, 5 May 1989, Rosebud Sioux Tribal Office.
96. "Smoke Signals: License May Open Way for Legal, Political Relief," *Todd County Tribune,* 10 May 1989.

project would proceed without either side attempting to settle the juris-dictional question.[97]

It had not been easy for the tribal council to agree to this. At a meet-ing at which the arrangement proposed by the state was discussed, it was clear that council members were suspicious of the language pro-posed by the state, and saw the proposed agreement as an attempt to erode the tribe's sovereignty. Only after heated discussion and deletion of language stating "that purchase of a business license [would] not in-voluntarily subject the contractors...to Tribal jurisdiction" did the council consent to the agreement.[98] Ultimately the tribe amended the business-license provision of the commercial code to remove the re-quirement of a signed statement of consent to tribal court jurisdiction for all business licensees.[99] The understanding was that tribal jurisdic-tion was a matter of inherent tribal sovereignty, and was not condi-tioned upon consent; another provision in the code, in any event, stated that each licensee "shall comply with all applicable tribal laws" and "consents to the jurisdiction of the Tribal Court."[100]

ROSEBUD SIOUX TRIBE V. WALSH

The matter of local businesses ignoring the license requirement, how-ever, was still unresolved. "[M]ore business people than not [had] de-clined to buy the license,"[101] and in May 1989 the tribal attorney gen-

97. Special Provision Regarding Tribal Business License, 7 July 1989, South Dakota Department of Transportation. In an interview with the author, a tribal official at the time recalled the circumstances of the dispute:

> [A]ll that time the contractors were telling [the tribe] it wasn't them that didn't want to buy the license. They were willing to do it. They wanted to go to work. It was the state that was...calling them "our contractors."... [S]o we finally asked whether these people are state employees.... The state department of transportation had to admit that they were not state employees, that they were in-dependent contractors.... [T]hey ended up putting that notice [of the business li-cense requirement] in the bids, so that they would know, because that was part of [the state's] argument..., that these poor contractors had no idea that they were going to have to do this, and it's not fair. And so we said, "alright, then, give them notice."...Well they bid on it anyway. They didn't care.

98. Special Provision Regarding Tribal Business License, 19 June 1989, South Dakota Department of Transportation; Tribal Attorney General to Secretary of Transportation, 13 June 1989, South Dakota Department of Transportation; Minutes and Tape of Meet-ing, Rosebud Sioux Tribal Council, 28 June 1989, Rosebud Sioux Tribal Office.
99. Resolution 89-101, Rosebud Sioux Tribal Council, 12 October 1989, Rosebud Sioux Tribal Office.
100. Rosebud Sioux Tribal Law and Order Code, 16-1-206.
101. Resolution 89-101, Rosebud Sioux Tribal Council, 12 October 1989, Rosebud Sioux Tribal Office.

eral filed motions with the tribal court for orders to show cause why the delinquent businesses should not incur civil penalties. The motions were granted by the tribal court, and the case of *Rosebud Sioux Tribe* v. *Walsh* was underway.[102]

The central legal question in the case was whether recent Supreme Court decisions granted the tribe authority to regulate the activities of the businesses involved. *Brendale* v. *Confederated Yakima Indian Nation,* a case decided by the Supreme Court in 1989,[103] distinguished between "open" or "integrated" reservation areas, in which fee-patenting had resulted in the influx of non-Indian residents, and "closed" areas, in which there had been no such integration of non-Indians. *Brendale* reiterated the Court's general assumption in *Montana* v. *United States* (1981) that tribal jurisdiction over non-Indians did not extend to fee lands in integrated reservation contexts. *Brendale* also raised the threshold of the *Montana* exceptions by holding that tribal jurisdiction over non-Indians was valid only if the non-Indian activity is "demonstrably serious" and actually imperils "the political integrity, economic security or the health and welfare of the tribe."[104]

The decision in *Rosebud Sioux Tribe* v. *Walsh* was handed down in October 1991.[105] After establishing that it had jurisdiction over the case, the tribal court considered "whether the Rosebud Sioux Tribe has the authority to make laws governing the conduct of non-Indians on the Rosebud Reservation." The court started by reading the *Montana* exceptions broadly—as had been urged by the tribal attorney general in the tribe's brief[106]—to cover most activities of non-Indians normally regulated by a municipal or state government. The delinquent businesses contended that the *Montana* exceptions did not apply to them because

102. Motions for Orders to Show Cause, filed May 1889, *Rosebud Sioux Tribe* v. *Walsh et al.,* Civ. 89-210-216, Rosebud Sioux Tribal Court, Rosebud, S. D.

103. 492 U. S. 408. The attorney for the defense in the *Walsh* case filed an amicus brief in the *Brendale* case on behalf of a group of rural counties, including Todd (Brief for Mendocino County *et al.,* as Amici Curiae, filed 3 September 1998, *Brendale* v. *Yakima,* 87–1622 [U. S.]). The South Dakota attorney general's office also filed an amicus brief in the *Brendale* case (Brief of the State of South Dakota as Amicus Curiae, filed 2 September 1988, *Brendale* v. *Yakima,* 87–1622 [U. S.]).

104. 492 U. S. at 431.

105. Memorandum Decision and Order, 22 October 1991, *Rosebud Sioux Tribe* v. *Walsh,* Civ. 89-210-216, Rosebud Sioux Tribal Court. In addition to briefs filed by the tribal attorney general and the attorney for the defendants, the court considered an amicus brief submitted by the South Dakota attorney general. Brief of Amicus Curiae, filed 2 August 1989, *Rosebud Sioux Tribe* v. *Walsh,* Civ. 89-210-216, Rosebud Sioux Tribal Court.

106. Brief of Petitioner in Opposition to Motion to Dismiss, filed 7 August 1989, *Rosebud Sioux Tribe* v. *Walsh,* Civ. 89-210-216, Rosebud Sioux Tribal Court. Three

they were located on deeded land within a *Brendale*-type "integrated community." In denying the businesses' motion to dismiss,[107] the tribal court held that the argument had been answered directly by the holding in *United States* v. *Mission,* in which the federal district court determined that Mission was not a non-Indian community, notwithstanding its integrated character.[108] The tribal president called the decision affirming jurisdiction over non-Indian businesses "a victory" for the tribe, and the tribal revenue director announced that the tribe would file suit against other delinquent businesses not included in the original case.[109]

JURISDICTION OVER NONMEMBER INDIANS

In 1990 the Supreme Court handed down its opinion on tribal jurisdiction over nonmember Indians in *Duro* v. *Reina.*[110] The case involved a member of another tribe who killed an Indian on the Salt River Reservation in Arizona. After federal charges against him were dismissed, the defendant was charged in tribal court with illegal firing of a weapon on the reservation. He filed a petition for a writ of *habeas corpus* in United States District Court, which granted the writ, holding that assertion of criminal jurisdiction by the tribe over a non-member Indian would violate the equal protection guarantees of the ICRA. Since the Supreme Court had held in *Oliphant* that non-Indians were not subject to tribal criminal jurisdiction, "to subject a nonmember Indian to tribal jurisdiction where non-Indians are exempt would constitute discrimination based on race."[111]

Many parties, including both the state of South Dakota and the Rosebud Sioux Tribe, had an interest in this case. The legal and policy

---

dissenting justices in the *Brendale* case had made the same argument. They argued strongly against a narrow interpretation of *Montana* that would rely on that case's "anomalous" general holding (that tribes lack jurisdiction unless delegated it by Congress or justified by the "exceptions"). *Montana*, the dissent argued, "must be read to recognize the inherent authority of tribes to exercise civil jurisdiction over non-Indian activities on tribal reservations where those activities...implicate a significant tribal interest." When put into the context of a hundred-and-fifty years of Indian case law, it is clear, the dissenting justices went on to say, that *Montana* must be read with a recognition that "tribes *retain* their sovereign powers over non-Indians on reservation lands" unless inconsistent with national interests or expressly divested by Congress (450 U. S. at 450).

107. Memorandum Decision and Order, 22 October 1991, *Rosebud Sioux Tribe* v. *Walsh,* Civ. 89-210-216, Rosebud Sioux Tribal Court.

108. 548 F. Supp. 1177 (D. S. D., 1982). See pp. 88–89.

109. "Tribe Wins Business License Case," *Todd County Tribune,* 13 November 1991.

110. 495 U. S. 676.

111. Ibid., 682 (paraphrasing the holding of the district court).

arguments surrounding *Duro* had clear implications not only for tribal jurisdiction over nonmember Indians but also for tribal jurisdiction over *non-Indians.* The Court of Appeals for the Eight Circuit noted in a 1988 case involving the same question as *Duro* that "because [nonmember Indians], like the non-Indian residents of the Devil's Lake Reservation, cannot vote in tribal elections, hold tribal office, sit on tribal juries, become members of the Devil's Lake Sioux Tribe, nor significantly share in tribal disbursements . . . the powers that may be exercised over them are appropriately limited."[112] Not surprisingly, South Dakota filed an amicus brief (with New Mexico and Washington) in the *Duro* case.

The Supreme Court determined that "[i]n the area of criminal enforcement . . . tribal power does not extend beyond internal relations among members."[113] Since a nonmember Indian could not "vote, hold office, or serve on a jury," her or his situation was the same as that of the non-Indian examined in *Oliphant,* and thus a tribe's powers over a nonmember Indian "are subject to the same limitations."[114] Tribal courts possess "only the powers of *internal* self-governance."[115] "Criminal trial and punishment is so serious an intrusion on personal liberty that its exercise over non-Indian citizens was a power necessarily surrendered by the tribes in their submission to the overriding sovereignty of the United States. . . . We hesitate to adopt a view of tribal sovereignty that would single out another group of citizens, nonmember Indians, for trial by political bodies that do not include them."[116] Indian people, the Court ruled, are citizens of the United States and thus have the same rights as all citizens under the supreme authority of the "overriding sovereign." Under such circumstances, the Court reasoned, tribal governments may not act as if that overriding sovereign, and the rights it guarantees, did not exist.

Judicial interpretation of the law was one thing; the politics surrounding national Indian affairs and the practical realities of reserva-

---

112. *Greywater v. Joshua,* 846 F.2d 468, 493 (8th Cir. 1988). The court of appeals also pointed out (ibid., 493) that "there are significant racial, cultural, and legal differences between the Devils Lake Sioux Tribe and the Turtle Mountain Band of Chippewa Indians [the petitioners' tribe]. These non-member Indian Petitioners thus face the same fear of discrimination faced by the non-Indian petitioners in *Oliphant:* they would be judged by a court system that precludes their participation, according to the law of a societal state that has been made for others and not for them."

113. 495 U.S. at 688.

114. Ibid.

115. Ibid., 692 (emphasis in original).

116. Ibid., 693.

tion law enforcement were quite another. In the wake of concerns about a law-enforcement "gap" created by *Duro,* Congress delegated temporary criminal jurisdiction over non-member Indians to tribal governments in 1990 by amending the ICRA to specify that the "powers of self-government" include "the inherent power of Indian tribes, hereby recognized and affirmed, to exercise criminal jurisdiction over all Indians."[117]

This amendment was temporary,[118] however, and a permanent congressional "*Duro* override" or "*Duro* fix" was a serious political question, both in South Dakota and beyond. In 1991 the South Dakota legislature adopted a resolution—introduced by a senator from Mission who was also a Rosebud Sioux tribal member—noting that *Duro* had "created an entire class of people over whom neither the federal, state or tribal governments have jurisdiction for misdemeanor crimes." The resolution commended Congress for giving temporary jurisdiction to tribes and urged a permanent law.[119] The resolution was presented at a hearing of the Select Committee on Indian Affairs of the U. S. Senate by the state senator who had introduced it as "the official position of the State of South Dakota."[120]

There were, however, interests that opposed a congressional *Duro* override. In 1990 the Conference of Western Attorneys General adopted a resolution brought by the South Dakota attorney general urging "Congress to reject any attempt to subject nonmember Indians to the criminal jurisdiction of the tribal courts... as contrary to the United States Constitution."[121] A staff attorney for the government of South Dakota explained for me the concerns of the attorney general's office regarding a *Duro* override in quite direct terms: If tribes could go to Congress and get a lawful delegation of jurisdiction over nonmember

117. 104 Stat. 1892, sec. 8076 (b). The statute also specified that "Indian means any person who would be subject to the jurisdiction of the United States as an Indian under section 1153 of title 18 if that person were to commit an offense listed in that section in Indian country" (104 Stat. 1892, sec. 8077[c]).

118. 104 Stat. 1893, sec. 8076 (d); 105 Stat. 616. Permanent extension of tribal jurisdiction over nonmember Indians was postponed because of Senate concerns over "whether additional protections are needed in the Indian Civil Rights Act that affect the administration of justice in tribal courts. The major issues cited for exploration in the criminal law context are the right to court-appointed counsel and the right to jury selected from other than solely tribal members" (U. S. Congress, Senate 1991b, 12).

119. Senate Concurrent Resolution 15, 19 March 1991.

120. U. S. Congress, Senate 1991a, part 2:14.

121. Resolution No. 90-01, 3 August 1990, Conference of Western Attorneys General, in U. S. Congress, Senate 1991a, part 2:96–97.

Indians, they could also seek legislative delegation of jurisdiction over non-Indians. Congress, of course, has complete "plenary" authority to delegate to tribes power as it sees fit. As a matter of policy the state had good reason to protect the civil rights of nonmember Indians, but from the perspective of the attorney general's staff's the implications of a *Duro* override were of greater import than the override itself. Tribes had full territorial sovereignty on their "agenda," the attorney explained, and getting past *Duro* with a congressional override would be a first step in fulfilling that aim.

In 1991 the Senate Select Committee on Indian Affairs held hearings on a permanent *Duro* override. A prepared statement from a staff attorney from the South Dakota attorney general's office argued that delegating tribal jurisdiction over a class of people barred from participating in tribal government set a dangerous precedent. Such a delegation would be "contrary to the belief which animated the founding of the nation." The statement referred to the Declaration of Independence on the derivation of government powers from the consent of the governed. "In addition, the Civil War may be seen as a struggle to guarantee self-government for all persons, regardless of race. This idea is captured in Abraham Lincoln's teaching that 'no man is good enough to rule another man without that other man's consent.'" Tribal governments, the statement reasoned, necessarily lost the power to control *external* relations when they were incorporated as dependencies into the United States: a line of federal cases made this plain, and *Duro* was "simply the logical outcome of these cases."[122]

An attorney from Winner testified at the same Senate hearings on behalf of four county governments,[123] and set out the representation argument against a congressional override of *Duro*—the same reasoning that was central in arguments against tribal jurisdiction over non-Indians:

[WITNESS:]   [N]onmembers do not have the right to participate in [the tribal] political process and they should not have their Constitutional rights diminished by that process.

                          . . .

THE CHAIRMAN: In other words, since I do not participate in the political process of South Dakota, the courts of South Dakota should not exercise jurisdiction over me?

122. Statement of South Dakota Chief Deputy Attorney General, in U. S. Congress, Senate 1991a, part 2:84–86.
123. The counties were located in Idaho, Montana, Utah, and Washington. See U. S. Congress, Senate 1991a, part 1:265.

[WITNESS:] ...As a resident and a citizen of the State of Hawaii, you could come to South Dakota and you would be subject to the jurisdiction of the State of South Dakota. However, unlike the system that we are talking about here today, in South Dakota if you chose to do so you could become a voting member of that electorate, you could participate in that government.... Second, and more importantly, even if you chose not to, you would still have the full protection of the Federal Constitution in the State of South Dakota, which you would not have in the system that we are talking about.

Echoing the position of the tribes, the chairman then suggested that the interstate analogy might not be appropriate to understanding Indian sovereignty, and that an international analogy might be more useful:

THE CHAIRMAN: What about a nonresident alien?

. . .

Let us say that I am from Singapore and I go—

[WITNESS, INTERRUPTING:] We're not talking about people—excuse me, Mr. Chairman. We're not talking about people in this legislation who are from Singapore. We're talking about people who are citizens of the State and citizens of the United States.[124]

The witness concluded by moving from the nonmember question to the non-Indian question, articulating the ultimate concern of the counties, states, and local non-Indians regarding a *Duro* override: "We have had 100 years of Congressional policy in this country that has encouraged non-members to reside on Indian reservations. We have approximately 50 percent of the total population within the exterior boundaries of Indian reservations who are non-Indians."[125] In a prepared statement entered into the record, the witness pointed out that *Duro* was an affirmation of "fundamental Constitutional rights." While it is "one thing for an individual to voluntarily belong to an Indian tribe and give up his or her constitutional rights in this manner...[i]t is entirely another matter for anyone to subject other individuals, who are citizens of the United States, to this jurisdiction."[126] The witness interpreted the controversy around *Duro* against the larger background of tribal jurisdiction over nonmembers—Indian or non-Indian—and expressed the hope that

124. U. S. Congress, Senate 1991a, part 1:72.
125. Ibid., 73.
126. Ibid., 265.

Congress would not seek to undue *Duro* and the solid principles of law upon which it was based.

One of South Dakota's senators also put the matter of tribal jurisdiction over nonmember Indians into a larger context that clearly included the matter of tribal jurisdiction over non-Indians:

> I have heard the argument made that because we choose to live somewhere we give up certain prerogatives related to that choice.... Love it or leave it. Go onto a reservation and love it. If you don't like what you see or what's done to you, and you're not a tribal member, leave it. I can't accept that in the year 1991. That just does not seem to me to be an acceptable approach to the Constitutional liberties for which the very people subjected to this kind of double standard died in Kuwait, in Vietnam, in World War II, and in other situations. I think that with the responsibility of jurisdiction comes obligation, an obligation to make sure that those people who fall under the jurisdiction of tribal leaders have the opportunity to be heard, have the opportunity to dictate their destinies. We should not, on the basis of to whom you were born, determine whether or not they have that right.[127]

Although the senator supported a *Duro* override because of "people... taking complete advantage of the lawlessness that exists because no one has jurisdiction or because the jurisdictional lines are too gray," he refused to concede that such an action by Congress reflected willingness "to allow those who are non-members, to allow those who are non-Indians, to be subjected to a system that I feel is as un-American as anything can be."[128]

The matter came down to more than abstract principles of governance or representation. One of the arguments of those opposed to the *Duro* override was that the U.S. Commission on Civil Rights had faulted the tribal courts for laxity in guaranteeing due process and other rights under the ICRA. Bad press regarding tribal courts at a 1986 hearing of the Civil Rights Commission was brought forward at the Senate hearings. It was even suggested by those opposed to tribal jurisdiction that release of the Civil Rights Commission report on the ICRA was being purposely held up for public relations purposes until Congress could push through the *Duro* override.[129]

Although the June 1991 Civil Rights Commission report conceded problems in the adjudication of ICRA claims in tribal courts, it suggested that these problems could be remedied with federal funding for tribal courts and training for tribal court and tribal government per-

127. U.S. Congress, Senate 1991a, part 2:32–33.
128. Ibid., 33.
129. See ibid., 19–20.

sonnel. The report recommended against considering federal court review of ICRA claims until the funding and training avenues had been exhausted as solutions.[130]

The Rosebud Sioux Tribe, of course, had its own opinion. In a resolution, the tribal council called the *Duro* decision "a direct and flagrant violation of the Tribe's inherent sovereignty." Although federal legislation had been introduced to "reaffirm the Tribe's inherent authority to arrest and prosecute non-member Indians," some legislators had "suggested that as a condition to the Tribe's exercise of misdemeanor jurisdiction over nontribal member Indians and/or non-Indians that nontribal members and/or non-Indians should have the right to vote in tribal elections to tribal government office, which is the equivalent to termination." The tribe supported making the temporary *Duro* fix permanent without imposing additional burdens on the tribe.[131] The *Duro* override was enacted into law in 1991, but with specific assurances and exceptions: that the legislation did not apply to non-Indians, that it was not a prelude to a congressional override of *Oliphant*, and that Congress would undertake an investigation of tribal courts.[132]

130. U. S. Commission on Civil Rights 1991.

131. Resolution 91-189, 11 July 1991, Rosebud Sioux Tribal Office.

132. 105 Stat. 646. Permanent *Duro* override began with a House bill. On the floor of the House of Representatives the question of tribal jurisdiction over non-Indians arose again. An Arizona representative asked: "Does the legislation affect the tribes' jurisdiction over non-Indians?" and "Is this legislation a precursor to overturning the Oliphant decision in which the Supreme Court precluded tribal court jurisdiction over non-Indians?" Only after being assured that this was not the case did the congressman agree to support the bill (*Congressional Record*, 14 May 1991, vol. 137:H2989). The House passed, without amendment, a bill that simply acknowledged tribal jurisdiction over nonmember Indians (ibid., H2992).

Senate deliberations on the House bill began with assurances by the chair of the Select Committee on Indian Affairs that subjecting "Indians" to tribal jurisdiction was not a matter of treating some people differently because of race. Rather, Indianness was a *political* status based on membership in a political community, a tribe, or nation. Nonmember Indians subject to tribal jurisdiction were Indians not because of their race but because of their membership in other tribes (*Congressional Record*, 23 September 1991, vol. 137:S13469-70). Another senator, however, was not convinced and feared that congressional override of *Duro* would subject some American citizens (nonmember Indians) to a reduction of civil liberties simply because of *race*: "Congress cannot ... allow the exercise of whatever laws are passed by a tribe to infringe on the fundamental civil rights of an American just because of Indian ancestry." In his view, "Federal court review of Indian Civil Rights claims is an absolute necessity before any Duro overturn legislation is made permanent." He could not support the bill without such a guarantee (ibid., S13470). While this senator had not directly raised the issue of tribal jurisdiction over non-Indians, the implication was clear, and the chair of the committee responded directly: "I would like to assure the Senator that this legislation does not address the issues raised by Oliphant versus Suquamish Indian Tribe, and nothing in this bill is intended to alter or affect the holding in that case." The Senate amended the House bill to substitute a

CONTRADICTION YET AGAIN

No one involved has any doubt that in discussing the question of tribal jurisdiction over non-Indians, we are contemplating profound legal contradiction. Frederick J. Martone was so convinced of the aberrant nature of special Indian rights over non-Indians on American soil that, in a 1979 law journal article, he predicted the inevitable disappearance of tribal jurisdiction over non-Indians. The resolution of the contradictions in federal law, Martone argued, would come about gradually as the non-Indian silent majority stood up for its own *inalienable* constitutional rights: "The curious position of the American Indian tribe in the federal system is evolving toward a precise definition. This is chiefly caused by the politics of Indian country which has forced otherwise quiet observers to take note of the tribal presence. The resulting congressional, judicial, and administrative activity has enormously advanced the timetable within which legal issues of substantial importance are resolved."[133] As an advocate of the non-Indian position, Martone believed the resolution of a precise definition of tribal rights involved *no* rights of jurisdiction over non-Indians. Such an eventuality was not farfetched in 1979, when a "backlash" against tribal sovereignty was apparent even in some corners of Congress.[134]

Tribal advocates, of course, had their own vision of the character of (and remedy for) the contradiction in federal Indian law. Although contemplating tribal jurisdiction over resident non-Indians may have defied common sense for non-Indian advocates, denying tribes the same rights

---

continuing temporary override of *Duro,* for the permanent override contained in the version passed by the House (ibid.).

The House opposed the amendments, however, and a conference committee was called to resolve the disagreement (*Congressional Record,* 26 September 1991, vol. 137:S13749). The conference committee recommended that the Senate amendment be withdrawn, leaving the *Duro* override permanent. A South Dakota senator issued a statement separate from the conference committee report regarding his concerns about subjecting nonmember Indians to tribal court jurisdiction without guarantees of civil liberties and without rights of representation in tribal government (U.S. Congress, House 1991). The chief Senate opponent of the override advised his colleagues that he "decided to allow the permanent extension of the Duro overturn to pass in spite of strong reservations regarding... inadequate civil rights protections for Native Americans on this country's Indian reservations" because he had obtained a commitment from the chair of the Indian Affairs Committee to explore the matter further. He looked forward to hearings that would "fully examine the issue of tribal sovereignty, tribal courts, and Federal review of Indian civil rights claims" (*Congressional Record,* 17 October 1991, vol. 137:S14931). The hearings were held in November 1991 (U.S. Congress, Senate 1992).
    133. Martone 1979:829.
    134. See U.S. Commission on Civil Rights 1981.

that any *local* government—let alone a sovereign nation with treaty rights—possessed was equally absurd for tribal governments: should a sovereign nation, for example, be prohibited from issuing a traffic ticket to a non-Indian? This political and litigatory standpoint, and the precedents and rationale it was able to find in its reading of the law, prevented any resolution of the contradictions in the direction envisioned by Martone.

The fundamental contradiction involved here is between two inconsistent regimes of rights-claims. Under the tribal reading of federal Indian law enunciated by Felix Cohen in 1934 and espoused by tribal governments to this day, tribes are sovereign governments with inherent powers to exercise jurisdiction over their territory. In the other regime of rights-claims—which upholds the rights of non-Indians and non-tribal members—tribes are domestic dependent polities allowed by Congress to govern their internal affairs, but without full territorial sovereignty. Territorial sovereignty is diminished because the "integrated" communities resulting from allotment created a class of reservation residents who are not tribal members, and because tribes are "domestic" and "dependent" they have no inherent right to violate the constitutional rights of American citizens. They may have had sovereign authority to exercise jurisdiction lawfully over outsiders at one time, but that sovereignty was necessarily diminished by the tribes' "dependent status within our scheme of government."[135] Tribes necessarily lost powers "inconsistent with their status" (in the language of the *Oliphant* court), such as the power to exercise general jurisdiction over nonmembers because this would conflict with "overriding sovereignty of the United States" and its guarantee of civil rights to all citizens. Tribes may be, in some senses, "nations" (and the quotation marks are emphasized in this reading of Indian "nationhood"), but they are, ultimately, *incorporated* "nations"; their limited "sovereignty" must necessarily conform to the larger sovereignty of the United States. As one business-person in Mission put it to the governor in 1988, the tribal constitution "exists only under ours."[136] To advocates of tribal sovereignty, this amounts to making tribes into "Boy Scout troops" in the words of one of my informants.

To some extent, the conflict is a matter of fundamentally inconsistent statute law enacted in different historical periods, as in the boundary,

---

135. *Duro v. Reina*, 495 U. S. 676, 684.
136. Correspondent to Governor, 20 June 1988, Indian Affairs, General, General Files, Mickelson Papers.

liquor-store, and highway-jurisdiction cases examined earlier in the book. Here the conflict is, to some degree, between justifiable expectations arising out of the checkerboarding of the reservation. Checkerboarding was a direct effect of the removal of federal trust status from Indian allotments under law enacted by Congress during the "civilization" period on the one hand, and, on the other, support for tribal government grounded in the IRA of the New Deal period and in the more recent "self-determination" period. In 1992, the governor of South Dakota, paraphrasing a law review article that was circulating among the state executive branch,[137] told the House Committee on Interior and Insular Affairs that the federal government had made "two promises"—one to the tribes that they would have control over tribal territory, and one to non-Indians who settled in Indian country that they would not be subject to tribal control. "It's clear to me," the governor said, that "those who were invited to homestead wouldn't be subject to tribal regulation.... We're both [the tribes and the state] in a position of having to settle these issues in court because the law isn't settled, and that's a waste of resources for all of us."[138]

But beyond the historical overlay of conflicting statutes, the struggle examined in this chapter is also about the general principles that inform the logic of federal Indian law—the perennial conflict between the principles of uniqueness and uniformity, between treaty rights and constitutional rights. These are not simply policy goals that informed Congress at various times, or textual impulses on which the courts drew during different periods. They are *moments* in the recurrent dialectic within federal Indian law. This conflict was present at the creation of Indian law and has been repeatedly rehearsed in the debates in Congress and in the majority and dissenting opinions of the federal courts. Although one or the other of the general principles may take on some degree of political or judicial institutionalization during particular periods, the alternative argument is always waiting in the wings and pressing itself forward as a principled minority opinion. The exemplary instance of this was the AIPRC Final Report and its corresponding dissenting minority opinion. Indian law is, from first principles, contradictory.

The coexistence of the conflicting principles—especially regarding tribal jurisdiction over non-Indians—is particularly apparent in the

---

137. Furber 1991.
138. "Reservation Jurisdiction Gets Debated," *Todd County Tribune,* 12 February 1992; [Testimony,] Governor George S. Mickelson, State of South Dakota, n. d., Indian Affairs, General, General Files, Mickelson Papers.

compass of Supreme Court opinions. In *Montana* v. *United States* (1981), the Court announced "the general proposition that the inherent sovereign powers of an Indian tribe do not extend to the activities of nonmembers of the tribe."[139] "[I]t defies common sense," the Court insisted, "to suppose that Congress would intend that non-Indians purchasing allotted tribal lands would become subject to the tribal jurisdiction."[140] In *Iowa Mutual* v. *LaPlante* (1987), on the other hand, the Court stated: "Tribal authority over the activities of non-Indians on reservations is an important part of tribal sovereignty. . . . Civil jurisdiction over such activities presumptively lies in the tribal courts unless affirmatively limited by a specific treaty provision or federal statute."[141] The *Brendale* (1989)[142] decision is even more telling regarding fundamental contradiction. Six justices adopted the reasoning in *Montana,* two justices in effect split the difference between *Montana* and *Iowa Mutual* by distinguishing between "open" and "closed" reservation areas with respect to jurisdiction over non-Indians, and three justices insisted that *Montana* was an anomalous holding, a ruling that contradicted a hundred-and-fifty years of case law supporting the general principle that "tribes *retain* their sovereign powers over non-Indians on reservation lands" unless inconsistent with federal interests or expressly divested by Congress.[143]

The Supreme Court has recently insisted that there is no conflict here. In *Strate* v. *A-1 Contractors,* a unanimous Court reconciled the apparent conflict between *Montana* and *Iowa Mutual* (and *National Farmers Union*)[144] by declaring that when read carefully *Iowa Mutual* does not alter the "pathmarking" holding in *Montana* that tribes do not have jurisdiction over non-Indians on fee lands, but for two narrow exceptions. *Iowa Mutual*'s passage on tribal jurisdiction was, the *Strate* Court insisted, really about nothing more than allowing the tribal court to have the first crack at testing a jurisdiction question. Similarly, *Iowa Mutual* really only said that non-Indians must exhaust tribal remedies in challenging tribal jurisdiction before turning to the federal courts. The federal courts, however, would have ultimate say in questions of jurisdiction, and *Iowa Mutual* did not expand tribal jurisdiction over

139. 450 U.S. 544, 565.
140. Ibid., 560 note.
141. 480 U.S. 9, 18.
142. 492 U.S. 408.
143. Ibid., 450. See Frickey 1997 on conflicts in Supreme Court holdings regarding tribal jurisdiction over non-Indians.
144. 471 U.S. 845 (1985).

non-Indians beyond the narrow scope laid out in *Montana*. The *Strate* Court recognized that there had been confusion over what the apparently liberal language of *Iowa Mutual* meant for the bleak holding—from a tribal point of view—of *Montana*, and *Strate* was meant to clarify the controlling role of *Montana*'s narrow scope for tribal jurisdiction over non-Indians.[145] Notwithstanding this clarification of what *Iowa Mutual* "really" meant—to the Court—questions of tribal jurisdiction will continue to exercise the federal courts because of the opening allowed by the *Montana* exceptions.[146]

Given this conflict-laden universe of available legal theory, it comes as no surprise that, as in the other cases that have been explored in this book, both sides in the tribal jurisdiction dispute have compelling legal and political arguments, and that the losing side always believes it still has the law on its side, whatever the ruling of the judiciary (arbitrarily, it must seem to the losing side) in the particular case at hand. Recall the irate letter of the Mission businessman to his state legislator asking how it could be that his basic constitutional rights could be violated. Consider also the repeated references by non-Indians to "taxation without representation" and the "consent of the governed," as well as the citation of foundational texts—the Declaration of Independence, the Constitution—and reference to "our forefathers," the Revolution, the Civil War, and the "constitutional liberties" for which Americans died in World War II, Vietnam, and Kuwait. A veiled reference to racial injustice in South Dakota—by Indians against whites—cast the conflict in terms as objectionable as white racism toward African-Americans in Alabama. This cannot be merely rejected as political hyperbole, since some of it ended up in a brief to the Supreme Court written by an skilled attorney experienced in federal Indian law. The repeated references to foundational ideas and texts are an indication of how deep the contradiction runs, and how profound the disharmony is between the two regimes of rights-claims.

As in the other cases explored in this book, both sides have good law on their side in their rights-claims, and the possibility remains that a minor change in the fact situation will open windows for litigation. One

---

145. 520 U.S. 438, 456–59 (1997). It seems unlikely that *Strate* would have been a unanimous decision had Justice Blackmun, who wrote the vigorous *Brendale* dissent—calling into question the "general principle" in *Montana*—been a member of the Court. Blackmun retired before *Strate* was decided. On the other hand, Blackmun seems to have accepted the reasoning of *Montana* in his dissent in *South Dakota v. Bourland* (508 U.S. 679 [1993]), in which he conceded that allotment diminishes the inherent sovereignty of a tribe (ibid., 701).

146. *Strate* was also intended to clarify what the *Montana* exceptions do and do not include.

of my Indian informants, a trained attorney, is concerned about the "integrated" reservation concept announced in *Brendale*. The problem is that there is a heavy concentration of non-Indian residents on the east side of Rosebud Reservation, perhaps sufficient to argue that this area must be seen as "open" in *Brendale*'s terms. "If you took that to court," my informant speculated, "I think you'd have a good chance of getting ...your [tribal] regulatory power really knocked down.... I'm sure the court's going to say, 'well, we're not going to let you regulate that part, those are all non-Indians.'"

And then there is always the fear of a statutory fix, an act passed by Congress that would clarify precisely how far tribal jurisdiction extends. Both sides can see the value of ending litigation by settling the question once and for all, but both sides also worry that a legislative fix might grant too much to the other side. There is even concern among some non-Indians, as we saw, that tribal advocates might be able to obtain serious congressional consideration of an *Oliphant* override in the wake of their success with the *Duro* override—a congressional "delegation" of tribal criminal jurisdiction over non-Indians. While this is not politically likely at present, the concern itself is an indication of the indeterminacy of the jurisdictional situation in both judicial and political terms.

It is telling that Charles Wilkinson, a legal scholar who has long worked in *defense* of tribal sovereignty and who has had a critical role in articulating the discourse of federal Indian law, could write in a 1987 treatise of the anomalous nature of tribal sovereignty from the point of view of broader civil rights: "even if separate lands were promised to tribal control more than a century ago, how can the United States, consistent with its democratic ideals, allow race-based Indian tribes to govern the non-Indians who have lawfully entered those lands to live and do business over the course of ensuing generations?"[147] The contradiction between rights-claims based on treaties and tribal sovereignty and those based in the Constitution and equality before the law could not be phrased more aptly.

The conflict directly drives racial tension in Indian country. Both Indian and white people experience the other as immediate opponents in a zero-sum rights-game. Tribal sovereignty means—from the point of

147. Wilkinson 1987:6. Along the same lines, Wilkinson argues: "The tribes have reasserted their inherent powers during the modern era and seek to fulfill their prerogative of self-rule almost as though the opening of the reservations had never occurred" (ibid., 21).

view of local whites—infringement of their basic rights: their *constitutional* rights. From the point of view of tribal advocates, however, the protection of "constitutional rights" means infringement of the tribal right to self-government: treaty rights. Thus, it is not surprising that an Indian witness from South Dakota testifying at a Senate hearing on the *Duro* override might characterize whites claiming their constitutional rights on the reservation as "burglars":

> The Indian tribes did not invite the non-Indians into their reservation. They were forced into the reservation, and the non-Indians that came there, the non-Indians that are there now, fully realized—and the courts have so recognized—that they did not have access to the political processes of the tribe. There was a tacit understanding that they had no right to participate in those governments. The same is true of the nonmember Indians that we are dealing with here today. . . . I think it is not a good enough argument for the non-Indians and nonmember Indians who, like burglars, have intruded into the tribal household and when caught, raise the defense that they should not be subject to punishment since they have no right to formulate the rules of the household.[148]

We turn in the next chapter to a closer examination of how federal Indian law produces Indian-white relations.

148. U. S. Congress, Senate 1991a, part 2:24.

CHAPTER 6

Making Indian-White Relations

The earlier chapters of this book laid out the central contradiction in the Indian law discourse between moments of uniformity and uniqueness and charted how this contradiction has been manifested historically as political struggles between Indian and non-Indian people on and around Rosebud Reservation. To some extent the contradiction emerges from conflicting statute law, enacted under profoundly incongruent historical periods but equally "on the books," effective, and available for quite legitimate—but fundamentally opposed—rights-claims. The contradiction also manifests itself as a recurring conflict between first principles of law and justice—first principles argued in the public sphere of Indian law, which includes judges, legislators, and common citizens, both Indian and non-Indian. The perennial conflict here is between first principles drawn from the letter and spirit of treaties signed with Indian nations (what has been called the uniqueness reading), and first principles drawn from American constitutional rights and equality before the law (uniformity). Both treaties and the United States Constitution are, after all, organic documents. Are "we" all *one* nation, or are there distinct nations involved here, a reality that non-Indians in Indian country simply have to accept? The answer to this question—both when it is politically claimed or imagined and when it is enforced—profoundly affects the public articulation and exercise of rights. Local people are necessarily "interested"—in the most political sense—in what is to be lost or gained in the struggle over rights. Put differently, political subjects in Indian country are formed in the process of struggle over conflicting regimes of rights-claims. And as we have seen, because of the particular legal discourse involved here and the rights it both gives and takes away, the political subjects formed are inescapably *racial* subjects.[1] In the Rosebud Country, one's rights—the rights that matter, materially, in the local scene—are inseparably tied to one's race. This chapter will examine how this process of political subject-formation works in, and through, the discourse of Indian law.

THE DISCURSIVE REGULATION
OF INDIAN-WHITE RELATIONS

During the 1970s, as a result of the efforts of AIM[2] and Indian politicians, as well as high-profile litigation, sovereignty was disseminated as a new political ideology and basis of rights-claims.[3] In concrete terms for Lakota people, sovereignty refers to special jurisdictional arrangements: tribal members' exemption from state law on the reservation and the authority of tribal government over *all persons* on the reservation. Although jurisdiction was a concern and even a target of political mobilization among the Lakota people before the 1970s, it was the concept of sovereignty—which, as we have seen, was read out of the corpus of federal Indian law—that crystallized political struggle and focused it squarely on jurisdiction. The jurisdictional question has become the central political front in the struggle for empowerment by Lakota people of all political stripes: "activists," "traditionalists," tribal officials,

---

1. One of the central tenets of federal Indian case law is that the particular rights of Indian people vis-à-vis non-Indians are not "racial" but rather political rights that derive from Indian people being "members of quasi-sovereign tribal entities" (*Morton* v. *Mancari,* 417 U.S. 535, 554 [1977]). The unique laws that apply to Indians are "rooted in the unique status of Indians as 'a separate people' with their own political institutions" (*United States* v. *Antelope,* 430 U.S. 641, 646 [1977]). These holdings are useful in trumping "egalitarian attacks on Indian policy" (Clinton, Newton, and Price 1991:105), that is, in defending the uniqueness principle from uniformist critiques. For present purposes, however, the root fact is that tribal membership requires "one-fourth (1/4) or more Sioux Indian blood" (Constitution and By-Laws of the Rosebud Sioux Tribe, art. II, sec. 1[c]). From the point of view of people on and around Rosebud Reservation, when one speaks of rights of Indians and non-Indians, one is talking about "race" relations.

2. Joanne Nagel analyzes the disseminating role of AIM activity as "publicity" (1997:225).

3. One elderly Lakota man, recognized on Rosebud Reservation for his knowledge of treaty rights, hosted a Lakota language program on the local radio station (KINI, St. Francis, S.D., and Crookston, Neb.) He told me that since there is no Lakota word for sovereignty, he would simply use the English word when discussing the matter in Lakota on the radio. The concepts of sovereignty and independent nation are, he told me, "a recent thing."

and just plain patriotic *Lakota* citizens.[4] Sovereignty is regularly invoked in meetings and in political campaigns, and it always implies the background of the ongoing struggle against injustice and the (non-Indian) forces opposed to Lakota sovereignty—much as the concept of "democracy" in the wider society implies the background of constant vigilance against antidemocratic forces. In 1991 I asked a Lakota activist to identify the "biggest issues" in Indian-white relations. She answered, "In South Dakota? . . . We're continuously in battle against the state for jurisdiction issues, sovereignty. . . . [T]hey just won't acknowledge that we're sovereign and [that] we do have a dual citizenship."

But why are "jurisdiction issues" the central struggle, and what are the consequences of this? To get at an answer to this question, it is useful to begin with the totality of "lived identities" (to use Raymond Williams's term)[5] or (as E. P. Thompson might describe the phenomenon)[6] the concrete, social "experience" of Lakota people. People on Rosebud Reservation do not experience race relations merely—or even mainly—in terms of legal briefs about sovereignty and jurisdiction—even when they know and can recite the arguments contained in those briefs and those arguments become part of their "practical consciousness."[7] To examine how they *do* experience race relations, let us examine the transcript of a 1989 meeting between the Rosebud Sioux Tribal Council and the director of the South Dakota highway patrol. The purpose of the meeting was to explore the possibility of working out an agreement with the state to settle the highway jurisdiction conflict (chapter 4). In the midst of that discussion, one of the tribal council representatives rose and addressed the highway patrol officer on the matter of "respect":

> [Y]ou know nothing about our cultures and our traditions. [P]eople think we live in tipis. . . . That is because throughout history we have defended . . . our home ground, protected our families. . . . Throughout history . . . we have had families, innocent men, women and children, actually murdered, and [the] officers in them battles are "heroes," there's things named after them. . . . We have always been portrayed throughout history as the hostiles . . . as the enemy. [T]he war has never ended. You look at what the court done for the Japanese-Americans who were imprisoned during World War II, and what they got. You look at the Jews, what was done to them by the Nazis, and

4. Lakota people often maintain that they have dual citizenship—in the United States and in the Sicangu, Lakota, or Great Sioux, Nation.

5. Raymond Williams 1977:110.

6. Thompson 1978:7–9.

7. Raymond Williams 1977:110.

where they're at today. Them people all have respect in this country.... [But w]e're still on the bottom of the pole. No one wants to respect us.... No one even wants to recognize that we have rights like everybody else does.... We was threw onto what everybody calls reservations.... We're still in prison. We're still chained today because we got the Bureau [of Indian Affairs] over here that got to ask them every time we want to do something. We got to ask permission to do things. We're locked in here, we can't go nowhere because everybody's got the control over us. We don't get the resources that we need to actually try to bring ourselves out of the situation that we're in now so we can build ourselves to where we can show people that we can do just what you can do. Given the chance, we can do the exact same thing that every other race in this country does. We deserve respect that is not given to us.... [I]t all boils down to respect....[8]

At the risk of being overly analytic, let us itemize some of the elements of oppression touched on in this remarkably passionate and eloquent articulation of a "structure of feeling"[9] generated out of racial inequality in America:

1. Indians are subjected to racist stereotypes.

2. Indians have been victims of genocidal wars.

3. Indians have always been portrayed as America's enemy, and are still.

4. Indians have fared poorly in comparison to other minorities.

5. Indians were confined to reservations without their consent.

6. Indians are denied basic human and constitutional rights.

7. Indians are subjected to colonial, bureaucratic domination.

8. Indians are the victims of economic deprivation.

What is particularly noteworthy about this statement for present purposes is that it came up in the context of a *jurisdictional* dispute, even though the forms of oppression itemized do not seem to have anything directly to do with jurisdiction. If racial oppression is experienced in the form of racial stereotypes, to take one example from the above, why would Indian people choose to make *jurisdiction* the locus of the struggle for justice? Why, if the struggle for racial justice is to address the forms of oppression enumerated by the representative of the tribal council, is jurisdiction—rather than something else—the political issue?

8. Tape of Meeting, 26 May 1989, Rosebud Sioux Tribal Office.
9. Raymond Williams 1966:48.

Another question also presents itself. Not only is the *content* of the dispute waged in the pursuit of justice worthy of our close scrutiny, but so also is the identity of the oppressors. *Who* is called to account for the lack of "respect" in the account above is worth noting in the original words: "The state, especially, this state, right now, does not respect us. We have no respect, we're just considered savages out here, basically by this state. And until this state can come and show that 'we're gonna treat you as equals, we're gonna show you some respect, we appreciate what you've been through, and we know you deserve more than where you're at and what you've been through,' when they can come here with that attitude and treat us that way, at that point I may want to sit down and try to talk to my colleagues into saying 'let's talk to the state'...."[10] How and why is the state of South Dakota, or its citizens, "especially" implicated in the lack of "respect" to which Indian people are subjected?

The argument of this book is that the discourse of federal Indian law creates a narrow and specific range of rights-claims that are actionable—both legally and politically—for Indian people. It creates a determinate channel of allowable grievances that must suffice for those grappling with a much larger range of systemic domination and social injustice. The discourse of federal Indian law defines what are and are not "reasonable" rights-claims. This clearly hegemonic effect aside, because the rights allowed provide a degree of relatively effective protection against domination, the discourse is used effectively by Indian people and espoused by them, even if it is not a complete "remedy." Thus it is not surprising that jurisdictional struggles end up bearing remarkable burdens for wide-ranging oppressions, as we saw in the statement above.

REGULATING THE CONTENT OF INDIAN-WHITE RELATIONS

As is clear by now, sovereignty and jurisdictional rights-claims were not invented out of whole cloth by Indian people. The intellectual, cultural, and historical origins of sovereignty are much more complex, implicating not only autonomous indigenous resistance,[11] but also the institution of federal Indian law: sovereignty can only be formulated as an articulate rights-claim on the discursive terrain of federal Indian law as it has evolved. The federal court opinions, the treaties, the acts of

10. Tape of Meeting, 26 May 1989, Rosebud Sioux Tribal Office.
11. For an analysis that gives autonomous, indigenous agendas priority over legal discourse in native claims of sovereignty, see Asch 1993b [1984]:30, 31, 34; 1995.

Congress have a great deal to do with how Indian people articulate—
and, to an extent difficult to measure, think about—sovereignty. Although this regime of rights-claims is clearly in part generated by
Lakota people (and their allies)—indeed, it requires great intellectual
creativity and hard intellectual work on their part—the regime is also
heavily shaped by discursive regularities not under their control.
Sovereignty in particular and Indian rights in general are, after all, a
reading of legal texts not authored by Indian people (although it may be
possible to argue that Indian people had some role in authoring the
treaties and agreements, and we often have the transcripts of the negotiations). Furthermore, the practical political effectiveness of Indian
rights-claims—their concrete usefulness for Lakota people—derives ultimately from the admissibility of the claims in legal or quasi-legal contexts not controlled by Indian people. Not surprisingly, given the con-
straining and channeling power of the discourse of federal Indian law,
the rights that are produced and claimable are quite limited. In the history described in this book, the rights-claims articulated by Indian people are their right not to be subjected to state jurisdiction within Indian
country and the tribal government's right to regulate (some) non-Indian
activities in Indian country. Both of these classes of rights are allowed to
tribes and tribal members in federal statute and case law and are
claimed by Lakota people as inherent rights (even if from an arguably
more autonomous Lakota point of view they do not exhaust the vision
of sovereignty).

The rights of sovereignty are extremely particular—even merely
"technical"—when considered against the full context of racial domination faced by Lakota people and articulated dramatically in the transcript quoted above. The articulable rights offer only narrow protections, around which escape egregious forms of oppression—forms of
oppression that are directly linked to the position of the Lakota people
in the history of the larger society. In other words, the current political
front on which the struggle against non-Indian domination is waged by
Lakota people does not seem to have been determined directly by the
social reality of the Lakota situation. The site of struggle, and those implicated as opponents and allies, might have been different were it not
for the hegemonic effect of the discourse of federal Indian law, which allows some rights to be articulable, others not. That is, if Indian law
were different, or if there was no Indian law, "Indian-white relations"—
particularly the tensions and struggles involved—in the United States
might have been profoundly different.

There is a great deal of slippage between the totality of Lakota racial disempowerment in America and the remedies sought in Lakota political action as orchestrated by the discourse of Indian law. If we were to take what Alan Freeman has called a "victim perspective"[12] on the situation of the Lakota—a perspective that starts with the social reality of their concrete situation and not with the violation of specific legal rights as defined in law—we would need to start with the historical and structural origins of the oppression of the Lakota people. The disempowerment of the Lakota and other American Indian peoples is not a historical accident or merely the product of individual or local acts of "discrimination" or "racism," or individual or local violations of Indian rights (such as the violations identified in the lawsuits described in this book), but rather the result of larger, more systemic processes. Although there is much debate in American Indian studies about how these processes work, the very use of the term "colonialism" insists upon a larger regularity of oppression in the history and structure of Indian-white relations. Colonial processes include the historic expropriation of Lakota resources[13] and political colonization of the Lakota people,[14] the harnessing of wealth from aboriginal Lakota lands for the benefit of people other than the Lakota,[15] the displacement of labor and disruption of community in rural hinterlands by capital-intensive agriculture,[16] the inability of capitalism to generate full employment and the associated reproduction of a reserve army of labor, and the accelerating tendency of capital to be increasingly unattached to place and the resulting differentiation of the fortunes of human communities across global space.[17] The processes relevant to understanding the oppression of Lakota people would also include the "cultural" side of colonialism: the centrality of race in the emergence of hierarchy and privilege in the United States, and the inescapable role of racist representations in producing the status of "whiteness" itself.[18] These racist representations are, of course, not confined to the "minds" of white people but have

12. Freeman 1982:98. This phraseology has an unfortunate ring to it in the present, but it would be silly indeed to suggest that capitalism and "modernization" have not produced victims.

13. Hoxie 1984: chap. 5; McDonnell 1991.

14. Thomas 1966a, 1966b; Biolsi 1992, 1995.

15. On American Indians generally, see Jorgensen 1972; on the Lakota in particular, see Mathiessen 1983.

16. Biolsi 1993.

17. Harvey 1989.

18. In general, for example, Roediger 1991:36, 56–57, 95; Frankenberg 1993:17; Haney Lopez 1996:28–31, 58, 167, 174. On American Indians, see Berkhoffer 1978.

been disseminated in increasingly public media and reverberate back on Indian—and other non-white—people through many channels.

The everyday consequences of this dense colonial and racial situation for Lakota people and their communities are legion. Let us take one concrete example for the purposes of the argument here: Lakota people face a serious public health crisis in the form of pervasive alcoholism and an alarming incidence of fetal alcohol syndrome (FAS). According to a 1983 tribal resolution (in the midst of the liquor store suit), 67 percent of the tribal population were "alcohol abusers," and 27 percent were "chronic alcoholics."[19] One of the motivations for pursuing the liquor store matter was the desire to bring down the high incidence of alcoholism and FAS on the reservation. When the tribal liquor commission held hearings in 1984 on a license for the Mission liquor store, for example, several tribal members testified about problems associated with alcohol abuse. A passage from the minutes of that hearing testifies to the seriousness of these concerns: "There is no way that alcohol damage can be measured. [The witness] especially wanted the grandmothers and the older people who ended up taking care of the kids of alcoholics to talk out against the destruction of the family caused by alcohol. He indicated that the problem does not stop in Mission, because the sale of alcohol in the City of Mission [a]ffects White River, Norris, Parmelee, Rosebud, St. Francis, and all other parts of the reservation. It is common knowledge that most Indian people come to Mission to buy the liquor."[20] A member of the tribal council at the time the liquor store was refused a tribal license told me that the rationale was "let's try a little prohibition and see what that does."

When the liquor store was finally closed, however, the effect on the alcohol crisis was insignificant. Off-reservation stores and reservation bootleggers easily met the continued demand. In fact, the mayor of Mission himself was arrested for bootlegging a few months later.[21] In 1986, more than a year after the store was closed, the tribal council still identified alcohol abuse as "the number-one health problem" on the reservation.[22] In fact, in 1996 the Rosebud Sioux Tribal Council "declared war on all that is associated with alcohol and drug abuse" after

19. Resolution 83-21, 12 May, Rosebud Sioux Tribal Office.
20. Record of Proceedings, Rosebud Sioux Tribal Liquor Commission, 19[28] September 1984, *In the Matter of the Appeal City of Mission and Mission Golf Course from Denial of Licenses*, Civil Case 84-45, Rosebud Sioux Tribal Court, Rosebud, S.D.
21. "[Mayor] Charged with Selling Liquor Illegally," *Todd County Tribune*, 30 January 1985.
22. Minutes, 30 January 1986, Rosebud Sioux Tribal Office.

noting that of all the "many problems which threaten our survival as Lakota people . . . none has such a devastating effect on our communities and families as does the problem of alcohol and drug abuse."[23] Freedom from alcoholism, however, is not a "right" that Indian people have been allowed by law; indeed, neither civil rights nor the discourse of federal Indian law allow such a freedom to be articulated as a right, since alcoholism is "nonactionable experience."[24] Although alcoholism is a substantive effect of colonialism and racism faced by Lakota people and a concern about which they are in fact socially mobilized,[25] it is not definable as a *political* problem within the prevailing universe of thinking on social justice for American Indians—a universe undergirded by the discourse of Indian law. Indian alcoholism is not definable as an injustice that Congress or the larger society has a responsibility to remedy. Alcoholism is a site of "personal" and even social struggle, but not of *political* struggle; it is not commonly or clearly seen as an "Indian-white" problem. The liquor store case was the closest the Lakota people of Rosebud Reservation came to politicizing alcoholism as a race-relations matter, but the political struggle ended with the assertion of tribal jurisdiction over the Mission liquor store.

To engage in a bit of counterfactual history, let us imagine that in addition to the right of sovereignty—understood narrowly as technical jurisdictional arrangements—Lakota people also had the right to be free from alcoholism. This right could be based on a social-citizenship or human-rights claim regarding public health. More concretely, it could be based on the recognition that alcoholism and other addictions or dependencies are closely connected to class and racial positioning in a society stratified by class and by race,[26] and are therefore inherently *political* problems requiring political solutions. That is, the right to be free from alcoholism could be based on the recognition that the wider social order is inescapably implicated in Indian alcoholism. Under this thinking, the incidence of alcoholism on the reservation could enter into the way people—Indian and non-Indian—pursue justice and fight injustice, and people could "reasonably" demand that the wider society take the

23. Resolution 89-33, as amended 21 February 1996, Rosebud Sioux Tribal Office.
24. MacKinnon 1982:705.
25. Alcoholics Anonymous meetings and sobriety dances and walks are common on Rosebud Reservation, and discussion of problems related to alcohol often emerges in traditional Lakota and Christian religious contexts. Many students at Sinte Gleska University (indeed, the institution itself) are outspoken proponents of sobriety, and the issue often arises in political campaigns on the reservation.
26. See Duran and Duran 1995.

necessary steps and expend the necessary resources to address the problem. The outcome of such demands would not, of course, be pre-
dictable, but at least the political argument would be admissible in the
public sphere—in the media, in political campaigns, on the floors of legislatures, and possibly in the courts. Alcoholism per se would be a political front in Indian-white relations, and it might not be *local* whites—
some of whom go to the same Alcoholics Anonymous meetings as the
Lakota people—who turned out to be the deadliest enemies.

But freedom from poverty, from systemic racial inequality, and from
alcoholism are not rights Lakota people have been allowed in law and
thus are not claimable rights in the practical consciousness of Lakota
people or their allies. The point is that the kinds of rights that the discourse of Indian law has allowed Indian people to claim are very specific.
They involve jurisdictional arrangements and have direct bearing on
only *some* of the modes of oppression that Indian people face on a daily
basis. With the substitution of a few words, what Alan Freeman says of
federal civil rights law is applicable to federal Indian law: "As surely as
the law has outlawed racial discrimination, it has affirmed that Black
Americans can be without jobs, have their children in all-black, poorly
funded schools, have no opportunities for decent housing, and have very
little political power, without any violation of antidiscrimination law."[27]
As surely as Indian tribes are held in law to be sovereign entities with
special jurisdictional rights, it is affirmed that Indian people can live in
poverty and political subjection without any violation of their rights of
sovereignty. How many of the matters alluded to in the transcript quoted
above will be addressed effectively by jurisdictional arrangements?

It may be that Indian people can "imagine" alcohol as a political front
in the struggle for racial justice. As will be recalled from chapter 3, many
Indian people recognized that "it's those white people in Mission that
are selling booze to the Indians out in the communities and getting them
drunk"; some saw the liquor store revenues as "blood money." This
would seem to come very close to politicizing alcohol as a systemic
Indian-white matter, but it lacks the final push that clearly articulates the
political nature of alcohol in race relations. And the final push is missing
because such a position is not arguable or admissible within the discourse of Indian law at present. The discourse of Indian law does indeed
set limits on what Indian people "can imagine as *practical* options."[28]

27. Freeman 1982:210.
28. Gordon 1984:111 (emphasis added).

In fact, the discourse of Indian law operates powerfully to prevent Lakota people from demanding freedom from poverty and its effects. The rights of sovereignty are easily construed as inconsistent with claims to social justice within the larger social order. Treaty rights are not social-citizenship, or universal/human, rights. Claiming sovereignty is a matter of imagining and asserting (national) political *boundaries*,[29] and in the prevailing neoliberal regime, each sovereign nation—like each sovereign individual—is responsible for its own welfare. Thus, the emergence of sovereign status for autonomous, indigenous *nations* must inescapably result in the undermining of "legitimate" claims they can make, legally and politically, as *American citizens* entitled to a piece of the larger American "pie," or as human beings with human rights and a claim on the social surplus.[30] "Autonomy" for native nations is politically incompatible with economic subsidization of tribal governments and of reservation economies and social programs by the United States. Many Indian people recognize that this is precisely why Congress is supporting "self-determination"; one Lakota man told me "You can't spell 'self-determination' without 'termination.' " Indeed, it is difficult to imagine why sovereignty would be given such a legitimate, if contestable, place in American law, recognized—even if not the way Indian people would "recognize" it if they were truly authorized to—repeatedly by Congress, the courts, and even presidents, if it were not inherently limiting and deradicalizing[31]—in a word, hegemonic.

Of course, financial support for indigenous nations under specific treaty provisions in the form of "foreign aid" might provide some minimal support for reservation economies and tribal programs in the face of an emerging independent-nation status for American Indians, but the pursuit of sovereignty—as it is orchestrated by the discourse of Indian law—clearly has inherent negative consequences for the pursuit of a broader empowerment and social justice for and by Indian people. Non-Indians are, in fact, quite fond of pointing out to Lakota people the incompatibility of tribal sovereignty and federal subsidization. In 1985, for example, the *Todd County Tribune* editorialized:

> [T]he Rosebud Sioux Tribe is *either* a ward of the federal government, subject to federal law and inheritor of the U. S. Government's treaty promises of free health, free education, free welfare, free housing, ad infinitum

29. Levin 1993.
30. Regarding the dependence of Rosebud Reservation upon the social surplus, see Biolsi 1993.
31. On the deradicalizing effects of law, see Klare 1978.

or
    it should abrogate its treaties with the U. S. Government, declare itself a
sovereign nation, pass its own laws and levy taxes with an eye toward self-
sufficiency without federal or state monies.
    But not both.[32]

More recently, the *Tribune*'s editor has expressed the hope that "as
tribal people continue to rise to the millennial challenges of true [in]de-
pendence and sovereignty, they will eventually realize that they no
longer need money from the other jurisdiction."[33] Within the dominant political worldview of neoliberalism, "true independence and
sovereignty" purportedly means fiscal self-reliance. As the governor of
Minnesota recently put it to Indian tribes, "[i]f you're your own
sovereign nation, then take care of yourselves."[34]

Indian people sometimes have difficulty denying the "logic" of this assertion. One of my Lakota informants has spoken to me on more than one
occasion about "solvrency"—a conflation of the words "sovereignty" and
"solvency." He obviously sees an inescapable connection between political
independence and fiscal self-reliance: to be a sovereign nation is to be a sol-
vent nation. In a similar vein, a Native American academic recently criticized "colonial tribal governments" in a column in *Indian Country Today*,
a paper widely read on Rosebud Reservation:

> Another form of dependence is financial dependence. Almost all Indigenous
> nations today are dependent upon the United States for some funding of
> their government operations. While we might look upon these transfers as a
> treaty obligation and a payment on America's debt to us, taking money from
> a foreign government compromises freedom and choice. The extent to which
> federal funds constitute a share of an Indigenous nation's financial resources
> is the extent to which the United States is able to keep that nation under its
> control.[35]

Obviously, in this reasoning, sovereign nations should expect to address
their "own" problems with their "own" resources, just as an individual
should take "personal responsibility" for his welfare.
    It is now widely recognized by scholars interested in class, race, and
gender that although the constitutional rights of equal protection and

    32. "Smoke Signals," *Todd County Tribune*, 17 July 1985.
    33. "Smoke Signals: Indian People Winning Three of Three," *Todd County Tribune*,
24 February 1999.
    34. "Governor 'The Body' Gets Pinned," *Indian Country Today*, 15–22 March 1999.
    35. "Colonial Tribal Governments Promote Weakness," *Indian Country Today*, 19
January 2000.

private property provide certain protections for the subaltern, they also make it next to impossible to allow concrete injuries rooted in class, racial, or gender experience in the United States to be *admitted* into court or mainstream politics. "Equality before the law" deradicalizes the law by excluding class, race, and gender inequalities from its cognizance and from the practical political struggles it underwrites.[36] If such "bourgeois" equality and property rights thus amount to a "coded denial of experience,"[37] so does "sovereignty" as constructed in federal Indian law. By the logic of Indian self-determination and autonomous nationhood as structured by the discourse of Indian law, the more tribal sovereignty is formally realized under existing federal Indian law, the more difficult it is for Lakota people to make credible legal and political claims regarding the full range of daily forms of oppression they are subjected to. To the extent that tribal sovereignty is achieved as a legal fact and a political arrangement, it becomes more difficult to articulate local problems as connected to larger—ultimately continental and global—*colonial* processes. Indeed, the logic of sovereignty threatens to challenge the vision that sees local problems as part of the functioning of a larger social formation.

The question then presents itself: why *do* Lakota people espouse sovereignty if it is so limiting—if it is a form of hegemony? The answer is that, as we have seen in earlier chapters, they have good practical reasons to draw on and defend the rights-regime of sovereignty, even if it may "in the last instance" limit what they can realistically claim and struggle for politically. Indian people stand to protect, or even gain, concrete things from winning jurisdictional conflicts. Because of the precariousness of rights in Indian country, Indian rights are always at risk, and losses in the jurisdictional realm are one of the recurrent threats to Indian individuals and communities. Thus, this analysis is not meant as a "trashing" of the rights-strategy pursued by Lakota people under the discourse of Indian law.[38] In 1993 I interviewed a Lakota man who had been active in the highway jurisdiction case (see chapter 4). With my tape recorder running I asked him why he had been willing to go to jail for contempt of court simply to keep the highway patrol off

36. Thompson 1975; Balbus 1977; Corrigan and Sayer 1981; Stubbs 1986:66; Flagg 1998.

37. Corrigan and Sayer 1981:33.

38. For minority critiques of the "trashing" of "bourgeois rights" strategies by scholars in the Critical Legal Studies movement, see Patricia Williams 1987 and Crenshaw 1988.

the reservation. It was easy, I said, to understand in principle why African-Americans might go to jail or even risk injury or death in order to vote, go to a state university, or ride in the front of a bus, but how did preventing state jurisdiction serve justice for Indian people? The man asked me to turn off my tape recorder because the answer to my question involved saying some "harsh" things about white people. He then explained that because the whites had killed their own god, there was nothing to prevent them from killing wantonly. The Wounded Knee massacre, for him, was symptomatic of this inhuman condition of the whiteman. The man laid out for me a scenario—actually, a nightmare—in which a scraggly Indian was beaten by a white policeman who thrived on absolute power over others, especially minority others. He spoke about being roughed up as a young man by white policemen and told me that even as an older man he still feels apprehension about white policemen off reservation.

The point is not that jurisdictional struggle under the terms of sovereignty is an inauthentic form of struggle—indeed, far from it—but rather that it is a profoundly partial or piecemeal form of struggle: it apprehends only part of the picture, a real part, but far from complete. Jurisdictional struggle is not pointless, but it is *regulated* struggle, which might look very different if it was not fought out upon the terms laid down by the discourse of Indian law.

Since jurisdictional rights-claims are the only practical way to address *any* of the whole picture of Indian oppression—at least as of yet—they *represent* the struggle against all oppression and its structure of feeling for many Indian people. This is why in the account above on "respect" one has the impression of a dam breaking, of a flood of grievances engulfing an apparently narrow and specific—even technical legal—issue. And this is why Indian people respond aggressively to even apparently minor assertions of local self-government by subdivisions of the state, which are seen as *racism* by Indian people.

REGULATING GUILT AND INNOCENCE

Let us examine now what is at stake for non-Indians in Indian country—or in areas that might, because of a court decision, *become* Indian country. While the phrase "taxation and government without representation" to describe tribal jurisdiction over non-Indians might seem an abstract grievance, very concrete matters are involved. A non-Indian resident of Rosebud Reservation vividly recounted for me the feelings of some non-Indians during the liquor store conflict: "there was a fear of losing the entire municipal government because there were those kind of threats, 'we're gonna get you, whiteman.'" During the liquor store dispute, the *Todd County Tribune* ran this editorial:

> About ten weeks ago, a federal judge told the people of Mission that their community was no longer a non-Indian community.... I see this as being more than merely a liquor control issue. It seems we are being presented with the distinct possibility of the loss of liberty and freedom for both Indians and whites who live in Mission. Any time we find a decree or an opinion forced onto us by authorities who haven't bothered to learn first how it will affect human life, we're conceivably facing a kind of dictatorship. It isn't just the City of Mission who is affected by [the district court's] decision—Indian people could lose something too. We are in danger of losing the most important freedom there is—*the right to govern*.[39]

Some non-Indians clearly worry that they will have increasingly less control over what happens locally because of tribal sovereignty and their lack of representation in tribal government. They worry about becoming second-class citizens in their own community.

Some non-Indians also fear that they will be abused by an unresponsive, undemocratic tribal government or tribal court. When I asked one of my Indian informants whether non-Indians had a right to live in Todd County, she responded: "No, I don't think they do.... [A]nd if they're going to live here a long time then they need to get a visa...so they know that they're in our territory, in our nation, and that they're here at our discretion." While this is probably a fairly "radical" point of view, non-Indians occasionally have it enunciated for them, if more commonly in the retort, "if you don't like it here, there are four roads off the reservation...." Some non-Indians fear that they will be taxed or regulated out of business, or that private property or personal income will eventually be taxed to the point of forcing non-Indians to leave. What is to prevent tribes from going to extremes, these people ask; what check is there on tribal authority over whites? Some non-Indians believe that they are in danger of losing everything they and their families have worked for and being "run out" by tribal government.

Indian people, as well, have a great deal more than "principle" at stake in the contests over what appear to be simply matters of jurisdiction. We have seen many Indian people express fear about how they would fare in the state law enforcement and judicial systems. In its re-

39. "The Liquor Thing," *Todd County Tribune,* 29 December 1982.

port on a 1999 U. S. Civil Rights Commission hearing in Rapid City, the South Dakota Advisory Committee to the commission concluded that "there is a widespread perception among Native Americans that there is a dual system of justice...." In fact, "the lack of confidence in the justice system among Native Americans has reached crisis proportions" in the state.[40] While some in South Dakota claim that these fears are unfounded,[41] it is not difficult to understand where Indian people might get the idea that they have reason to be afraid. While only 8 percent of the state's population was Indian in 1999, Indians made up 21 percent of the male prison population in South Dakota.[42] In 1985 the South Dakota Supreme Court upheld the decision of a circuit court in Winner, sentencing a Rosebud Lakota man to five years in the penitentiary on a finding of his being a habitual offender after he was arrested for entering an unlocked car while intoxicated and stealing and eating a can of beans.[43] This notorious—to Indian people[44]—court case was referred to by the Legal Services lawyer who made me aware of it as the "Beanie Weenie case." In 1988 the state supreme court had no choice but to reverse the "preposterous" decision of the same circuit court when it held an eleven-year-old Lakota girl guilty of second-degree burglary and found her to be a juvenile delinquent for eating a chocolate Easter egg taken from an off-reservation store without paying for it.[45] In 1990 a state prosecutor in a county with a substantial Indian population stated at a public hearing that the "Native American culture as we know it now...is a culture of hopelessness, godlessness, of joblessness and lawlessness."[46] The attorney general refused to consider removing the prosecutor from office.[47] Clearly Indian citizens would not seem to be without their reasons for wondering whether they can expect fair treatment under state law in South Dakota.

40. U. S. Commission on Civil Rights 2000: chap. 3, pp. 6, 4.

41. "[Governor]: Civil Rights Report Offers No Proof," *Press and Dakotan*, 5 April 2000. The advisory committee admitted that its report is concerned with Native American perceptions, not discriminatory patterns in law enforcement and the courts. Documenting discrimination would require systematic data collection, which the committee recommended (U. S. Commission on Civil Rights 2000: chap. 3, p. 5; "[Committee Member]: [Governor] Missed Point of Civil Rights Report," *Press and Dakotan*, 6 April 2000).

42. U. S. Commission on Civil Rights 2000: chap. 1, p. 6.

43. 377 N. W.2d 141.

44. One Lakota informant recalled how "bad" he felt about the incarceration of the defendant: "I went to school with him. He's the most generous and the most harmless person you ever want to meet."

45. *Matter of T. J. E.*, 426 N. W.2d, 23, 26.

46. "Slam of Indians Challenged," *Sioux Falls Argus Leader*, 6 September 1990.

47. "A. G. Won't Investigate Comments," *Press and Dakotan*, 8 September 1990.

For many Indian people, attempts by the state to assert jurisdiction over the reservation are a threat to their very homes. As we saw in chapter 2, termination has long been a fear of Indian people who envision the loss of their land if it ever becomes subject to state jurisdiction and thus taxable (this, remarkably, is a mirror image of the non-Indian fear of getting "run out"). An elderly resident of the reservation recalled for me the nightmare of the terminated Indian walking off the former reservation along the section line with his coat thrown over his shoulder. Section lines are public property, and the implication here is that all the Indian land on the reservation would become private (white) property, and the only place a homeless Indian could walk, if termination were to transpire, would be down the section line.

Many tribal members also realize that the continued survival of the Sicangu Lakota people as a culturally distinct entity in the modern world is dependent upon asserting sovereignty in a context of traditional Lakota values. This is one reason why Indian people resist the idea of "naturalizing" non-Indians. One Lakota man explained the problem of letting non-Indians into tribal government: "You . . . can't change their cultural thinking, and the whole point of having a reservation and Indian people being able to live here in one place is for us to be able to continue with our culture, to be able to protect ourselves, to be able to protect our culture, our language, our religion." Either allowing non-Indians "in" or "integrating" tribal government into the state system, Indian people fear, would undermine the basis for cultural survival because Lakota values would no longer have a privileged space and would wither in the face of "majority rule" and "the bottom line." But a sovereign tribal government can develop, say, economic development policy that not only serves the interests of "everyone" in the region but that also serves the interests of cultural preservation. Closely related to this is the matter of revenue for tribal government. One of the motives for the liquor store suit, for example, was obtain a portion of the revenues from the Mission Liquor Store in order to address tribal needs.

Many Indian people also see critical matters of identity behind what appear to be mere jurisdictional conflicts. For many Indian people sovereignty is a direct challenge to the racist culture of white dominance. One Indian resident of Rosebud Reservation described "internalized oppression" for me in the following terms:

I know that most Indian people don't think of themselves as being oppressed. I certainly don't, educated and all that. But every so often it comes back to haunt me that I grew up in a government boarding school, that my parents and my grandparents were Christianized in spite of themselves, and that we still carry these feelings that we're not good enough. Todd County has ... 8,000 Indian people and 1,000 non-Indians. It's the non-Indians who run the city government, who run the county government, who run the school system, ... they own all the businesses. And I believe that that is a product of internalized oppression, that Indian people still don't believe that we're good enough, smart enough to do all these things that we let non-Indians do.

For this person sovereignty is about nothing less than reclaiming human dignity. In 1993 I attended an Antelope Community meeting at which the prospect of the tribe "638-contracting"[48] law enforcement from the BIA was discussed. The argument in support of the proposal was that the tribe could do a better and more efficient job than the BIA, but there was some hesitation among tribal members about whether the tribal government was ready for this serious undertaking. One man who was in favor of the tribalization of law enforcement insisted, "[o]ur people are just as capable as the *wasicu* [whites] out there." He wondered why Indian people so commonly believed that "the only person who can do something right is a white man." When the tribal police were actually sworn in at an impressive ceremony, the president of Sinte Gleska University told the crowd, "We can do anything." For many Indian people on Rosebud Reservation, the tribal police force is an affirmation of the competence, indeed, the full humanity, of Indian people in the face of racist stereotypes of Indians.

Another Indian man directly linked sovereignty to the personal empowerment of Indian people who had been harmed by racism: "My personal goal is to let our people know that you don't need to be afraid of anyone, and what you do here on this reservation, ... that is your decision.... [W]e need to start standing up and start speaking. Don't be afraid to do that, because over the years because of Christianity and because [of] prejudice, we were so used to having someone else telling us what to do. You know, our thinking is in that direction, but now we're telling people, 'Hey, you need to make those decisions.'"

For both Indian and non-Indian people, then, a complex mix of costs and benefits—tangible and intangible, material and cultural, real and imagined—are at stake in jurisdictional arrangements. These stakes all involve local, zero-sum struggles: it is local non-Indians who stand to

48. The reference is to a procedure under the Indian Self-Determination Act (88 Stat. 2203 [1975]) by which a tribe may contract to deliver reservation services administered by the federal government, such as law enforcement, health care, etc.

lose if Indians win, and vice versa. This is a direct result of the vested interests that have built up around rights claims defined in certain—regulated—terms and contestable on certain regulated terms. Put differently, it is the discourse of federal Indian law that has created these zero-sum games. It may be that Indian and non-Indian people on and around Rosebud Reservation *are* deadliest enemies, but they have been made that way through the evolution of rights-games not of their own choosing.

One of the outcomes of the local Indian-white political struggle generated out of the federal Indian law discourse is that alternative political configurations of alliance and struggle are ruled out of court, as it were. There are many commonalities between Indians and whites in places like Todd County, commonalities that could conceivably be much more compelling than the assumed differences between them. Indian and white people are coparticipants in rural economies marginalized by global capitalism that disadvantages both races on a regional basis.[49] Although Indian-white differences—cultural, linguistic, political-economic—are potential separators, class/regional situation is a potentially strong unifier: in Todd County in 1989, although per capita income for whites was $10,150 compared with $4,005 for Indians, 19 percent of white households had incomes below $10,000.[50] Certainly these poor white rural families must have a great deal in common with poor Lakota families. "Welfare reform" and the lack of child-care services, unemployment, and the general defunding of social programs for rural areas are issues that come to mind immediately. Is it not reasonable to wonder why Indian and non-Indian people in "satellite" regions such as South Dakota do not seriously entertain the interests that they have in common against powerful forces emanating from outside?

Indeed, it is surprising that this has *not* happened, and requires explanation. Looking at class and region, there are good historical reasons to predict that South Dakota Indians and whites would be not be "deadliest enemies" but rather *allies*. Let us examine a period when interregional conflicts loomed larger than intraregional, "racial" tensions. In 1924, near the end of the Progressive Era,[51] the non-Indian editor of the *Todd County Tribune* applauded the governor for declaring that "the East does not feel any common interests with the West and that the tendency of all laws passed by Congress in the past has been 'to create

49. See, for example, Jorgensen 1971, 1972; Hoover, 1983, 1988; Klein 1993; Biolsi 1993; Sider 1993; Pommersheim 1995:29.
50. U. S. Department of Commerce 1992, 1990.
51. On the Progressives in South Dakota, see Schell 1975:chap. 18; Hoover 1983.

a more prosperous East at the expense of the agricultural West.' " "Here in South Dakota," the editor went on, "farmers, bankers, merchants, in short—all, are feeling the effects of the financial stringency. The East is rolling in prosperity and wealth.... Fifty years of careful legislation has brought this about."[52] Practically paraphrasing more contemporary notions of "metropolis and satellite,"[53] the editor wrote: "I don't pretend to be a shark at financial matters, but I have heard men say that if the money sent East to buy automobiles and coal had been paid to manufacturers and miners within our own and sister states hard cash wouldn't be so scarce here."[54] Indeed, the governor took on the major oil companies in 1924 by ordering the South Dakota highway department to offer fuel to the public at a below-market price, and some South Dakotans took seriously the idea of state-owned grain elevators, mills, and packing plants.[55] Although Indian people had not been inserted into the regional economy in precisely the same way that non-Indians were during the 1920s, many, if not most, Indian families on Rosebud Reservation were either directly or indirectly dependent upon the agricultural economy; all of course, were affected by the prices of manufactured goods.[56] Thus, one might think that the regionally based Progressive thinking articulated in the *Tribune* would be as widespread among Indian people as it was among whites in South Dakota, and that it would bring to the foreground for both whites and Indians what they have in common, opening up possibilities for political coalition that crossed—or more precisely, *ignored*—race lines.

This kind of populist, transracial consciousness is not absent from South Dakota; indeed, there are recurring examples of it. At this writing a mixed Indian-white coalition of people in Mellette County are challenging, on environmental grounds, the construction of a corporate hog farm on Rosebud Reservation.[57] At a public seminar on Rosebud Reservation in 1993, for example, a well-known Rosebud Sioux tribal member after a series of speakers who had openly criticized whites, had this to say about Indian-white relations: "Sometimes we get mad at white people.... [But the] real enemy is in Washington, and that enemy is many colors, it's not just whites." Sometimes, he contin-

---

52. "The East vs. the West," *Todd County Tribune,* 21 February 1924.
53. Frank 1967.
54. Editorial, *Todd County Tribune,* 5 June 1924.
55. Schell 1975:chap. 18.
56. See Biolsi 1992:chap. 1
57. "Hog Farm Protest Draws Act, Others," *Todd County Tribune,* 24 March 1999.

ued, we take it out on white people because "the color of their skin" represents Washington. At the risk of putting words in this man's mouth, he certainly seemed to be saying that Indian-white relations in South Dakota do not *originate* in local "racial" tensions but rather are matters of a large-scale organization of power that is determined elsewhere.

Three Rosebud Sioux tribal members made a similar point clearly in a recent paper written for a course at Sinte Gleska University: "The Federal government, as a result of its special relationship to Indian tribes, has often been central in creating these jurisdictional issues but seldom seems involved in their solution. For example, in the boundary case it was the failure of Congress, in the three County Acts of 1904, 1907 and 1910, to make clear its intent as to whether or not they were diminishing the Rosebud Reservation that led to the boundary issue. Yet in the court case . . . [Congress] did not get involved. . . . This [brings to mind] an old [local] saying, they make laws . . . but they don't have to live here with the problems they have created."[58]

In his 1975 inaugural address, the governor of South Dakota characterized the serious problems of Indian-white relations in South Dakota in the following terms:

> The problems we face are not necessarily of our own making and we cannot solve them alone. Federal decisions made well before statehood, as well as today, by authority far removed from the plains of Dakota continue to complicate the daily lives of both Indian and non-Indian people. Because of these decisions, costly and complicated litigation is going forward today to determine even such fundamental questions as the boundaries of South Dakota reservations, and also to resolve the attendant questions of the relative rights and obligations of state government, its subdivisions and those of tribal and federal governmental authority. This litigation and the uncertainty it fosters for all people living in the disputed areas has brought in its wake unrest— and even fear. . . . [W]e must foster an effort to inform the people of South Dakota, the nation, and the world that our problems are not as simple as they may seem. . . .

Indeed, the governor said, those problems go beyond "racial intolerance" and "cultural conflict."[59] In a 1975 message to the legislature, he elaborated on the point: "I am convinced that much of the hostility and

58. Marlon Leneaugh, Rhonda Leneaugh, and Robert Moore, "Tribal Law Enforcement and Jurisdiction" (research paper in author's possession).

59. Inaugural Message, 7 January 1975, Indian Affairs Coordinator File, Box 86, Kneip Papers.

mistrust which permeates the current Indian/non-Indian scene is the result of an abdication of responsibility on the part of the federal government."[60]

A white attorney who has worked in state government characterized
the situation of jurisdictional disputes between Indian and non-Indian
people in South Dakota this way: "I always think of it as two metal
balls...on strings...[Y]ou can see Uncle Sam up here holding it. Well,
what happens is...the tribe's as hard-headed as the state, but then all
of a sudden we start clacking on something, and we're always bumping
into each other. The highway jurisdiction deal: Congress could have
passed a law and said, 'this is what we mean.... You guys didn't know
what we mean? This is what we mean.' Never happens."

A non-Indian resident of Mission insisted that the problems stemmed
from "two different government systems ['the federal-state-county-
municipal system' and the 'federal-tribal system'], with the federal government at the head of both. That's where a lot of the jurisdictional confusion has come in over the years. We have laws that...non-Indians are
required to live by, just as laws that Indians have to live by. They try to
obey theirs, we try to obey ours. [But, t]he laws are written in such a
convoluted way that frequently they cross each other.... And then
where's the fight? It's down here at the local level. We don't know what
to do." The problem was simply "two different systems both emanating
from the same head." Certainly none of these people was speaking of
"the discourse of Indian law," but all of them recognized that they were
being made into enemies by forces not of their own choosing—and that
is the central argument of this book.

These astute penetrations by local people, however common they
might be, are not sufficient to trump the material reality of the opposed
interests between Indians and non-Indians on Rosebud Reservation—a
material reality directly produced by the zero-sum game of Indian law.
Although people in South Dakota may well be able to see the discourse
of Indian law for what it really is—an arrangement of power, largely determined by others, that orchestrates local politics in ways local people
cannot control—they cannot ignore the concrete order of things that
follows from that discourse. *Everyday* political threats come from *local*
opponents, and thus "everyday resistance"[61] is understandably directed
toward local "deadliest enemies," not more distant, and less distinct,

60. Executive Communication, 12 March 1975, Indian Affairs File, Box 11, Kneip
Papers.
61. Scott 1985.

enemies "far removed from the plains of Dakota." Indeed, it is difficult to name precisely the external threat—"lawyers," "federal judges," "Congress," "Washington," "the East"? Thus it is not surprising that no sustained "coalition" politics crosses the race line in South Dakota.

This raises another dimension of the discursive regulation of Indian-white relations. It is not just that the discourse of Indian law has generated local, zero-sum games that make deadliest enemies out of people who might otherwise be regional allies. The "geography" of Indian-white relations—under the hegemonic effects of the Indian law discourse—leaves certain parties *out* of the deadliest enemies equation: those non-Indians not implicated in the local jurisdictional disputes. This is an important part of the construction of white political innocence regarding Indian people in the United States.

As world attention focused on race relations in South Dakota in the wake of the 1973 occupation of Wounded Knee, the governor spoke of the problem of Indian-white relations in his state during his 1975 inaugural address: "Whether it is right or wrong—fair or unfair—the eyes of the world are on South Dakota and history seems to have chosen us as a testing ground for the ingenuity of man and his democratic institutions to resolve a most complex and emotional situation. How we respond to that test...can make South Dakota a model for the world—or it can make our name synonymous with intolerance."[62] To many "outsiders"—and to many Indian people who live in South Dakota—the state has come to stand for racial injustice toward Indian people in America at large, and even American racism in general. In a 1971 journal article, for example, a New Zealand historian asked, "Why are race relations in New Zealand better than in South Africa, South Australia or South Dakota?"[63] Here, South Dakota clearly stands for American racism on the global stage; it was, in the clever alliteration of the article's title, even more "southern" than the American South, and racism toward American Indians was depicted as even more paradigmatic than racism toward African-Americans.[64]

Indeed, the South Dakota governor received correspondence from all over the world regarding injustices in his state during the mid-1970s, when civil unrest on and around South Dakota reservations (especially

62. Inaugural Message, 7 January 1975, Indian Affairs Coordinator File, Box 86. Kneip Papers.
63. Sinclair 1971.
64. See Frankenberg 1993:79 on the representation of the "South" as distant in white representations of innocence.

Pine Ridge) was making international headlines and was carried on television and radio news broadcasts worldwide. Here is a Catholic priest from Indiana, writing to the governor in 1974:[65]

> I sincerely hope that you can forego any "political" crap and find it in your heart to try to help these people that have been inhumanely treated and subjected to treatment that I am afraid and ashamed of.... The time is closely approaching where the Indians, as a people, I fear will be morally right in their civil disobedience against the practices of your state.... I do feel strongly about this Governor. So much so that I have decided to cancel my vacation in South Dakota.... I cannot "enjoy" myself in an atmosphere that is contrary to Christian values and humanitarian justice.[65]

An Illinois resident was incensed at the idea of South Dakota having a role in the upcoming United States Bicentennial celebration—given the "depridations [sic], holding out and general 'lazy attitude' toward Indian problems in your state." "If South Dakota can get away with mistreating the Indians along with the Government and can have gall enough to celebrate a 200th birthday for land you don't even own," the writer asked, "what scruples does this country possess?" He advised the governor that he would visit South Dakota "only to see the Indians and spend my money for them," driving "through Nebraska and directly onto the reservation to keep from giving revenue for gas" (referring apparently to the state sales and gasoline taxes). He could not condone all the activities of AIM, but he could "agree with nothing the whites have done in the past 200 years." South Dakota here bore a heavy representational load, standing in for two centuries of the oppression of Indian people.[66]

A Michigan resident, enclosing fundraising literature he had received from a Catholic Indian school in South Dakota, asked the governor "*Why* can't our schools get aid or help to educate and feed the Indians. They are the most mistreated, misguided, segregated group of people in this [sic] United States. The white man invaded their homeland, stold [sic] their land mass, murdered old men, mothers, young and old, and children. They fought back for what was theirs yet they were classified as ignorant heathens. They were over powered by mass murder and put on reservations.... The reservations are confined to the most useless land.... We help the Black man that is not a native of

65. Priest to Kneip, 29 November 1974, Indian Affairs Coordinator File, Box 86, Kneip Papers.
66. Correspondent to Kneip, 29 July 1975, Indian Affairs File, Box 11, Kneip Papers.

this land but damn little help for our native Indians."[67] A Virginia correspondent had this to say to the governor: "Why have they [Indians] been neglected? Their lands were taken from them and now they are in poverty. They deserve better treatment than they are receiving. What are you as Governor doing to relieve these poverty stricken people? May God forgive you."[68]

The governor also received a form letter from a Minnesotan seeking to organize a boycott of the South Dakota tourist trade: "As an American Citizen, Wife, Mother and Human being, I just cannot believe or understand what has happened and is still happening to our Native Americans in this country and especially in the state of South Dakota. Beatings, harrasings [sic], and yes, even murderings." After recounting American misadventures in attempting "to force our type of government and our ways on the Vietnamese people as we have done to the American Indian," the author of the letter searched for the origins of American racial injustice: "I will never place all American people in the roles of bad, racist, etc., etc., because it just isn't so."[69] South Dakota was clearly the racist exception: "we must soon learn that hate such as has been shown and witnessed on many occasions in South Dakota toward Indian people has ... got to stop and now."[70] South Dakota was the "pocket of racism" that exculpated America at large.[71]

More scholarly examinations have targeted South Dakota as the clear site and source of injustice against Indian people. Task Force Four of the American Indian Policy Review Commission, which released its report on reservation jurisdiction in 1976, saw local whites as culpable and clearly rejected what it called "the innocent victim thesis" as a characterization of local whites in Indian country. It quoted the Rosebud Sioux tribal president approvingly: "We have problems with people ... who have come into Indian country understanding that they are coming into Indian county, because it is cheap to live there. It's cheap to lease land. It's cheap land to be purchased."[72] In other words, whites came to Indian country for the same

67. Correspondent to Kneip, n. d. [1974], Indian Affairs (Misc.) File, Box 27, Kneip Papers.

68. Correspondent to Governor, 12 June 1974, Indian Affairs (Misc.) File, Box 27, Kneip Papers.

69. Correspondent to Kneip, 5 April 1975, Indian Affairs (Misc.) File, Box 51, Kneip Papers.

70. Correspondent to Kneip, 5 April 1975, Indian Affairs (Misc.) File, Box 51, Kneip Papers.

71. See Ross 1990:311.

72. American Indian Policy Review Commission 1976:99.

reason Europeans went to the colonies—to benefit personally at the expense of indigenous people.[73]

In 1981 the United States Commission on Civil Rights released its report, *Indian Tribes: A Continuing Quest for Survival*. The report sought the origins of the backlash against emerging Indian sovereignty and the reclaiming of other treaty rights, and found it, largely, in the vested interests of local non-Indians on and around Indian reservations: "non-Indian interests, both governmental and private, that have been unfairly profiting at Indian expense have found their individual advantages disrupted by Indian legal and political victories and have organized to recapture their preferential position. In this view, the backlash is identified as *a vocal minority of vested interests*." (The report quoted with approval *United States* v. *Kagama* on "deadliest enemies.") Although the report conceded that the backlash was national in scope and had some connection with mass public ignorance and stereotypes of Indians among "common citizens,"[74] its focus was in fact narrow: the anti-fishing rights movement in Washington and Civil Liberties for South Dakota Citizens, as well as the national organization to which CLSDC gave birth: the Interstate Congress for Equal Rights and Responsibilities (organized in Salt Lake City in 1976).

What is critical in these narratives of South Dakota racism is the degree of separation—the *self*-separation—of the (guiltless) outsiders articulating the narratives and the (guilty) whites in South Dakota who are the object of the narratives. Innocence and guilt are a clear binary in all the above accounts.

In the face of these narratives, it is instructive to consider the South Dakota governor's response to the irate Indiana priest quoted above: "We have racial intolerance in South Dakota as you do in Indiana and everywhere else in the world where peoples of different races live together.... [But, o]ur problem in South Dakota is ... complicated by a very complex legal situation involving treaty rights, reservation boundaries, responsibilities and rights of citizenship and other forms of jurisdiction. One result of this complicated, and to a great extent unresolved, legal situation has been the understandable fears of non-Indians living on reservations and in disputed areas that their property and other rights are in jeopardy."[75] Put differently, although South

73. For a clear statement of colonial relations in this vein, see Memmi 1965.
74. U.S. Commission on Civil Rights 1981:1.
75. Governor to Indiana Priest, 29 November 1979, Indian Affairs File (21), Box 11, Kneip Papers.

Dakota is no more free of racism than any other place in America, the reason tensions between Indians and whites are so serious in South Dakota has less to do with local perpetrators of racism and more to do with the particular form of the rights-games—Indian versus non-Indian rights—orchestrated by what we are here calling the discourse of Indian law.

What the governor did not say, but which deserves our very careful attention, is the exculpation of non-Indians outside of South Dakota from any responsibility in the historic and ongoing oppression of Indian people. This, too, is a concrete form of social relations orchestrated by the discourse of Indian law. It is not a mere "mystification" that local non-Indians appear as the deadliest enemies of Indian people and that other non-Indians are not implicated or even appear as the "allies" of Indian people. This is a social fact, but it is a social fact directly engineered by the discourse of Indian law that makes jurisdictional arrangements—which are always local—the primary terrain for the struggle for justice by Indian people. White people outside of South Dakota can picture themselves as the "friends" of Indians—consider the long history of *that* self-serving fiction[76] —and opposed to the oppression of Indian people because they are not legally implicated in the struggles as constituted.

This neat arrangement of guilt and innocence is not unlike the "perpetrator perspective" in antidiscrimination law, which identifies racism as the "action of individuals." Alan Freeman frames the matter in the following terms: "The perpetrator perspective, which is the principal model of contemporary antidiscrimination laws, assumes that apart from the misguided conduct of particular actors the rest of society is working.... All we need to do is root out the villains. Having done so, we can say with confidence that it was all their *fault*. A corollary of this fault notion is that those who...are not labeled perpetrators have every reason to believe in their own innocence and their separation from the problem. If one is not a perpetrator, one must be just an innocent bystander. And why should one be called to account or implicated at all in the business of eradicating the past?"[77] The discourse of Indian law calls certain parties to court—both figuratively and literally—over certain matters but leaves the vast majority of non-Indians

76. See, for example, Prucha, ed., 1978.
77. Freeman 1982:99. On the legal production of innocence, see also Lawrence 1987; Ross 1990; Harris 1993; Flagg 1998. See Freeman 1988:339–40 on the "southernization" of racism as it is constructed in civil rights law.

out of the indictment of oppression. This allows most whites to understand "racists ... as either historical figures or aberrational and iso-
lated characters,"[78] "rednecks" in (distant) South Dakota. We turn in
the conclusion to the role of this arrangement in the construction of
whiteness in America.

78. Ross 1990:312.

Conclusion

Whiteness and the Legal
Imagination

While I was doing fieldwork on Rosebud Reservation some years ago, a Lakota man harangued me on one occasion about what "the white-man" had done to the Lakota people. I do not recall the specifics of the discussion, but I do recall being a little uncomfortable (indeed, offended) by what seemed to me the "over-generalization" of the phrase *the whiteman.* I distinctly recall feeling that he was too "closed-minded" to realize that "not all whitemen are alike," and that, indeed, I was his "ally," not his enemy—if only he was "smart enough" to "see" that. Had current critical terminology been in vogue at the time, I probably would have responded (to myself, anyway), "(racial) essential-ism!" History is simply too complex, I thought, for the phrase "the whiteman" to have any political or intellectual value (except as an undeniable "native category"). Is race, after all, the only, or even the most important, system of domination? What about capitalism, and what it has done to people and culture on the planet in the last two hundred years? What about, for instance, my grandfather, a displaced northern Italian miller who came to the United States in 1916 and worked in a factory in New York and eventually struggled to buy and make a go of a family truck farm on eastern Long Island? Was he the same kind of "whiteman" as the Vanderbilts or the Rockefellers, and was he equally accountable for the oppression of Indian people? And, more to the point, what about me, a "whiteman" from a blue-collar family (my father was a plumber, my mother a "milk lady" in a school cafeteria) who had studied for a Ph. D. in anthropology precisely because of my interest in seeing justice done in Indian-white relations? Was I the same kind of "whiteman" as somebody in South Dakota who does not respect Indian culture or Indian sovereignty?

After writing this book and doing the thinking that writing it forced me to do, I now have profound doubts about my initial reaction to the category *the whiteman* and about my (white) *innocence*. Indeed, the full range of ways that history has privileged[1] people like me while simultaneously harming (racial) others is, for lack of a better word, breathtaking. In this regard, Gerald Sider's description of the direct connections between his privilege on the one hand, and the domination of African Americans on the other hand, is instructive here: As African Americans were "starved and bludgeoned into" racial subordination, "I was, inescapably and by the very same violence, made White; neither one without the other."[2]

This is not to minimize the importance of class in complicating the position of everyone who must live within systems of racial privilege. But it does underscore the material advantages most whites have accrued from their positions in the prevailing order—at the expense, of course, of people who are not white. Innocence, in this scheme of things, is both a produced cultural fiction, and a valuable political and legal status. Racial innocence for people like me, in other words, like the transparency of whiteness itself and the "invisibility" of white privilege, is a *political achievement,* not a natural state of having stood "outside" a system of oppression.

How does the collective achievement of white innocence come about in America, and what role does law play in its production? In 1823 Chief Justice John Marshall criticized the doctrine of discovery in *Johnson* v. *McIntosh*. Marshall called the colonizers' assumption of their *ownership* of the *inhabited* country they encountered in the New World an "extravagant... pretension."[3] This book has argued that the deadliest enemies hypothesis, most clearly articulated in *United States* v. *Kagama*, but deeply rooted in federal Indian law, is also an extravagant pretension. The assumption that the deadliest enemies of Indian people are their non-Indian *neighbors,* against whom they must be protected by the federal government (or by "the rest of us"), elides the role of the

---

1. For a concise outline of white privilege, see McIntosh 1989.
2. Sider 1993:114.
3. 21 U.S. (8 Wheat.) 543, 590. As we saw in the introduction, however, Marshall also accepted this extravagant pretension as the law of the land.

law itself in *making* Indian and non-Indian people on and around reservations into deadliest enemies. The discourse of Indian law does not reduce Indian-white conflict any more than, as Foucault showed, the prison reduces crime.[4] To the contrary, it is *productive* of racial conflict. It multiplies conflict by interposing racial discord where there might otherwise be social solidarity. Indian law is an *incitement* to racial struggle.[5] In short, the discourse of Indian law "cannot fail to produce" racial conflict—as the prison positively produces delinquency.[6]

The political work of the Indian law discourse, however, does not lie merely in positioning local people as deadliest enemies of each other. A discourse "works"—in the Foucaultian sense—by strategically *regulating,* or *managing* an object. One way a discourse does this is by rendering *visible* certain dimensions of an object so as "to leave in the shade those that one wishes to—or must—tolerate."[7] By making local white[8] and Indian people highly visible deadliest enemies, the discourse of Indian law leaves in the shade we *other whites* who might otherwise be called to account in the native struggle for racial justice. The most critical effect of the Indian law discourse, then, is the *production of white innocence.*

The importance of this material exculpation of most whites in "the social construction of whiteness"[9] in America should not be underestimated. *Innocence* is an important component of white privilege because it convincingly denies the reality "that white people generally have benefited from the oppression of people of color, that white people have been advantaged by this oppression in a myriad of obvious and less obvious ways."[10] But it must be understood that white innocence is not a mere "ideological" matter of white "representation" or of the white "imaginary." Whiteness is also a *social position* that involves freedom from accountability in certain political struggles—at least for most whites. And that social position is a direct product of the discourse of

4. Foucault 1979.

5. Foucault 1978.

6. Foucault 1979:266.

7. Ibid., 1979:277. See James Ferguson's analysis of international development as an "anti-politics machine" (1990).

8. See Hartigan 1997 on the possibility that marginalized whites may be necessary to make a privileged whiteness possible.

9. On the analysis of whiteness, see Takaki 1982; Ross 1990; Roediger 1991; Ford 1992; Frankenberg 1993; Harris 1993; Haney Lopez 1996; Frankenberg 1997; Hartigan 1997; Lawrence 1997; Flagg 1998.

10. Ross 1990:301. See also Lawrence 1987:325; Frankenberg 1993:47, 188; Harris 1993; Haney Lopez 1996:58; Flagg 1998.

Indian law that makes certain forms of oppression "nonactionable," as we saw in the last chapter, and that leaves certain forms of white privilege "in the shade" while singling out others for "justice."

But if, as suggested in the introduction, a discourse is not a prison-house, notwithstanding its formidable power-effects, how might race relations be organized differently, so as to disrupt white innocence? As has been mentioned repeatedly in this book, Indian people *do* seem able to imagine a different order of culpability for racial injustice than the regime of guilt and innocence produced by Indian law, one that is at odds with the common sense understanding of racism held by most whites "far removed from the plains of Dakota." In this regard the following case is revealing. In 1993 the estate of Tasunke Witko, a.k.a. Crazy Horse, sued—in Rosebud Sioux Tribal Court—the corporate brewers, bottlers and distributors of "The Original Crazy Horse Malt Liquor," Heileman Brewing Co. of Wisconsin, and Hornell Brewing Co. of New York. The complaint charged, among other things, that the defendants were violating Lakota "customary rights of privacy and respect owed to a decedent and his family." The complaint further asserted that the defendants were illegally appropriating the commercial publicity value of the good name of Tasunke Witko, a piece of property that under Lakota customary law remains part of the estate for seven generations. The estate asked the court for an injunction against continued use of the name by the defendants, compensation from the defendants under Lakota customary law *(Lakol Woope)* in the form of tobacco braids, blankets, and horses, and monetary damages in excess of one hundred million dollars.[11]

The tribal court dismissed the complaint on the grounds that it lacked personal jurisdiction over the defendants because they had neither committed a tort on Rosebud Reservation (which would have brought the tribal long-arm statute into play) nor engaged in activities that brought them under the *Montana* exceptions (see p. 156).[12] The Rosebud Sioux Supreme Court, however, reversed this jurisdictional holding. In a unanimous, six-member decision, the court held that the Rosebud Sioux Tribal Court does have jurisdiction and remanded the case to the tribal court for hearing. The tribal supreme court reasoned

11. Amended Complaint, filed 21 September 1993, *In the Matter of the Estate of Tasunke Witko, a.k.a. Crazy Horse v. Heileman Brewing Co. et al.,* Civ. No. 93-204, Rosebud Sioux Tribal Court, Rosebud, S. D.

12. Memorandum Opinion, 25 October 1994, *Estate of Tasunke Witko,* Civ. No. 93-204, Rosebud Sioux Tribal Court.

that even though the defendants had not physically marketed their objectionable product on Rosebud Reservation (or even in South Dakota), the *harm* to the plaintiffs had taken place on Rosebud Reservation, and the product, which mentioned the "Black Hills . . . , home of Proud Indian Nations," was "specifically directed to" the Great Sioux Reservation, of which Rosebud is a part. Thus, under the tribe's long-arm statute, the tribal court clearly had jurisdiction to hear the tort.[13]

The Court of Appeals for the Eighth Circuit found in January 1998 that the tribal court did not have personal jurisdiction over the defendants under the terms of the U. S. Supreme Court's *Montana* holding.[14] Nevertheless, what is important in this case is the use of the law by a tribal member to summon into court not a local non-Indian, but a powerful New York corporation.[15] Even in its "failure" regarding jurisdiction, this high-profile case successfully politicized the traffic in racist representations by a kind of perpetrator not usually the subject of indictment by reservation Indians. This is certainly a disruption of the prevailing geography of political struggle described in chapter 6. Furthermore, while jurisdiction came up in the case, what is at issue here is something much more global—racist representations of Indian people and the freedom of powerful non-Indians in places distant from Indian country to traffic in those representations. Because the Eighth Circuit's opinion specifically mentioned the availability of federal district court as a suitable forum for the estate to take up the specifics of its case against Hornell, we can anticipate that the larger issue here—the one beyond jurisdiction—will remain in political as well as legal play.

The *Crazy Horse* case is not alone in challenging racist stereotypes circulating in the dominant culture. In 1999 the federal Trademark Trial and Appeal Board canceled the trademark registration of the "Washington Redskins." The case, *Harjo v. Pro-Football, Inc.,* was brought by seven prominent Native Americans in 1992 who argued that the word "redskin(s)" "was and is a pejorative, derogatory, denigrating and racist designation for the Native American person," and that the associated logos constitute material that "disparages Native American persons, and brings them into contempt, ridicule, and disrepute," and are

13. Memorandum Opinion and Order, 1 May 1996, *Estate of Tasunke Witko*, Civ. No. 93-204, Rosebud Sioux Supreme Court.

14. *Hornell v. Rosebud Sioux Tribal Court,* 133 F.3d 1087.

15. It is also worth noting the irony that one of the strategies originally used to colonize ("civilize") Indian people—"teaching" them about, and allotting them, *private property*—has been turned around by Indian people as a weapon of resistance.

therefore violations of the Trademark Act.[16] In April 1999 the Trademark Trial and Appeal Board held that the Redskins trademark "may disparage Native Americans and bring them into contempt or disrepute,"[17] and it cancelled the trademark registration.

Of course legal challenges to white representations of Indians in the popular culture can also be said to be *partial* and *piecemeal* forms of struggle, just as are the jurisdictional disputes examined in this book. But *Crazy Horse* and *Harjo* v. *Pro-Football* make a form of white racism that has long been "invisible" (to many whites, at least) politically visible and legally actionable. These cases challenge white "innocence" in ways that go beyond the regime of guilt and innocence produced by the discourse of Indian law.

It would certainly be difficult not to conclude from the history narrated in this book that law—especially Indian law—is a "racial politics machine"[18] with powerful—hegemonic—ideological and political effects. We must always remain alert to the critical fact that there is no will to racial justice that stands behind the discourse of Indian law and guarantees its humane unfolding. It is also the case, however, that Native American people have a long history of reading and using the law in ways unintended and unforeseen by the elites who wrote and thought they controlled that law. We should expect nothing less in the future. The law—federal Indian law or some other kind—will continue to be at the center of the struggle for justice for native people, and for us all.

16. U.S. Department of Commerce 1999, 5–6.

17. Ibid., 145. See also Johnson and Eck 1995–96; " 'Redskins' Trademark Revoked," *Indian Country Today,* 19–26 April 1999.

18. The allusion, of course, is to James Ferguson's argument that the development discourse is a powerful "anti-politics machine" (Ferguson 1990).

References

PUBLISHED FEDERAL GOVERNMENT DOCUMENTS

Congressional Record
Constitution
Federal Register
Statutes at Large of the United States
United States Code
United States Code Annotated
U. S. American Indian Policy Review Commission
    1976. *Report on Federal, State and Tribal Jurisdiction* (Task Force Four)
    1977. *Final Report*
U. S. Commission on Civil Rights
    1977. *Liberty and Justice for All,* Report Prepared by the South Dakota Advisory Committee
    1978. *American Indian Issues in the State of South Dakota.* Hearing Held in Rapid City, S. D. 27–28 July
    1981. *Indian Tribes: A Continuing Quest for Survival*
    1986. *Enforcement of the Indian Civil Rights Act,* Hearing Held in Rapid City, S. D., 31 July–1 August and 21 August, Hearing before the United States Commission of Civil Rights, no. 44
    1991. *The Indian Civil Rights Act. A Report of the United States Commission on Civil Rights*
    2000. *Native Americans in South Dakota: An Erosion of Confidence in the Justice System* (March) (http://www.usccr.gov/sdsac)

U. S. Congress, House of Representatives

  1975. *Jurisdiction Indian Reservations in South Dakota,* H. Rept. 2704, 57th Cong., 1st sess.

  1991. *Power of Indian Tribes to Exercise Criminal Jurisdiction over Indians,* H. Rept. 261, 102d Cong., 1st sess.

U. S. Congress, Senate

  1890. *Message from the President of the United States,* S. Rept. 1724, 51st Cong., 1st sess.

  1901. *Agreement with Indians of Rosebud Agency, S. Dak.,* Doc. 31, 57th Cong., 1st sess.

  1975. *Tribal Judicial Reform,* Hearings before the Subcommittee on Indian Affairs of the Committee on Interior and Insular Affairs, 94th Cong., 1st sess.

  1991a. *Impact of Supreme Court's Ruling in Duro* v. *Reina,* Hearing before the Select Committee on Indian Affairs, S. Hrg. 102-158, 102d Cong., 1st sess.

  1991b. *Making Permanent the Legislative Reinstatement, Following the Decision of Duro against Reina (58 U.S.L.W. 4643, May 29, 1990), of the Power of Indian Tribes to Exercise Criminal Jurisdiction over Indians,* S. Rept. 102-153, 102d Cong., 1st sess.

  1992. *Federal Court Review of Tribal Court Rulings in Actions Arising under the Indian Civil Rights Act,* Hearing Before the Select Committee on Indian Affairs. S. Hrg. 102-599, 102d Cong., 1st sess.

U. S. Department of Commerce

  1990. *Census of Population and Housing*

  1992. Summary Tape File, CD 90-3A-52, South Dakota (laser disk)

  1999. *Harjo et al.* v. *Pro-Football, Inc.,* Trademark Trial and Appeal Board, Patent and Trademark Office

U. S. Department of the Interior

  Annual Report of the Commissioner of Indian Affairs

  Annual Report of the Secretary of the Interior

  1979 *Opinions of the Solicitor of the Department of the Interior Relating to Indian Affairs, 1917–1974,* two volumes

PUBLISHED STATE OF SOUTH DAKOTA GOVERNMENT DOCUMENTS

Biennial Report of Attorney General (various years)

Commissioner of Immigration

  1890. *Facts about South Dakota: An Official Encyclopedia*

Constitution

House Journal

Interim Investigating Committee, South Dakota Legislature

  1962. *A Report of an Investigation of the South Dakota Department of Public Welfare*

Legislative Research Council

Session Laws

Senate Journal
South Dakota Code, 1939

ROSEBUD SIOUX TRIBE

Constitution and By-Laws
Law and Order Code

CANADA

Shortt, Adam, and Arthur G. Doughty, eds.
    1918. *Documents Relating to the Constitutional History of Canada,*
    1759–1791. 2d ed., pt. 1. Ottawa: Canadian Archives

ARCHIVAL AND MANUSCRIPT SOURCES

Assumption Abbey Archives, Richardton, N. D.
    James McLaughlin Papers, microfilm
City of Mission Office, Mission, S. D.
    A Record of the Organization and Incorporation of Mission Townsite
      Company
    Liquor Store file
    United States v. *Mission* file
Dakota Plains Legal Services, Mission, S. D.
    Rosebud Sioux Tribe v. *South Dakota* file
Federal Records Center, Denver, Colo.
    Rosebud Sioux Tribe v. *Kneip* (Civ. 86-3019) file (D. S. D.)
Finch, Viken, Viken and Pechota, Attorneys-at-Law, Rapid City, S. D.
    United States v. *Mission Golf Course and City of Mission* file
Institute for Indian Studies, University of South Dakota, Vermillion
    A Report on the Bureau of Indian Affairs Fee Patenting and Canceling Poli-
      cies, 1900–42
Lakota Archives and Historical Research Center, Sinte Gleska University, Rose-
    bud, S. D.
    Frank LaPointe Papers
    Jurisdiction file
    Miscellaneous files
    Opening of the Rosebud Indian Lands
    Rosebud Sioux Herald
Lyman County Courthouse, S. D.
    Case files
National Archives and Records Administration, Washington, D. C.
    Microfilm Publication M595 (Indian Census Rolls)
    Microfilm Publication M1011 (Superintendents' Annual Narrative and Sta-
      tistical Reports)
    Record Group 75 (Records of the Bureau of Indian Affairs)

National Indian Law Library, Boulder, Colo.
    Rosebud Sioux Tribe v. *Kneip* files
Richardson Archives, I. D. Weeks Library, University of South Dakota, Vermil-
    lion, S. D.
    Sigurd Anderson papers
    Archie Gubbrud papers
    Richard F. Kneip papers
    George S. Mickelson papers
    Cato Valandra papers
Rosebud Sioux Supreme Court, Rosebud, S. D.
    In the Matter of the Estate of Tasunke Witko, aka Crazy Horse, v. *Heileman
        Brewing et al.,* Civil Case 93-204
Rosebud Sioux Tribal Court, Rosebud, S. D.
    *In the Matter of the Appeal City of Mission and Mission Golf Course from
        Denial of Licenses,* Civil Case 84-45
    In the Matter of the Estate of Tasunke Witko, aka Crazy Horse, v. *Heileman
        Brewing et al.,* Civil Case 93-204
    Rosebud Sioux Tribe v. *Walsh et al.,* Civil Case 89-210-16
Rosebud Sioux Tribal Office, Rosebud, S. D.
    Mission Golf Club file
    Rosebud Sioux Tribal Council Records
John Simpson Law Office, Winner, S. D.
    Fire v. *Winner* file
South Dakota Department of Transportation, Pierre
    Miscellaneous files
 South Dakota Legislative Research Council, Pierre
    Minutes of Legislative Committees
South Dakota State Historical Society, Pierre
    Indian Affairs Commission Records
    Task Force on Indian-State Government Relations Records
    Todd County Tribune, microfilm
    Winner Advocate, microfilm
Stanford University Law Library, Stanford, Calif.
    The Indian Civil Rights Act, Five Years Later (American Indian Lawyers As-
        sociation, 1973)
Tobin Law Office, Winner, S. D.
    Rosebud Sioux Tribe v. *Kneip* files
Tripp County Courthouse, Winner, S. D.
    Case files
United States Court of Appeals for the Eighth Circuit, United States Court-
    house, St. Louis, Mo.
    United States v. *Mission Golf Course and City of Mission* file (Civ. 82-1516)
United States District Court for the District of South Dakota, United States
    Courthouse, Pierre, S. D.
    Rosebud Sioux Tribe v. *South Dakota* (Civ. 86-3019) file
United States Supreme Court, Washington, D. C.
    Brendale v. *Yamika* (87-1622) records, microfiche

Mission v. *United States* (83-606) records, microfiche
Oliphant v. *Suquamish Indian Tribe* (76-5729) records, microfiche

PUBLISHED SOURCES

Abraham, Kenneth S.
  1988. Statutory Interpretation and Literary Theory: Some Common Concerns of an Unlikely Pair. In *Interpreting Law and Literature: A Hermeneutic Reader*, ed. Sanford Levinson and Steven Mailloux, 115–29. Evanston, Ill.: Northwestern University Press.

Asch, Michael
  1993a. Aboriginal Self-Government and Canadian Constitutional Identity: Building Reconciliation. In *Ethnicity and Aboriginality: Case Studies in Ethnonationalism,* ed. Michael Levin, 29–52. Toronto: University of Toronto Press.
  1993b [1984]. *Home and Native Land: Aboriginal Rights and the Canadian Constitution.* Vancouver: University of British Columbia Press.
  1995. Comment on Bringing the Law Back In, by Thomas Biolsi. *Current Anthropology* 36(4):559.

Balbus, Isaac
  1977. Commodity Form and Legal Form: An Essay on the "Relative Autonomy" of the Law. *Law and Society Review* 11:571–88.

Bee, Robert L.
  1992. Riding the Paper Tiger. In *State and Reservation,* ed. George P. Castile and Robert L. Bee, 139–64. Toronto: University of Toronto Press.

Berkhoffer, Robert F., Jr.
  1978. *The White Man's Indian: Images of the American Indian from Columbus to the Present.* New York: Vintage.

Biolsi, Thomas
  1992. *Organizing the Lakota: The Political Economy of the New Deal on Pine Ridge and Rosebud Reservations.* Tucson: University of Arizona Press.
  1993. The Political Economy of Lakota Consciousness. In *The Political Economy of North American Indians,* ed. John Moore, 20–42. Norman: University of Oklahoma Press.
  1995. The Birth of the Reservation: Making the Modern Individual among the Lakota. *American Ethnologist* 22(1):28–53.

Brennan, William, J., Jr.,
  1988. The Constitution of the United States: Contemporary Ratification. In *Interpreting Law and Literature: A Hermeneutic Reader,* ed. Sanford Levinson and Steven Mailloux, 13–24. Evanston, Ill.: Northwestern University Press.

Brest, Paul
  1988. The Misconceived Quest for the Original Understanding. In *Interpreting Law and Literature: A Hermeneutic Reader,* ed. Sanford Levinson and Steven Mailloux, 169–96. Evanston, Ill.: Northwestern University Press.

Burnette, Robert, and John Koster
    1973. *The Road to Wounded Knee.* New York: Bantam Books.
Calhoun, Craig, ed.
    1992. *Habermas and the Public Sphere.* Cambridge, Mass.: MIT Press.
Canby, William
    1998. *American Indian Law in a Nutshell.* 3d ed. St. Paul, Minn.: West Pub-
        lishing Co.
Casey, Robert J, and W. A. S. Douglas
    1948. *Pioneer Railroad: The Story of the Chicago and North Western Sys-
        tem.* New York: McGraw-Hill.
Caton, W. H.
    1984 [1913]. Indian Lands and Leases. In *A Rosebud Review, 1913, 39.*
        Gregory, S. D.: *Gregory Times-Advocate.*
Chambers, Opie
    1984 [1913]. The Early History of the Rosebud Country. In *A Rosebud Re-
        view, 1913, 5–9.* Gregory, S. D.: *Gregory Times–Advocate.*
Clinton, Robert N.
    1975. Development of Criminal Jurisdiction over Indian Lands: The Histor-
        ical Perspective. *Arizona Law Review* 17:951–91.
    1976. Criminal Jurisdiction over Indian Lands: A Journey through a Juris-
        dictional Maze. *Arizona Law Review* 18:503–81.
Clinton, Robert, Nell Jessup Newton, and Monroe E. Price
    1991. *American Indian Law: Cases and Materials.* 3d ed. Charlottesville,
        Va.: Michie.
Clow, Richmond Lee
    1981. State Jurisdiction on Sioux Reservations: Indian and Non-Indian Re-
        sponses. *South Dakota History* 11:171–84.
Cohen, Felix
    1942. *Handbook of Federal Indian Law.* Washington: Government Printing
        Office.
Collins, Richard B.
    1979. Implied Limitations on the Jurisdiction of Indian Tribes. *Washington
        Law Review* 54:479–529.
Colson, Elizabeth
    1974. *Tradition and Contract: The Problem of Order.* Chicago: Aldine.
Conference of Western Attorneys General
    1998. *American Indian Law Deskbook.* 2d ed. Niwot: University Press of
        Colorado.
Corrigan Philip, and Derek Sayer
    1981. How the Law Rules: Variations on Some Themes in Karl Marx.
        In *Law, State, and Society,* ed. B. Fryer, 21–53. London: Croom and
        Helm.
Crenshaw, Kimberle Williams
    1988. Race, Reform and Retrenchment: Transformation and Legitimation
        in Antidiscrimination Law. *Harvard Law Review* 101(7):1331–87.
Deloria, Vine, Jr.,
    1985 [1974]. *Behind the Trail of Broken Treaties: An Indian Declaration of
        Independence.* Austin: University of Texas Press.

1992. The Application of the Constitution to American Indians. In *Exiled in the Land of the Free: Democracy, Indian Nations, and the U. S. Constitution*, ed. Oren Lyons et al., 281–315. Sante Fe: Clear Light Publishers.

Deloria, Vine, Jr., and Clifford M. Lytle
1984a. *American Indians, American Justice*. Austin: University of Texas Press.
1984b. *Nations Within: The Past and Future of American Indian Sovereignty*. New York: Pantheon Books.

Dippie, Brian W.
1982. *The Vanishing American: White Attitudes and U. S. Indian Policy*. Middletown, Conn. Wesleyan University Press.

Drinnon, Richard
1986. *Keeper of Concentration Camps: Dillon S. Myer and American Racism*. Berkeley and Los Angeles: University of California Press.

Duran, Eduardo, and Bonnie Duran
1995. *Native American Postcolonial Psychology*. Albany: State University of New York Press.

Escobar, Arturo
1995. *Encountering Development: The Making and Unmaking of the Third World*. Princeton: Princeton University Press.

Everett, Margaret
1997. The Ghost in the Machine: Agency in "Poststructural" Critiques of Development. *Anthropological Quarterly* 70(3):137–51.

Ferguson, James
1990. *The Anti-Politics Machine: "Development" and Bureaucratic Power in Lesotho*. New York: Cambridge University Press.

Fields, Barbara
1990. Slavery, Race and Ideology in the United States of America. *New Left Review* 181:95–118.

Fish, Stanley
1980. *Is There a Text in This Class?: The Authority of Interpretive Communities*. Cambridge, Mass.: Harvard University Press.

Fixico, Donald L.
1986. *Termination and Relocation: Federal Indian Policy, 1945–1960*. Albuquerque: University of New Mexico Press.

Flagg, Barbara J.
1998. *Was Blind, but Now I See: White Race Consciousness and the Law*. New York: New York University Press.

Foley, Douglas
1995. *The Heartland Chronicles*. Philadelphia: University of Pennsylvania Press.

Ford, Richard T.
1992. Urban Space and the Color Line: The Consequences of Demarcation and Disorientation in the Postmodern Metropolis. *Harvard Blackletter Journal* 9:117–47.

Foucault, Michael
1972. *The Archaeology of Knowledge and the Discourse on Language*. New York: Pantheon Books.

1979. *Discipline and Punish: The Birth of the Prison.* Translated by Alan Sheridan. New York: Vintage.

1980. *The History of Sexuality,* vol. I: *An Introduction.* Translated by Robert Hurley. New York: Random House.

Frank, Andre Gunder

1967. *Capitalism and Underdevelopment in Latin America: Historical Studies of Chile and Brazil.* New York: Monthly Review Press.

Frankenberg, Ruth

1993. *White Women, Race Matters: The Social Construction of Whiteness.* Minneapolis: University of Minnesota Press.

1997. Introduction: Local Whitenesses, Localizing Whiteness. In *Displacing Whiteness: Essays in Social and Cultural Criticism,* ed. Ruth Frankenberg, 1–33. Durham, N. C.: Duke University Press.

Freeman, Alan

1982. Antidiscrimination Law: A Critical Review. In *The Politics of Law: A Progressive Critique,* ed. D. Kairys, 96–116. New York: Pantheon.

1988. Racism, Rights, and the Quest for Equality of Opportunity: A Critical Legal Essay. *Harvard Civil Rights–Civil Liberties Law Review* 23:295–392.

Frickey, Philip P.

1990. Congressional Intent, Practical Reasoning, and the Dynamic Nature of Federal Indian Law. *California Law Review* 78:1137–1239.

1997. Adjudication and Its Discontents: Coherence and Conciliation in Federal Indian Law. *Harvard Law Review* 110:1754–84.

Furber, Bradley

1991. Two Promises, Two Propositions: The Wheeler-Howard Act as a Reconciliation of the Indian Civil War. *University of Puget Sound Law Review* 14:211–82.

Getches, David H., Charles F. Wilkinson, and Robert A. Williams, Jr.

1993. *Cases and Materials on Federal Indian Law.* 3d ed. St. Paul, Minn.: West Publishing Company.

Gillingham, John W.

1993. Pathfinder: Tribal, Federal, and State Court Subject Matter Jurisdictional Bounds: Suits Involving Native American Interests. *American Indian Law Review* 18:73–132.

Goodbeer, Richard

1999. Eroticizing the Middle Ground: Anglo-Indian Sexual Relations along the Eighteenth-Century Frontier. In *Sex, Love, Race: Crossing Boundaries in North American History,* ed. Martha Hodes, 91–111. New York: New York University Press.

Gordon, Robert W.

1984. Critical Legal Histories. *Stanford Law Review* 36:57–125.

Gotanda, Neil

1991. A Critique of "Our Constitution is Color-Blind." *Stanford Law Review* 44:1–68.

Gramsci, Antonio

1971. *Selections from the Prison Notebooks.* New York: International Publishers.

Green, Charles Lowell
    1940. The Administration of the Public Domain in South Dakota. *South Dakota Historical Collections* 20:11–280.
Gregory Times-Advocate
    1984 [1913]. Winner. In *A Rosebud Review, 1913,* 100. Gregory, S. D: *Gregory Times–Advocate.*
Haney Lopez, Ian
    1996. *White by Law: The Legal Construction of Race.* New York: New York University Press.
Harmon, Alexandra.
    1995. Lines in the Sand: Shifting Boundaries between Indians and Non-Indians in the Puget Sound Region. *Western Historical Quarterly* 26:429–53.
Harris, Cheryl I.
    1993. Whiteness as Property. *Harvard Law Review* 106:1709–91.
Harrison, Faye V.
    1988. Introduction: Expanding the Discourse on Race. *American Anthropologist* 100(3): 609–31.
Hartigan, David
    1997. Locating White Detroit. In *Displacing Whiteness: Essays in Social and Cultural Criticism,* ed. Ruth Frankenberg, 180–213. Durham, N. C.: Duke University Press.
Harvey, David
    1989. *The Condition of Postmodernity: An Enquiry into the Origins of Cultural Change.* Cambridge, Mass.: Blackwell.
Higginbotham, A. Leon, Jr.
    1978. *In the Matter of Color: Race and the American Legal Process, The Colonial Period.* New York: Oxford University Press.
Hodes, Martha, ed.
    1999. *Sex, Love, Race: Crossing Boundaries in North American History.* New York: New York University Press.
Hoover, Herbert T.
    1983. Farmers Fight Back: A Survey of Rural Political Organizations, 1873–1983. *South Dakota History* 13:122–57.
    1988. South Dakota: An Experience of Regional Heritage. In *Heart Land: Comparative Histories of the Midwestern States,* ed. James H. Madison, 186–205. New York: Pantheon.
Hoxie, Frederick E.
    1984. *A Final Promise: The Campaign to Assimilate the Indians, 1880–1920.* New York: Cambridge University Press.
Hughes, John T., and Tom Tobin
    1973. New Town et al.: The Future of an Illusion. *South Dakota Law Review* 18:85–128.
Hunt, Alan, and Gary Wickham
    1994. *Foucault and Law: Towards a Sociology of Law as Governance.* Boulder, Colo.: Pluto Press.
Institute for the Development of Indian Law
    1974. *Treaties and Agreements and the Proceedings of the Treaties and*

Agreements of the Tribes and Bands of the Sioux Nation. Washington,
D. C: Institute for the Development of Indian Law.

1975. *Proceedings of the Great Peace Commission of 1867–1868.* Washington, D. C: Institute for the Development of Indian Law.

Iron Shield, Harold
1990–91. Reconciliation: The Next 100 Years. *South Dakota Law Review*
36(2): ix–xi.

Jackson, F. H.
1984 [1913]. Homesteading on the Rosebud. In *A Rosebud Review, 1913,*
17–18. Gregory, S. D.: *Gregory Times-Advocate.*

Johnson, Kim Chandler, and John Terrence Eck
1995–96. Eliminating Indian Stereotypes from American Society: Causes
and Legal and Societal Solutions. *American Indian Law Review*
20(1):65–109.

Jordon, Winthrop D.
1974. *The White Man's Burden: Historical Origins of Racism in the United
States.* New York: Oxford University Press.

Jorgensen, Joseph G.
1971. Indians and the Metropolis. In *The American Indian in Urban Society,* ed. J. Waddell and O. Michael Watson, 67–113. Boston: Little, Brown.
1972. *The Sundance Religion: Power for the Powerless.* Chicago: University
of Chicago Press.

Kairys, David
1982. Legal Reasoning. In *The Politics of Law: A Progressive Critique,* ed.
David Kairys, 11–17. New York: Pantheon Books.

Kappler, Charles J., ed.
1903. *Indian Affairs: Laws and Treaties.* Volume 2. Washington: Government Printing Office.

Kennedy, Duncan
1979. The Structure of Blackstone's Commentaries. *Buffalo Law Review*
28:205–382.

Klare, Karl
1978. Judicial Deradicalization of the Wagner Act and the Origins of Modern Legal Consciousness, 1937–1941. *Minnesota Law Review*
62:265–339.

Klein, Alan M.
1993. Political Economy of the Buffalo Hide Trade: Race and Class on the
Plains. In *The Political Economy of North American Indians,* ed. John
Moore, 133–60. Norman: University of Oklahoma Press.

Lawrence, Charles R., III
1987. The Id, the Ego, and Equal Protection: Reckoning with Unconscious
Racism. *Stanford Law Review* 39:317–88.

Lee, R. Alton
1974. Indian Citizenship and the Fourteenth Amendment. *South Dakota
History* 4(2):198–221.

Levin, Michael D., ed.
1993. *Ethnicity and Aboriginality: Case Studies in Ethnonationalism.*
Toronto: University of Toronto Press.

Lucas, S. F.
   1984 [1913]. Early History of the Old Part of Gregory County. In *A Rosebud Review, 1913,* 3. Gregory, S. D.: *Gregory Times-Advocate.*
MacKinnon, Catherine
   1982. Toward Feminist Jurisprudence. *Stanford Law Review* 34:703–37.
Macklem, Patrick
   1993. Ethnonationalism, Aboriginal Identities, and the Law. In *Ethnicity and Aboriginality: Case Studies in Ethnonationalism,* ed. Michael Levin, 9–28. Toronto: University of Toronto Press.
Martone, Frederick J.
   1979. Of Power and Purpose. *Notre Dame Lawyer* 54:829–45.
Matthiessen, Peter
   1983. *In the Spirit of Crazy Horse.* New York: Viking Press.
McDonnell, Janet A.
   1980. Competency Commissions and Indian Land Policy, 1913–1920. *South Dakota History* 11(1):21–34.
   1991. *The Dispossession of the American Indian, 1887–1934.* Bloomington: Indiana University Press.
McIntosh, Peggy
   1989. White Privilege: Unpacking the Invisible Knapsack. *Peace and Freedom* July/August:10–12.
Means, Russell [with Marvin J. Wolf]
   1995. *Where White Men Fear to Tread: The Autobiography of Russell Means.* New York: St. Martin's Press.
Mehta, Uday S.
   1996. Liberal Strategies of Exclusion. In *Tensions of Empire: Colonial Cultures in a Bourgeois World,* ed. Frederick Cooper and Ann L. Stoler, 59–86. Berkeley and Los Angeles: University of California Press.
Memmi, Albert
   1965. *The Colonizer and the Colonized.* Translated by Howard Greenfield. New York: Orion Press.
Merry, Sally Engle
   1985. Concepts in Law and Justice among Working Class Americans: Ideology as Culture. *Legal Studies Forum* 9:59–69.
   1986. Everyday Understandings of the Law in Working-Class America. *American Ethnologist* 13:253–70.
   1990. *Getting Justice and Getting Even: Legal Consciousness among Working-Class Americans.* Chicago: University of Chicago Press.
   1995. Wife Battering and the Ambiguities of Rights. In *Identities, Politics, and Rights,* ed. Austin Sarat and Thomas R. Kearns, 271–306. Ann Arbor: University of Michigan Press.
Nagel, Joane
   1997. *American Indian Ethnic Renewal: Red Power and the Resurgence of Identity and Culture.* New York: Oxford University Press.
Nash, Gary B.
   1999. The Hidden History of Mestizo America. In *Sex, Love, Race: Crossing Boundaries in North American History,* ed. Martha Hodes, 10–32. New York: New York University Press.

Norgren, Jill
   1996. *The Cherokee Cases: The Confrontation of Law and Politics.* New York: McGraw-Hill.
Otis, D. S.
   1973. *The Dawes Act and the Allotment of Indian Lands.* Edited by Francis Prucha. Norman: University of Oklahoma Press.
Philp, Kenneth R.
   1999. *Termination Revisited: American Indians on the Trail to Self-Determination, 1933–1953.* Lincoln: University of Nebraska Press.
Pommersheim, Frank
   1995. *Braid of Feathers: American Indian Law and Contemporary Tribal Life.* Berkeley and Los Angeles: University of California Press.
Pratt, Mary Louise
   1992. *Imperial Eyes: Travel Writing and Transculturalism.* New York: Routledge.
Price, Catherine
   1996. *The Oglala People, 1841–1879: A Political History.* Lincoln: University of Nebraska Press.
Price, Monroe E.
   1973. *Law and the American Indian: Readings, Notes and Cases.* New York: Bobbs-Merrill.
Prucha, Francis Paul
   1984a. *The Great Father: The United States Government and the American Indians.* Vols. 1 and 2, unabridged. Lincoln: University of Nebraska Press.
   1984b. *The Great Father: The United States Government and the American Indians.* Abridged ed. Lincoln: University of Nebraska Press.
   1994. *American Indian Treaties: The History of a Political Anomaly.* Berkeley and Los Angeles: University of California Press.
Prucha, Francis Paul, ed.
   1978. *Americanizing the American Indians: Writings by the "Friends of the Indian," 1880–1900.* Lincoln: University of Nebraska Press.
Roediger, David R.
   1991. *The Wages of Whiteness: Race and the Making of the American Working Class.* New York: Verso.
Ross, Thomas
   1990. Innocence and Affirmative Action. *Vanderbilt Law Review* 43(2):297–316.
Said, Edward
   1979. *Orientalism.* New York: Random House.
Schell, Herbert S.
   1975. *History of South Dakota.* 3d ed. Lincoln: University of Nebraska Press.
Schmeckebier, Laurence F.
   1972 [1927]. *The Office of Indian Affairs: Its History, Activities and Organization.* New York: AMS Press.

Scott, James C.
 1985. *Weapons of the Weak: Everyday Forms of Peasant Resistance.* New Haven: Yale University Press.
 1990. *Domination and the Arts of Resistance: Hidden Transcripts.* New Haven: Yale University Press.
Shattuck, Petra T., and Jill Norgren
 1991. *Partial Justice: Federal Indian Law in a Liberal Constitutional System.* Providence, R. I.: Berg.
Sider, Gerald M.
 1993. *Lumbee Indian Histories: Race, Ethnicity, and Indian Identity in the Southern United States.* New York: Cambridge University Press.
Sinclair, Keith
 1971. Why Are Race Relations in New Zealand Better than in South Africa, South Australia, or South Dakota? *New Zealand Journal of History* 5(2):121–27.
Smith, Paul Chaat, and Robert A. Warrior
 1996. *Like a Hurricane: The Indian Movement from Alcatraz to Wounded Knee.* New York: The Free Press.
Solum, Lawrence B.
 1997. Indeterminacy and Equity. In *Radical Critiques of the Law,* ed. Stephen M. Griffin and Robert C. L. Moffat, 44–66. Lawrence: University Press of Kansas.
Stoller, Ann Laura
 1989a. Rethinking Colonial Categories: European Communities and the Boundaries of Rule. *Comparative Studies in Society and History* 31(1): 134–61.
 1989b. Making Empire Respectable: The Politics of Race and Sexual Morality in 20th-Century Colonial Cultures. *American Ethnologist* 16(4): 634–60.
Strickland, Rennard, ed.
 1982. *Felix Cohen's Handbook of Federal Indian Law.* 1982 ed. Charlottesville, Va.: Michie.
Stubbs, Margot
 1986. Feminism and Legal Positivism. *Australian Journal of Law and Society* 3:63–91.
Takaki, Ronald T.
 1982. *Iron Cages: Race and Culture in Nineteenth-Century America.* Seattle: University of Washington Press.
Thompson, E. P.
 1978. *The Poverty of Theory and other Essays.* New York: Monthly Review Press.
Thornton, R.
 1998. The Demography of Colonialism and "Old" and "New" Native Americans. In *Studying Native America: Problems and Prospects,* ed. Russell Thornton, 17–39. Madison: University of Wisconsin Press.

Tilleman, Paul
   1976. In Law-Boundary Disestablishment through the Operation of Surplus
   Land Acts. *Wisconsin Law Review* 1305–31.
Wald, Priscilla
   1993. Terms of Assimilation: Legislating Subjectivity in the Emerging Nation. In *Cultures of United States Imperialism*, ed. Amy Kaplan and Donald E. Pease, 59–84. Durham, N. C.: Duke University Press.
   1995. *Constituting Americans: Cultural Anxiety and Narrative Form.*
   Durham, N. C.: Duke University Press.
Weil, Robert
   1975 [1888]. *The Legal Status of the Indian.* New York: AMS Press.
White, G. Edward
   1991. *The Marshall Court and Cultural Change, 1815–1835.* Abridged ed.
   New York: Oxford University Press.
White, Richard
   1991. *The Middle Ground: Indians, Empires, and Republics in the Great
   Lakes Region, 1650–1815.* New York: Cambridge University Press.
Wilkins, David E.
   1993. Transformations in Supreme Court Thought: The Irresistible Force
   (Federal Indian Law & Polity) Meets the Movable Object (American In-
   dian Tribal Status). *The Social Science Journal* 30(2):181–207.
   1995. Judicial "Masks": Their Role in Defining and Redefining the
   Tribal/Congressional Relationship 1870–1924. In *Issues in Native Ameri-
   can Identity*, ed. Michael K. Green, 81–165. New York: Peter Lang.
   1997. *American Indian Sovereignty and the U. S. Supreme Court: The
   Masking of Justice.* Austin: University of Texas Press.
   Forthcoming. The Reinvigoration of the Doctrine of "Implied Repeals": Re-
   quiem for Indigenous Treaty Rights? *American Journal of Legal History.*
Wilkinson, Charles F.
   1987. *American Indians, Time, and the Law: Native Societies in a Modern
   Constitutional Democracy.* New Haven, Conn.: Yale University Press.
Wilkinson, Charles F., and John M. Volkman
   1975. Judicial Review of Indian Treaty Abrogation: "As Long as Water
   Flows or Grass Grows upon the Earth"—How Long a Time is That? *California Law Review* 63:601–61.
Williams, Patricia
   1987. Alchemical Notes: Reconstructing Ideals from Deconstructed Rights.
   Harvard Civil Rights–Civil Liberties Law Review 22:401–33.
Williams, Raymond
   1966. *The Long Revolution.* Revised ed. New York: Harper.
   1977. *Marxism and Literature.* New York: Oxford University Press.
Williams, Robert A., Jr.
   1986. The Algebra of Federal Indian Law: The Hard Trail of Decolonizing
   and Americanizing the White Man's Jurisprudence. *Wisconsin Law Review* 219–299.

1988. Learning Not to Live with Eurocentric Myopia: A Reply to Professor Laurence's *Learning to Live with the Plenary Power of Congress over the Indian Nations. Arizona Law Review* 30:439–57.

1990. *The American Indian in Western Legal Thought: The Discourses of Conquest.* New York: Oxford University Press.

1996. "The People of the States Where They Are Found Are Often Their Deadliest Enemies": The Indian Side of the Story of Indian Rights and Federalism. *Arizona Law Review* 38(3):981–97.

Williamson, Joel

1980. *New People: Miscegenation and Mulattoes in the United States.* New York: The Free Press.

Willis, Paul E.

1977. *Learning to Labour: How Working Class Kids Get Working Class Jobs.* Farnborough, (U. K.): Saxon House.

Yngvesson, Barbara

1994 [1988]. Making Law at the Doorway: The Clerk, the Court, and the Construction of Community in a New England Town. In *Law and Community in Three American Towns,* ed. Carol J. Greenhouse, Barbara Yngvesson, and David M. Engel, 53–90. Ithaca, N Y.: Cornell University Press.

Zack, Naomi

1993. *Race and Mixed Race.* Philadelphia: Temple University Press.

NEWSPAPERS

Indian Country Today, Rapid City, S. D.

New Lakota Times (superseded by *Lakota Journal*), Rapid City, S. D.

New York Times, New York, N. Y.

Press and Dakotan, Yankton, S. D.

Rapid City Journal, Rapid City, S. D.

Rosebud Sioux Herald, Rosebud, S. D. (Lakota Archives and Historical Research Center, Sinte Gleska University, Rosebud, S. D.)

Sicangu Sun Times, Rosebud, S. D.

Sioux Falls Argus Leader, Sioux Falls, S. D.

Todd County Tribune, Mission, S. D. (microfilm copy, South Dakota State Historical Society, Pierre)

Washington Post, Washington, D. C.

Winner Advocate, Winner, S. D. (microfilm copy, South Dakota State Historical Society, Pierre)

Index

Thomas Biolsi is professor of Native American studies in the Department of Ethnic Studies at the University of California–Berkeley.

Text and display:	Sabon
Composition:	Impressions Book and Journal Services, Inc.
Printing and binding:	Edwards Bros.
Maps:	Bill Nelson
Index:	Barbara Roos